D1084618

The Making of National Money

The Making of National Money

Territorial Currencies in Historical Perspective

Eric Helleiner

Cornell University Press

Ithaca and London

First published 2003 by Cornell University Press

Printed in the United States of America

Library of Congress Cataloging-in-Publication Data

Helleiner, Eric, 1963–
    The making of national money : territorial currencies in historical perspective / Eric Helleiner.
        p. cm.
Includes bibliographical references and index.
    ISBN 0-8014-4049-1 (cloth : alk. paper)
    1. Money. 2. Money—Political aspects. 3. Currency question. I. Title.
    HG221 .H4855 2003
    332.4—dc21

                            2002009209

Cornell University Press strives to use environmentally responsible suppliers and materials to the fullest extent possible in the publishing of its books. Such materials include vegetable-based, low-VOC inks and acid-free papers that are recycled, totally chlorine-free, or partly composed of nonwood fibers. For further information, visit our website at www.cornellpress.cornell.edu.

Cloth printing   10 9 8 7 6 5 4 3 2 1

A modified version of chapter 10 of this book, "The Current Challenge to Territorial Currencies" appeared in *Governing the World's Money*, edited by David M. Andrews, C. Randall Henning, and Louis W. Pauly (Ithaca: Cornell University Press, 2002).

To Jennifer, Zoe, and Nels

Contents

Illustrations

Preface

This book provides a detailed history of a form of money that is unique to the modern age: territorially homogeneous and exclusive national currencies. My interest in this history was initially provoked by the challenges to "territorial currencies" in the contemporary age. By exploring the origins of these monetary structures across the world, my initial goal was to contribute to our understanding of contemporary transformations. Once I delved into the history, however, it soon became clear to me that territorial currencies had broader significance. As I show, this study of their origins sheds interesting light on the history of territoriality, national markets, macroeconomic policy, and state and nation building. It also contributes to our understanding of money not just as an economic phenomenon but also as a geographical, political, and sociocultural one.

Conducting the research for this book has been a fascinating experience. It involved not just the use of various libraries and archives, but also visits to many currency museums and coin shops in a number of countries. I am very grateful for the assistance I received from various librarians at the American Numismatic Society, the American Numismatic Association, and the Bank of Canada Currency Museum, as well as archivists at the Bank of England archives, Britain's Public Records Office, the Canadian National Archives, the League of Nations archives, the U.S. Mint archives, and the U.S. National Archives. A number of librarians and museum curators have also provided useful comments and other kinds of support, particularly Michael Bates, Paul Berry, Kevin Clancy, Richard Doty, Virginia Hewitt, Robert Wilson Hoge, James Hughes, Douglas Mudd, and James Zagon. My work was also helped by some very able research assistants: Rob Aitken, Ana Maria Vega Baron, Laura Chrabolowsky, Matt Griem, Derek Hall, Melissa Harnett, Andrea Harrington, Samuel Knafo, Margaret Moore, Sarai Nunez-Ceron, Vince Sica, Gita Sud, and Al Vachon. I am also grateful to the Social Sciences and Humanities Research Council of Canada for providing very useful support.

I thank other people who provided helpful comments and research assistance at various stages: John Agnew, David Andrews, Samuel Barkin, Phil Cerny, William Coleman, André Drainville, Marc Flandreau, Ed Friedman, Emily Gilbert, Gerry Helleiner, Randy Henning, John Hillman,

Nicolas Jabko, Tsuyoshi Kawasaki, Jonathan Kirshner, Andrew Linklater, Helen Milner, Don Moggridge, Julie Nelson, Lou Pauly, Randy Persaud, Andreas Pickel, Tony Porter, Susan Roberts, Jan Aarte Scholte, André Schmid, Beth Simmons, Jackie Solway, David Spiro, Kjell Stixrud, Charles Tilly, Christopher Tomlins, Bent Sofus Tranoy, Geoffrey Underhill, Amy Verdun, Robert Wolfe, Viviana Zelizer, one anonymous reviewer, and various participants in seminars at the University of Minnesota, Cornell University, Columbia University, Princeton University, Queen's University, Sciences Po, University of Oslo, University of Toronto, and York University. I extend a special thanks to Jerry Cohen, who has provided such helpful and detailed comments at various stages of the research, as well as to Roger Haydon for being such a helpful and understanding editor. Finally, I cannot imagine a better group of companions and friends while I have been engaged in this project than Jennifer, Zoe, and Nels. To them, I am forever grateful.

Eric Helleiner

Peterborough, Ontario

Introduction

We live in an era when conventional ideas about the relationship between countries and currencies are being called into question. Not so long ago, it was seen to be quite natural for each country to maintain its own territorially exclusive and homogeneous currency. Today, however, these "territorial currencies" increasingly are being challenged. In the European Union, most countries have recently replaced territorial currencies with a supranational form of money. In many poorer parts of the world, foreign currencies such as the U.S. dollar are used very widely within countries, and some governments have even adopted the dollar as the national currency. Challenges to territorial currencies also come from below as hundreds of subnational "local currencies" have been created since the early 1980s. In addition, many analysts predict the emergence of a multitude of competing electronic currencies issued by private corporations.

These various developments suggest that there is nothing "natural" about the existence of territorial currencies. In many regions of the world, money is already being organized in quite different ways. If territorial currencies face an uncertain future, what do we know of their past? When and why were territorial currencies created in the first place? Have territorial currencies faced challenges in the past similar to those they face today? In what ways might the history of territorial currencies help us to understand current developments?

To date, these historical questions have not received as much attention as one might expect in scholarly literature. Most economists and political economists analyzing contemporary monetary transformations have not tried to place these developments in a longer historical context.[1] The territorialization of currencies is also remarkably understudied in the large literature on the history of territoriality and state building.[2] Although historians of money provide answers to our questions for specific countries, they have not produced a more systematic history of territorial currencies.

[1] For some exceptions, see Cohen (1998, ch.2), Davies (1994), De Cecco and Giovannini (1989), Glasner (1989), Duncan and Rotstein (1991), Einaudi (2000), James (1997), Woodruff (1999), and Gilbert and Helleiner (1999).

[2] As David Woodruff (1999, xiii) recently put it, "Despite its centrality to economic state building, monetary consolidation has provoked virtually nothing in the way of studies."

As I show, the history of territorial currencies is important for three reasons. To begin with, it highlights that current monetary transformations are less novel than they appear. Because territorial currencies are commonly seen today as a traditional way of organizing money, challenges to them are frequently portrayed as a very dramatic development in long historical terms. I show that a close examination of the history of territorial currencies reveals how misleading this view can be. Territorial currencies are a modern creation, emerging for the first time in the nineteenth century and becoming a standard monetary structure in most countries only during the twentieth century. Moreover, even in this short life, territorial currencies were never as dominant or willingly accepted as conventional wisdom suggests. They were constantly contested in the various ways that we are witnessing in the current period.

Second, historical perspective encourages us to examine the relationship between political space and the organization of money in a much broader way. Economists overwhelmingly dominate scholarship on this relationship today. A study of the history of territorial currencies reveals how limiting a narrowly economic approach is. As I demonstrate, the construction of territorial currencies was an intensely political process involving domestic and international struggles over issues such as the nature of state building, the construction of national identities, the proper scale of markets, and the implementation of competing macroeconomic ideologies. It also was linked to deeper structural trends in the technology of money and changing state forms. This history suggests that a much broader and more interdisciplinary approach is required to explain the geography of money, both in the past and today.

Third, this study of the origins of territorial currencies also provides useful insights into some of the specific causes of challenges to territorial currencies in the current period. This is partly because some of the causes are very similar to those that have produced challenges in the past. In these cases, I show how a close examination of the past is directly useful in interpreting the present. At the same time, I argue that other causes of challenges to territorial currencies today have few parallels in the past. In these instances, historical perspective helps us to identify what is unique about monetary transformations in the current era.

How Dramatic Are Current Monetary Transformations?

Let us examine first the argument about the long historical significance of current monetary transformations. As noted above, challenges to territorial currencies are portrayed frequently as a very dramatic development in the long sweep of history. This portrayal has been most common in international relations scholarship where threats to the territorial state—including challenges to territorial currencies—are frequently said to be ushering in a new "post-Westphalian" world order.[3] This phrase refers to the 1648 Peace of Westphalia in Europe, a moment that many scholars think marked the origins of the modern territorial state. It suggests that a dramatic transformation in world politics is underway of a kind that has not been seen in three hundred years.

If that is the intended meaning of the phrase,[4] the history of territorial currencies does not support the case. Challenges to territorial currencies undermine a monetary structure that has been in existence for a much shorter time period than the "Westphalian" image infers. Before the nineteenth century, monetary structures in all parts of the world, including Europe, diverged from the territorial model in three ways: foreign currencies frequently circulated alongside domestic currencies, low-denomination forms of money were not well integrated into the official monetary system, and the official domestically issued currency was far from homogenous and standardized. Only in the nineteenth century did each of these features begin to be overcome in ways that allowed territorial currencies to emerge. In the decades leading up to 1914, the construction of territorial currencies was largely completed within some Western European countries, the United States, and Japan. Not until the interwar period, however, did most other independent countries in Europe, Asia, and Americas finish building homogeneous and exclusive territorial currencies. And for a few countries in Latin America and the Middle East as well as all African and Asian countries that had been colonized for much of the twentieth century, territorial currencies were not built until the early years after World War II.

Challenges to territorial currencies, thus, undermine a monetary structure that has not been in existence for long. Indeed, a number of these challenges simply re-create monetary conditions that were considered normal in many parts of the world well into the twentieth century. If this provides one reason not to overstate the long historical significance of current monetary transformation, the second reason is that territorial currencies remained contested throughout the nineteenth and twentieth centuries. Indeed, each of the challenges to territorial currencies today has important precedents during the past two centuries.

Before World War I, two challenges to the territorial currencies were particularly prominent. First, many European countries that had consoli-

---

[3] See, for example, Ruggie (1993), Rosenau (1989), Strange (1995).

[4] Some scholars who refer to territorial currencies as "Westphalian" money, such as Cohen, make it clear that they are aware of the nineteenth-century origins of this monetary structure as well as of its contested status throughout the nineteenth and twentieth centuries. Cohen uses the term in a more symbolic manner. See especially Cohen (1998, 173 fn.12).

dated other aspects of their monetary system along territorial lines chose to participate in regional "monetary unions" that endorsed the co-circulation of each other's coins. There was even considerable political support in the late 1860s for a worldwide monetary union, although such a union did not ultimately materialize. "Free bankers," whose liberal views were very similar to those of contemporary advocates of privately issued corporate electronic currencies, also challenged territorial currencies in the pre-1914 period. Arguing that the use of multiple privately issued bank notes was more compatible with liberal economic values, they encouraged governments to reject a single homogenous national bank note within their territories. Their recommendations found support among many groups, including private banks that did not want to abandon their note issue and regionalist groups who opposed the growth of the central government's power. In countries where these groups were politically powerful or where the structure and experience of private banking seemed to bolster the case for free banking, a homogeneous national paper note was often rejected.

In the interwar period, political support for currency unions and free banking collapsed, but two other challenges to territorial currencies emerged prominently. Some countries that had already consolidated territorial currencies found their monetary sovereignty undermined during periods of high inflation by a sudden growth of foreign currency use (or "currency substitution"). Just as is the case in many poorer countries experiencing "dollarization" today, their citizens lost trust in the national currency in these circumstances and sought refuge in the use of a more stable foreign currency. During the early 1930s, many countries around the world also experienced a sudden proliferation of subnational local currencies quite similar to those that have emerged in the current era. Although the phenomenon was short-lived, it involved many more people than are involved in local currency schemes today.

Between the late nineteenth and mid twentieth centuries, a further challenge to the hegemony of territorial currencies came from the monetary practices of imperial powers in their colonies. Imperial powers made enormous efforts to replace precolonial heterogeneous currencies with more homogeneous ones, but these reforms cannot be described as "territorializing." This was not just because they created homogeneous currencies in regions that were parts of empires rather than independent states. It was also because they often created large "monetary unions" that joined different colonial administrative units together. After World War II, most newly independent countries threw off their colonial monetary structures and ended these monetary unions. But even at this moment, some countries rejected the territorial model and retained monetary unions that had been constructed in the colonial period.

Each of the types of challenges to territorial currencies today was, thus, experienced at various times during the nineteenth and twentieth centuries: monetary unions, currency substitution, "local currencies," and competing privately issued corporate currencies. Many of these specific challenges were in fact more severe in the past. There is, for example, no serious talk today of a world monetary union as there was in the 1860s. The existence of competing privately issued corporate currencies within countries remains only a pipe dream today rather than the reality it was in many countries before 1914. Many more people in the early 1930s used local currencies than use them today.

Am I suggesting, then, that today's developments represent nothing new at all? No. Because they involve the full replacement of national currencies with a supranational currency, the kinds of monetary unions being proposed and implemented today are more ambitious in some ways than their pre-1914 predecessors. Although contemporary local currencies involve fewer people, their advocates see them as a permanent challenge to territorial currencies rather than simply as a temporary emergency measure, as was generally the case in the early 1930s. The use of foreign currencies is also much more extensive and long lasting today than any such use in the interwar period. I do believe, however, that a historical perspective encourages us not to overstate the significance of current trends.[5]

What Explains the Geography of Money?
The history of territorial currencies also encourages us to examine the relationship between political space and currency space in a different way than most contemporary analysts do. Economists dominate current academic debates on the future of territorial currencies. The theory on which they most commonly draw is the "theory of optimum currency areas."[6] This theory develops a sophisticated method for policymakers to evaluate the economic implications of creating a currency union within a given region. While assuming a union will produce microeconomic benefits in the form of lower transaction costs for cross-border commerce, the theory focuses its analytical attention on the potential costs involved in the loss of macroeconomic flexibility for each country. The costs are taken to be obvious: abandoning a territorial currency will mean the inability to pursue an

---

[5] My argument is similar to that of other international relations scholars who have also recently reexamined the history of territoriality in other sectors to highlight its recent origins and contested nature. See especially Krasner (1993, 1999) and Thompson (1994).

[6] The pioneering work in this theoretical tradition came from Mundell (1961).

independent national monetary policy or to use the exchange rate as a tool of macroeconomic adjustment. To evaluate how significant these costs are in each regional context, the theory examines criteria such as the nature of external shocks, the extent of factor mobility and wage and price flexibility, and the openness, size, and diversification of economies. If these criteria suggest that the costs are low, the region is said to approximate more closely an "optimum currency area" (OCA) that should be encouraged to create a monetary union.

Despite the prominence of this theory in analyses of current monetary transformations, it has limitations as a tool for explaining monetary geography. In the European context, many scholars have noted that the decision to create a common currency had little to do with the kinds of calculations outlined in OCA theory. Instead, political considerations appear to be more significant.[7] The theory is also not very useful in explaining other challenges to territorial currencies today, such as dollarization, the growth of local currencies, and the new interest in free banking. At a more profound level, Charles Goodhart has observed that countries themselves are rarely optimum currency areas despite the fact that most of them have created territorial currencies over the past two centuries. He concludes, as have others, that OCA theory has "relatively little predictive power."[8]

These criticisms are in some ways unfair. The pioneer of the theory, Robert Mundell, made it clear in his initial writings that he did not intend the theory to be used to explain or predict monetary developments. He assumed that political considerations would play the central role in determining currency structures.[9] The theory was simply advanced to provide economic advice to policymakers in contexts where political conditions made monetary change possible. The theory, in other words, was intended to be more normative than explanatory. Despite this caveat, the link between normative prescription and empirical explanation often appears blurred in recent writing in this tradition, and the theory remains the most influential way of analyzing the geography of money in economics.

If we seek to *explain* the spatial organization of money, it would be useful to have an alternative way of thinking about the determinants of the geography of money.[10] I suggest that an examination of the reasons why

---

[7] See Cohen (1998, ch.4).

[8] Goodhart (1995, 452).

[9] Mundell (1961).

[10] My book builds on Cohen's (1998) pioneering analysis, which examined the geography of money in a more interdisciplinary manner. His book concentrates more on the implications of challenges to territorial currencies in the contemporary period, while my goal is to develop an explanation of the geography of money in the context of the history of territorial currencies.

territorial currencies were created historically can be useful in identifying some of the key determinants. I begin by showing that the construction of territorial currencies was linked partly to two deep structural changes, one political and the other technological. With respect to the former, I develop a point that has been noted briefly by some historians: the emergence of the nation-state in the nineteenth century acted as a key precondition for the creation of territorial currencies. Many of the activities associated with the construction of territorial currencies relied on the nation-state's unprecedented capability to influence and directly regulate the money in use within the territory it governed. This capability stemmed from such features as its policing powers, its more pervasive role in the domestic economy, its centralized authority, and its stronger ability to cultivate the "trust" of the domestic population.

Territorial currencies could not be created, furthermore, without a technological transformation that has received less scholarly attention: the application of new industrial technologies to the production of coins and notes in the nineteenth century. This development dramatically and rapidly improved the uniformity of the money in circulation by enabling the production of standardized currency in mass quantities. For the first time, public authorities also found it possible and affordable to produce large quantities of high-quality, low-denomination coins that were linked in a stable fashion to the rest of the official monetary system. Equally important, the high quality of the new industrially produced money made counterfeiting a much more difficult proposition, a development that in turn strengthened the ability of state authorities to maintain stable national "fiduciary" forms of money on a mass scale. This latter development was of enormous significance in enabling states to create and maintain territorial currencies.

If new industrial technologies and the rise of the nation-state enabled territorial currencies to be created, why did state policymakers actively choose to create such currencies in these new conditions? Policymakers had not previously pursued this project with the kind of seriousness and consistency that began to appear in the nineteenth and twentieth centuries. The decision to create territorial currencies emerged in this era out of concrete political projects, and the authors of these projects grasped that this new monetary structure could serve goals that were broader than those identified in OCA theory. We can identify four sets of motivations that reappeared in many different country and historical contexts. My argument is not that these four sets of motivations provide an exhaustive list of the motivations that drove policymakers to territorialize money, nor that they were present in each country and each reform. Instead, I argue simply that they encompass the most prominent reasons why territorial currencies were created in many different countries in the nineteenth and twentieth centuries.[11]

The first, and often most important, motivation was the goal of fostering the emergence of national markets by altering transaction costs. Although the theory of OCA argues that currency unions will have the beneficial effect of minimizing transaction costs, the link between monetary reforms and transaction costs has received almost no analytical attention among economists working in that theoretical tradition. They have assumed this benefit and focused their attention on the macroeconomic roles of money.[12] This issue was, however, very prominent politically throughout the nineteenth and twentieth centuries. Policymakers were frequently driven by the desire to eliminate domestic transaction costs encountered by merchants operating in newly emerging nationwide markets where no standardized and exclusive currency existed. The emergence of national markets was not just the kind of spatial phenomenon that OCA theorists have in mind. It was also a "vertical" one in which the poor began to become incorporated within the larger market economy for the first time. In this context, creators of territorial currencies hoped to eliminate the transaction costs associated with the use of low-denomination money that was both heterogeneous and had an uncertain link to the official monetary systems.

The task of creating national markets involved bolstering not just the internal economic coherence of a country but also the economy's external territoriality by making a clear distinction between the domestic and international economy. Following World War II, some policymakers created territorial currencies with this latter goal in mind. They hoped a new territorial currency would *increase* international transaction costs by creating an exchange rate risk between the national and international economy as well as by strengthening the ability of the state to enforce controls on

---

[11] Specialist readers will note that in his analysis of the reasons why states may prefer territorial currencies in the modern age, Cohen (1998) also highlights four motivations, but his list is slightly different from mine. He does not mention the concern for transaction costs, and he adds another motivation that I do not include: the fact that this monetary structure can insulate the state from external coercion. There were a few instances where this latter concern did play a role in prompting policymakers to create territorial currencies, such as the cases of Guinea and Mali in the early 1960s that I describe in chapter 9 (see also Kirshner 1995, ch.4). Because I have been unable to find many more cases, however, I have not included this concern among the most important motivations for creating territorial currencies. The desire to exercise control over foreign countries also acted as a motivation for creating currency unions, as I examine in the case of France within the LMU in the nineteenth century, and Kirshner (1995, 60–62) notes in the case of Japanese monetary reforms in occupied China after 1937.

[12] An important recent exception is Andrew Rose (2000).

cross-border flows of money. These goals, designed to foster a more distinct and autonomous national economy, point to a further limitation of OCA theory as an explanatory theory. It assumes that policymakers see expanding intercountry commerce as desirable, while in fact this goal was highly contested in this period. Interestingly, this motivation was much less prominent in the nineteenth century and the 1920s when policymakers were more inclined to see their efforts to construct national markets as going hand-in-hand with the goal of strengthening economic links with the outside world. Indeed some key territorializing monetary reforms in many poorer countries during the late nineteenth and early twentieth centuries were driven by a desire to facilitate commerce with wealthier regions by adopting more "modern" territorial currencies that resembled those already established in these prosperous regions.

The desire to control the domestic money supply for macroeconomic purposes was the second motivation that drove territorializing monetary reforms. On the surface, this would appear to be a motivation that OCA theory anticipates well. In fact, the kind of macroeconomic theorizing represented in OCA theory was absent from policymakers' minds for much of the historical period in which territorial currencies were created. In the nineteenth and early twentieth centuries, policymakers inspired by classical economic liberalism often created note monopolies because of their desire to manage their country's growing supply of paper money in keeping with the automatic market-based principles of the gold standard. In these instances, the motivation for this "territorializing" monetary reform was the opposite of that predicted by OCA theory; policymakers hoped a more consolidated national monetary structure would allow them to guarantee that discretionary management of the domestic money supply and exchange rate did *not* happen. Their conception of macroeconomic management, thus, was extremely limited and sought simply to manage the domestic money supply in a way that simulated the automatic macroeconomic adjustment mechanisms of the gold standard.

In some countries—particularly less economically powerful ones—during this same time period, a second group of liberal policymakers had slightly more ambitious and nationalist macroeconomic objectives. These "liberal nationalists," as I call them, were also committed to the gold standard, but they hoped a central bank with a note monopoly could protect the country to some degree from the automatic macroeconomic adjustments of this standard. Rather than adjust a national exchange rate as OCA theory envisages, they had in mind more limited policy tools for this purpose such as foreign exchange market intervention. They also hoped a central bank with a note monopoly might strengthen the state's ability to intervene in the domestic economy. Again, the goal was not the ambitious one imagined in OCA of pursuing an activist domestic monetary policy. Instead, the objective was to use central banks to perform tasks such as reducing the monetary influence of foreign-owned banks, allocating credit to domestic firms, and fostering the growth of a money-based economy and domestic financial markets.

Only in the wake of the Great Depression did the macroeconomic rationale for territorial currencies become the ambitious one that is analyzed in OCA theory. Where territorial currencies did not yet exist, policymakers now often created them, inspired by what I call an ideology of "macroeconomic activism." In some instances, territorial currencies were created to allow a country to use exchange rate adjustments as a macroeconomic policy tool. More often, policymakers built territorial currencies so that the national money supply could be managed more effectively in a discretionary fashion to promote domestic goals of national full employment and industrial growth. Even in this period, however, the "macroeconomic activist" rationale for territorial currencies was politically contested, and many policymakers rejected it for a variety of reasons.

The third set of motivations driving policymakers to create territorial currencies related to the fiscal needs of the state. This motivation is absent from OCA theory, but it has received attention in other scholarship within economics and other disciplines. Some scholars have argued that territorial currencies were created *primarily* to maximize seigniorage gains and help finance the expanding fiscal needs of the state, particularly in the context of the emergence of mass warfare.[13] Whereas OCA theory assumes the primary goal of policymakers will be to maximize national economic welfare, these scholars emphasize the importance of state-building objectives. My historical analysis confirms that this fiscal motivation did play a key role in prompting some monetary reforms that created territorial currencies in the nineteenth and twentieth centuries. But I argue that its importance is easily overstated. This is partly because of the role of the other motivations I highlight. But it is also because the focus on seigniorage neglects another important way in which fiscal concerns drove monetary reforms. Policymakers were often less concerned with maximizing seigniorage than with reducing transaction costs associated with the administration of complex, modern public fiscal systems that were created for the first time in the nineteenth and twentieth centuries. The desire to reduce domestic transaction costs, in other words, reflected not just the goal of fostering national markets but also the objective of enabling new nationwide taxation, public accounting, and spending systems to operate efficiently in this period.

[13] See references in chapter 4.

Finally, territorial currencies were also often constructed to strengthen national identities. Although economists sometimes acknowledge the importance of the link between territorial currencies and national identities, the issue rarely plays any significant role in their analysis of the geography of money. Interestingly, the relationship between territorial currencies and national identities has also received almost no attention from scholars of nationalism or within new literature on the sociocultural dimensions of money. This issue, however, motivated nationalist policymakers throughout the nineteenth and twentieth centuries. They saw the construction of territorial currencies as fostering national identities in several ways. At the level of iconography and naming, policymakers recognized that exclusive and standardized coins and notes might provide an effective vehicle for their project of constructing and bolstering a sense of collective tradition and memory. By reducing transaction costs within the nation, a territorial currency was also seen to facilitate "communication" among citizens. Because trust plays such a large role in the use and acceptance of modern forms of money, it was thought that territorial currencies might encourage identification with the nation-state at a deeper psychological level. And finally, territorial currencies were increasingly associated with national sovereignty both in a symbolic sense and because they could be used to serve the national community as tools for activist national macroeconomic management.

To sum up, territorial currencies were created historically not because policymakers made a rational and carefully considered judgment one day that their country had become an "optimum currency area." Indeed, this point should be obvious from the fact that most countries are not optimum currency areas. Instead, the construction of territorial currencies was a much more complicated affair. Many of the key determinants of the rise of territorial currencies receive no attention in the theory. These include the role of structural changes in the technology of money and state authority as well as the fact that policymakers saw the geography of money linked to broader political objectives of nation and state building. This history also highlights the fact that macroeconomic flexibility is not always as highly valued as the theory suggests and that the link between transaction costs and monetary reform is much more important and contested than most scholars working in the OCA tradition have acknowledged. Equally apparent is the limitation of OCA theory's assumption that changing monetary geography is best evaluated according to its impact on national aggregate economic welfare. The creation of territorial currencies was an intensely political affair that often became the subject of intense domestic and international struggles because of its distributional consequences and because of conflicting ideas about the various goals outlined above. An explanatory theory of monetary geography must acknowledge and analyze how this kind of political conflict shapes monetary policymaking in this area.[14]

Can History Help to Explain Challenges to Territorial Currencies Today?

This historical analysis should be directly useful for those interested in examining the causes of contemporary challenges to territorial currencies. Existing scholarship offers many explanations for each specific challenge to territorial currencies. What has been missing, however, is a more general analysis explaining why territorial currencies are being challenged in so many different ways today. The history of territorial currencies suggests that such an analysis should not use OCA theory as its starting point. Instead, it highlights that the changing spatial organization of money may be determined by transformations in technological and state structures as well as by political projects in which money is seen to serve more than just the functions addressed by OCA theorists. Building from this premise, I give particular attention to whether territorial currencies are being challenged today by similar causes to those that prompted their contestation at various points over the past two centuries.

I show how some challenges to territorial currencies are being encouraged by a structural transformation in the technology of money that is unique to our era: the emergence of new forms of "electronic money." Transformations in state structures are also playing a role in encouraging monetary transformations, although they are less novel to our age. Currency unions, for example, are being fostered by intensifying patterns of interstate cooperation, just as has been true in the past. Many poorer countries are also experiencing growing currency substitution for the same reason some countries did in the interwar period: the state's ability to influence and directly regulate the money in use within its territory has eroded in contexts of economic and political instability. What is somewhat new, however, in the current era is the extent of this erosion. Whereas states in the interwar period were able to reverse foreign currency use by restoring their authority, the more pervasive weakening of the power of nation-states in many poorer countries today has caused them to experience much longer-lasting currency substitution than was true in that earlier period. In these contexts, as Cohen has pointed out, the geography of money becomes increasingly determined by market forces rather than the choices of state officials.[15]

---

[14] For this point more generally, see Kirshner (2000).
[15] Cohen (1998).

In addition to these structural developments, I argue that challenges to territorial currencies today also reflect some disillusionment with the various motivations that drove policymakers to create territorial currencies in the first place. Whereas territorial currencies were viewed as a tool to help construct national markets, today they are often seen as interfering with political projects aimed at furthering international economic integration. This perspective is not entirely new: it also encouraged currency unions to be created in various contexts during the nineteenth and twentieth centuries. But a more prominent goal today is the desire to eliminate exchange rate instability in the current environment of very high capital mobility. There are two other unique developments in the current era that relate to this motivation. One is the interest in free banking as a means to reduce transaction costs in one of the most rapidly growing sectors of the global economy: e-commerce. The other is the fact that supporters of local currencies, instead of embracing the project of international economic integration, are deeply opposed to it. As I show, local currencies are designed deliberately to increase transaction costs in order to defend economic localism in the face of globalization pressures, a goal that was not shared by creators of local currencies in the interwar period.

Disillusionment with the kind of national "macroeconomic activism" that had become prominent after the 1930s has also prompted many policymakers to support alternatives to territorial currencies. This disillusionment has stemmed partly from the resurgence of economic liberal ideology in macroeconomic affairs over the past two decades. We have seen how in the pre-1931 period economic liberals distrusted the ability of national governments to pursue discretionary national monetary management. In that era, however, only free bankers extended this distrust to a desire to reject territorial currencies altogether. In light of the experiences with national macroeconomic activism since the 1930s, more liberals today—though not all by any means—are inclined to adopt this stance and endorse either free banking, currency unions, or currency substitution as tools that can help to discipline national governments.[16]

Others have become disillusioned with national macroeconomic activism for different reasons. The growing power of global financial markets has led many to conclude that national macroeconomic activism, while perhaps still theoretically desirable, is no longer practical. This stance has encouraged some policymakers to be less resistant to the idea

---

[16] Interestingly, many of these liberals have called attention to the ideological assumption embedded in OCA theory that macroeconomic flexibility is a good thing and argue that the macroeconomic costs involved in abandoning a territorial currency are much less than those predicted by the theory (Tavlas 1993).

of abandoning territorial currencies in favor of monetary unions or dollar-ization. Many supporters of local currencies also view these forms of money as tools to address macroeconomic goals that they believe national governments are no longer capable of serving. In this respect, contempo-rary local currency advocates are similar to their counterparts in the 1930s, who were responding to the fact that national governments were doing little to help them in the desperate economic conditions of the Great Depression.

In the past, challenges to territorial currencies also reflected some fiscal goals. Some nineteenth-century economic liberals saw free banking as a way to ensure that states did not abuse the national monetary system for their own fiscal purposes. With the revival of liberal economic ideology today, it is not surprising to see this motivation reemerge as rationale to support not just free banking but also currency unions and dollarization. This motivation is not a very prominent one, though, because the relative significance of territorial currencies for public revenue has diminished since the nineteenth century. In the past, another fiscal rationale for reject-ing territorial currencies was put forward by colonial policymakers: they favored large colonial monetary unions as a means of reducing intra-em-pire fiscal transaction costs for the public sector. Today, there are few par-allels to this rationale, with the partial exception of the concern of Euro-pean policymakers about the impact of European exchange rate instability on the operations of EU-wide fiscal arrangements, most notably the Com-mon Agricultural Policy.

Finally, are alternatives to territorial currencies being supported as a means of fostering new forms of political identities? In the past, they sometimes were. Some policymakers saw the introduction of colonial cur-rencies as a tool to transform the identities of colonized peoples in ways that served imperial goals. Many nineteenth-century liberal advocates of currency unions also hoped that this monetary system would allow na-tionalist identities to be replaced by more cosmopolitan sentiments. The latter motivation is certainly present in Europe where the euro is often supported as a tool to foster closer European political union. In a different way, the "greens" who promote local currencies also hope their monetary reform will undermine national identities, although this time by fostering localist allegiances. In other contexts, however, advocates of monetary re-form are going out of their way to argue that national identities will not be threatened by the abandonment of territorial currencies. This phenome-non, I suggest, may in fact mark an interesting political initiative to ques-tion the historical link between national identities and territorial curren-cies that has existed since the nineteenth century.

In sum, I argue that the history of territorial currencies provides some useful insights for those trying to explain the widespread challenges to territorial currencies today. It does not, of course, help us to develop a comprehensive explanation of each challenge; but it does identify some key factors that have influenced the determinants of monetary geography in the past and continue to do so today. More specifically, this history suggests that some of the causes of challenges to territorial currencies in the past remain important today. At the same time, it reveals other causes of challenges to territorial currencies today that have few parallels in the past and illuminates the unique nature of some dimensions of contemporary monetary transformations.

Conclusion

This book is divided into two major sections. Part 1 explores the birth of territorial currencies in the nineteenth and early twentieth centuries. The exact nature of transformations that first produced territorial currencies in that era is described in chapter 1. The importance of the two preconditions for the birth of territorial currency, the presence of nation-states and industrial technology, are outlined in chapter 2. In chapters 3–5, the four principal motivations that drove policymakers to create territorial currencies in the nineteenth and early twentieth centuries are explained: the desire to construct national markets (chapter 3), the various macroeconomic and fiscal goals (chapter 4), and the objective of strengthening national identities (chapter 5).

The spread of territorial currencies in the twentieth century to most regions of the world and the contested nature of territorial currencies throughout the nineteenth and twentieth centuries are examined in part 2 of this book. Chapter 6 analyzes the two most prominent principled challenges to territorial currencies before World War I: the free banking movement and supporters of monetary unions. Chapter 7 explores the spread of territorial currencies in the interwar period as well as the challenges presented to them by the growth of foreign currency use and local currencies in some countries. In chapter 8, the monetary practices of colonial powers are studied. This is followed by an analysis in chapter 9 of the last wave of territorializing monetary reforms: those that took place in many Southern countries during the years after World War II. The concluding chapter of the book draws on this history to examine the causes of challenges to territorial currencies in the current age.

One final caution for the reader is necessary before launching into the book. This book examines the history of territorial currencies in countries across the world over the last two centuries. It cannot, however, pretend to provide a comprehensive history of the monetary experiences of every country over the time period. I inevitably give greater emphasis to the history of some countries over others. In some cases, these choices are well justified by the relative significance of each country's monetary history to the point being made. In others, however, it has simply reflected my knowledge or ability to access country-specific research sources. In the latter cases, I hope this book helps prompt future researchers to address holes I have not been able to fill and to demonstrate how their research supports or challenges my arguments.

Part 1

The Birth of Territorial Currencies in the Nineteenth Century

1

The Initial Transformation
From Monetary Heterogeneity to Territorial Currencies

How was money organized before the emergence of territorial currencies? When and how were territorial currencies first created? These questions have not been well addressed in existing literature. Even international relations scholars, who recently have shown growing interest in
the historical origins of territoriality, have neglected them. This neglect is
unfortunate because the monetary case calls into question a conventional
view about the origins of territoriality. Territoriality is often presented as
having had its roots in seventeenth-century Europe, around the time of
the birth of the sovereign state at the 1648 Peace of Westphalia. But it was
not until the nineteenth century that territorial currencies were first created. Before then, currency systems throughout the world departed from
the territorial model in three ways: foreign currencies often circulated
alongside domestic currencies, low denomination forms of money were
not well integrated into the official monetary system, and official domestically issued currency itself was far from homogeneous. Territorial currencies emerged only when public authorities began deliberately to
transform each of these three features of monetary system in the nineteenth century.

Money before Territorial Currencies

Is there really no sign of the origins of territorial currencies to be found in
seventeenth-century Europe, as conventional international relations
scholars would predict? It is true that important European theorists of
state sovereignty in the early modern era such as Jean Bodin did argue
that sovereigns must become the sole issuers of currency within the territories they each governed.[1] But the novelty and importance of Bodin's
views should not be overstated. In other parts of the world before the sev-

---

[1] Bodin (1992, 59, 78–79).

enteenth century, the exclusive authority to issue currency within a given territory was often seen as a sovereign privilege.[2] More important, Bodin's advice did not lead any European ruler—or any ruler elsewhere—actually to create a territorial currency in the seventeenth century. Not until the nineteenth century was Bodin's vision realized.

Before explaining how pre-nineteenth-century monetary systems departed from the territorial model, it is important to clarify the meaning of "money"—a term that I use interchangeably with "currency" in this book. Money is a notoriously difficult term to define precisely. Economists usually define money according to the functions it performs. Three are cited most frequently: a medium of exchange, a store of value, and a unit of account. Scholars from other disciplines have found this approach limiting. While modern money usually performs all three of these roles, historical forms of money have sometimes assumed only one or two of these functions. Money's functions are also often not just economic but also political (e.g., an instrument of power), social (e.g., facilitating various social relationships), and cultural (e.g., transmitting or reflecting cultural values).[3]

Rather than define money solely according to what it does, a second approach also defines money according to what it is, and has been, in concrete historical settings. This is what the historian Richard von Glahn calls a "typological" definition alongside the more "functional" one used by economists.[4] Following the French monetary historian Pierre Vilar, we can identify three important types of money that have been used in human societies historically.[5] The most common has been "commodity money," which refers to an object whose monetary value is similar to the value of the material from which it is made. Various commodities have been used as money in this way, particularly those that are portable, indestructible, homogeneous, and divisible such as cowry shells or precious metals, especially silver and gold. Before the nineteenth century, commodity monies were key elements in the monetary systems of most societies around the world. Indeed, as we shall see, their diminishing role was closely connected with the emergence of territorial currencies.

A second type of money is "nominal money," which refers to an abstract "money of account" and indicates a value that has no correspondence to a physical currency in circulation. This type of money performs only one of three economic functions cited above: a unit of account. Its use

[2] See China (von Glahn 1996, 1, 23–33) or Mughal India (Thakur 1972, 139–40; Mitra 1991, 19).

[3] Gilbert and Helleiner, eds. (1999).

[4] Von Glahn (1996, 15–23).

[5] Vilar (1984 [1969], 20–21).

has often become extensive in contexts where the value of other forms of money is changing rapidly and unpredictably, or where other forms of money are not homogeneous and standardized. Many monetary systems before the nineteenth century fit these criteria and thus nominal monies played a much more pervasive role in monetary systems in the past than they have during the last two centuries.

The third key type of money is "fiduciary money," which is money accepted to have a certain value unrelated to the value of the material from which it is made. It is sometimes said to be a modern invention, but fiduciary money was also common throughout much of human history in the form of various kinds of paper notes, "book money," and low-denomination coins made out of base metals such as copper or brass. During the nineteenth and twentieth centuries, the use of fiduciary money did dramatically expand in all countries as coins assumed this nature, and as paper notes and various forms of "book money" (especially bank deposits) took a central place in monetary systems. Today, fiduciary forms of money have come to dominate monetary systems around the world.

The Widespread Use of Foreign Currencies
These typological distinctions are useful in explaining how monetary systems around the world before the nineteenth century were organized. These monetary systems differed from territorial currencies in three principal ways. First, foreign currencies were commonly used alongside domestically issued currencies. In Europe, Fernand Braudel notes how "a mixture of foreign and domestic currencies was the rule" before the nineteenth century, despite the fact that Bodin had disapproved of the practice.[6] In many instances, this practice was even endorsed by European states, which set a rate at which foreign coins should be accepted vis-à-vis domestic coins. The European experience was quite typical of other regions during this period. In the United States, foreign silver coins—primarily Mexican and Spanish currency—formed the bulk of the domestic coinage up until the 1850s.[7] An enormous variety of foreign coins also played a key role in Canada's monetary system until 1870.[8] Across Latin America, foreign coins also were used widely well into the nineteenth century.[9] In East Asia, foreign coins circulated widely alongside domestically issued money into the nineteenth century, even within relatively

---

[6] Braudel (1990, 601). See also Cipolla (1956, 14). For Bodin's disapproval, see Monroe (1923, 64).

[7] Carothers (1930, ch.11).

[8] Helleiner (1999a).

[9] Hamilton (1944).

closed economies such as Tokugawa Japan.[10] Foreign currency was also in common use across the Middle East and the Ottoman Empire where their rating by local authorities even varied from place to place.[11]

Although their use was common across the world before the nineteenth century, foreign currencies were not accepted for widespread circulation by all states within the territories they governed. An important case was the Mughal Empire between the mid sixteenth and early eighteenth centuries in India. Like Bodin, the Mughal emperors saw the issuing of coin as their sovereign prerogative, and they made great efforts to keep foreign currencies from circulating within the regions they governed. Historians argue that they were in fact fairly successful in forcing merchants and foreigners to convert foreign coins into imperial coins at the borders of the empire, even placing mints in every frontier town for this purpose.[12] But this determined effort and the relative success of this highly centralized and absolutist empire was exceptional before the nineteenth century.

One of the key reasons foreign currency circulated so widely in domestic monetary systems before the nineteenth century was the pervasive nature of "commodity money." Because its face value derived simply from its commodity value, this kind of money was inherently quite cosmopolitan. The stable coins of leading economic powers in particular often circulated very widely. In the early modern period, the most famous of these was the Spanish "dollar." Produced primarily at Spain's colonial mints in Mexico and Peru, this coin circulated widely in monetary systems throughout the Americas and Asia in the seventeenth, eighteenth, and well into the nineteenth centuries.[13] "Commodity monies" other than coins also circulated in cosmopolitan ways before the nineteenth century. Uncoined gold, silver, and copper were forms of money that circulated across the world. Equally important were cowries. Issued—or more accurately "harvested"—exclusively in the Maldive Islands before the mid nineteenth century, cowries were transported around the world, often as ballast in ships, and used as currency in many parts of the world before the nineteenth century (including in the Mughal Empire, as noted below).

Although commodity monies were the most common form of "cosmopolitan" currency, some other types of money were also used widely beyond their home countries before the nineteenth century. Between the eleventh and fifteenth centuries, the Chinese state was the first to use issue

---

[10] Shinjo (1962, 10, 15).
[11] Himadeh (1953, 25–27), Issawi (1982), Frangakis-Syrett (1997, 265).
[12] For an overview of the Mughal monetary system, see Richards (1987).
[13] Andrew (1904). The international role of the Maria Theresa thaler also presents an interesting case. See Tschoegl (2000).

paper notes on a large scale and these notes circulated widely as a medium for international trade throughout the Indian Ocean as well as East and Central Asia.[14] Some "bank monies" created in leading European commercial cities, especially Amsterdam, in the early modern era also were used widely beyond their country of origin. Amsterdam's bank money was issued by a public bank as a way of coping with the presence of so many different foreign coins that were attracted to the city in its trading heyday. The Bank of Amsterdam accepted large deposits from merchants in any coin, which were credited to their account in a unit of "bank money" that was equivalent to that coin's value in unminted metal. Large-scale trade in the city was then largely conducted via credits and debits to merchants' accounts at the bank that were denominated in this bank money. Because of their stability and wide use, Einaudi notes that this bank money—and that of other public banks in cites such as Genoa and Venice—was then often used as currency "in traffic all over Europe."[15]

Distinctive Low-Denomination Money: "Tiered Monetary Systems"
Pre-nineteenth-century monetary systems also diverged from the territorial model because low-denomination money was linked in only a loose and uncertain way to the official currency. Low-denomination monetary instruments in many parts of the world consisted of "fiduciary" coins made of copper, bronze, or other base metals. These coins were often issued by local merchants or towns and were not easily convertible into officially sanctioned higher-denomination metallic coins both because of their uncertain value and because their circulation was often limited to small geographical areas. Before the nineteenth century, states made few concerted efforts to ban these "local currencies" and initiatives to replace them with government-issued petty coin were only partial. Moreover, when petty coins were issued by state authorities, they were usually poorly made and their value had no clear relationship to silver and gold coins. The authorities who produced these petty coins rarely tried to control their supply and, as noted in chapter 3, they often did not even consider them to represent "real" money.

These features of low-denomination coins were very common in Europe before the nineteenth century. They have been particularly well documented in the case of England where low-denomination private token coins made of copper, tin, and lead had been issued by merchants and towns since the thirteenth century. By the early 1600s, approximately

---

[14] Von Glahn (1996, ch.1). Tsuen-Hsuin (1954, 99) writes that Chinese paper notes even circulated as far as Persia by 1294.
[15] Einaudi (1953, 252).

three thousand London businesses issued unauthorized farthing token coins, which often circulated no farther than several city blocks. State authorities made occasional, half-hearted efforts in the seventeenth and early eighteenth centuries to produce low-denomination copper coins for the first time, but they did not consider these coins to be real money and widespread counterfeiting of the coins was hardly ever prosecuted during the eighteenth century. The production of privately issued tokens in England then grew so rapidly in the final decades of the eighteenth century that the Royal Mint reported in 1787 that only 8 percent of the copper coins in circulation resembled the king's coin. Production of private tokens by towns and merchants extended even to include small-denomination silver money during the Napoleonic wars when Britain's inconvertible currency produced an enormous shortage of official silver coins.[16]

Unofficial privately issued, low-denomination forms of money made of copper, lead, wood, leather, and even soap were also widespread in the Americas during the colonial period and early independence years. In colonial Mexico, for example, one report in 1766 notes that at least two thousand shopkeepers in Mexico City were issuing their own tokens made of base metals. The "tlacos" circulated widely in the city, but were not always acceptable with other merchants. During the nineteenth century, the Mexican state made periodic efforts to produce low-denomination copper coins, but more widely used were tokens issued by merchants, hacienda owners, mining companies, and even some municipalities.[17] Elsewhere in Latin America, the United States, and Canada, frequent shortages of official low-denomination coins also encouraged cities and merchants to issue private tokens well into the nineteenth century (see figure 1).[18]

Even in the sophisticated monetary order of Mughal India, low-denomination money was not well integrated with the rest of the official currency. In contrast to European authorities at the time, the Mughal emperors did in fact produce an enormous number of copper coins. But unlike the silver and gold coins they produced, the value of these copper coins was not uniform across the empire. It varied according to the cost of transportation from copper mines in the north, and the coins' value also was not fixed vis-à-vis silver and gold coins. Moreover, many low-denomination transactions in Mughal India were conducted in other commodities, such as almonds and especially cowries. Their value was also quite vari-

[16] Craig (1953, 140, 253), Peck (1970, 214), Doty (1987a).

[17] Pradeau (1958), Hamilton (1944, 36–38).

[18] Carothers (1930, 95), Helleiner (1999a), Romano (1984, 127–28), Hamilton (1944), Subercaseaux (1922, 51, 57).

Figure 1. South American token issued as currency by a private hacienda.
Photograph courtesy of The British Museum. © The British Museum.

able (it was usually higher in regions far from the coast), and their ex-change rate vis-à-vis higher-denomination money was not standardized within the empire.[19]

Cowries were widely used for low-denomination money not just in the Mughal Empire but in many other regions around the world before the nineteenth century such as China, Southeast Asia, Africa, the Pacific Islands, and part of the Americas (see figure 2). Hogendorn and Johnson

[19] Mitra (1991, 87), Habib (1961).

Figure 2. Cowry shells. Photograph courtesy of The British Museum.
© The British Museum.

point out that cowries were in fact one of the best commodities to be used for low-denomination transactions in the preindustrial age. Their value was much lower than any metallic coin, allowing them to serve important monetary needs in preindustrial contexts where incomes were very low. Cowries were also much more durable than preindustrial, low-denomination metallic coins; they were very hard to break and showed few signs of wear over decades of use. Equally important, the shells were much more difficult to counterfeit than coins, and their size and quality was uniform. Despite all these benefits of cowries, societies that used them experienced the same difficulties that the Mughal Empire had. The value of cowries usually fluctuated from place to place, according to transportation costs and local custom. Their value was also often difficult to link in a stable manner to that of official higher-denomination money.[20]

Monetary systems around the world before the nineteenth century thus were characterized by the lack of stable connection between the value of low-denomination money and that of high-denomination money. With a fluctuating or unclear exchange rate between these two types of money, a tiered monetary order was created rather than a coherent territorial one. Indeed, a number of monetary historians have highlighted how

[20] Hogendorn and Johnson (1986, 114–24). See also Polanyi (1966, 177, 187).

this tiered monetary order corresponded with the different spheres of economic life that the poor and rich primarily inhabited in the preindustrial era. In the European context, Cipolla notes how "in a stratified society different classes use different types of money."[21] Similarly, Habib notes how low-denomination money such as copper coin in the Mughal Empire was "the currency of the masses" that served popular needs in localized economic contexts, while higher-denomination gold and silver coins were used primarily by the wealthy and served the needs of large enterprises and long-distance trade.[22]

Heterogeneous Official Domestically Issued Currency
Domestic monetary systems differed from the territorial model before the nineteenth century in a third way: even the officially sanctioned domestically issued money of each country was not standardized. In regions of the world where state authority was very weak, the distinction between official and unofficial forms of money was hard to draw. In many parts of precolonial Africa, for example, Hogendorn notes how monetary systems were dominated by "informal" currencies put into circulation by private producers and merchants, as opposed to "formal" currencies issued or sanctioned by states.[23] These included cowries as well as commodities such as the copper rods ("manillas") that were used widely in West Africa. Their value varied from region to region and changed according to trade conditions and the availability of imports of the commodity.

In other regions where states took a larger role in declaring what money was officially sanctioned, official domestically issued money was rarely homogeneous. To begin with, domestically issued silver or gold coins in circulation were rarely of uniform quality. There were exceptions: the consistency of the purity and standard of the Mughal Empire's coins was very high. But in most countries, this was not the case. Not only were old and worn coins left in circulation without being regularly withdrawn, but the product of official mints within the country also varied considerably from mint to mint, from year to year, and even within a single coining session. In addition, it was not uncommon for the value of the same official coins to vary considerably region to region, or even from town to town, as in nineteenth-century Iran and the Ottoman Empire.[24]

In many regions of the world, multiple official coinage standards and

[21] Cipolla (1956, 56).
[22] Habib (1961, 10). See also Romano (1984, 12), Deyell (1987, 24), Guyer (1995), von Glahn (1996, 8).
[23] Hogendorn (1996, 111).
[24] For Iran, see Jones (1986, 44), Minai (1961, 164). For Ottoman Empire, see Frangakis-Syrett (1997, 265), Himadeh (1953).

systems also persisted within each country. This was particularly true of regions where central state authority was weak. In Tokugawa Japan, the central government's coinage circulated alongside coins issued by various lords according to various different standards. Indeed, at the time of the Meiji Restoration in 1868, the coinage had become quite chaotic, with approximately sixty different kinds of coins in circulation (including foreign coins).[25] In medieval Europe, many local lords and even religious leaders had also issued coins according to various standards. As European states acquired more centralized power in the early modern era, these coining rights were gradually withdrawn, although this process often took a long time. In the tiny German duchy of Oldenberg, for example, four independent coinage systems coexisted as late as 1810.[26] Even in the centralized Mughal monetary order, distinct coinages often persisted in parts of the empire.[27]

The Chinese monetary system presented a particularly dramatic example of multiple monetary standards and systems. When the central state lost its ability to maintain a uniform monetary standard and currency during the Ming (1368–1643) and Qing (1644–1911) dynasties, various kinds of privately issued coin, circulating at different rates, began to appear across the empire. Rounded silver bars ("sycees") increasingly became a dominant medium of exchange (see figure 3). Produced by private mints, their size and weight varied enormously across the country, between distinct commercial centers, and even within each center. Beginning in the late nineteenth century, governments at various levels—central, provincial, and local—also started to issue coins (and sometimes notes) in an unstandardized way. The result was a very heterogeneous monetary order—what Perlin refers to as "multimedia payments order"— that lasted up until the 1930s.[28]

In countries where paper money was used, it often contributed to the lack of uniformity in official monetary systems. Across Europe, many institutions—including different levels of government and a multitude of private banks—began to issue paper notes in the eighteenth and nineteenth centuries, and the denominations and appearance of these different forms of paper money often varied considerably. So too did their "quality" and thus the degree of their acceptance across the economic space of each country. Unstandardized paper money also became increasingly

---

[25] Spalding (1918), Shinjo (1962).

[26] Heckscher (1955, 123). For medieval Europe, see Spufford (1988).

[27] Habib (1961).

[28] Perlin (1994, 181). See also Perlin (1994a, 135–46), von Glahn (1996), Hao (1986, 34–71), Pomeranz (1993), Kahn (1926), Rawski (1989, 121–71).

Figure 3. Chinese sycees used widely as a medium of exchange in that country until well into the twentieth century. Photograph courtesy of The British Museum. © The British Museum.

common in Tokugawa Japan. By the end of the Tokugawa era, there were in fact as many as 1,694 different kinds of paper notes in circulation issued by various local lords.[29] An even more dramatic example of a heterogeneous paper note circulation existed in the United States during the first half of the nineteenth century. Just before the Civil War, as many as ten thousand different types of paper notes circulated in that country and merchants were forced to consult frequent newsletters that detailed the exchange rates between them.[30]

[29] Takaki (1903, 31), Maruyama (1999).
[30] Davis (1910).

Compounding the lack of uniformity in the quality of coins and notes was the large-scale counterfeiting of both forms of money before the nineteenth century. No country was insulated from this problem, even those with relatively powerful centralized states such as Britain where notes and coins were widely forged until the early nineteenth century.[31] Counterfeiting was particularly widespread where the monetary system was already very heterogeneous. At the start of the Civil War, as many as 50 percent of U.S. bank notes in circulation are estimated to have been counterfeit.[32] As explained in the next chapter, this problem was not addressed effectively until the new industrial manufacturing techniques were applied to the production of coins and notes in the nineteenth century.

One further important way in which the homogeneity of official domestic monetary systems was undermined was the absence of a stable relationship between the value of the various kind of currencies in use. In regions where paper money was widely used, its value vis-à-vis coins was not always stable. As the first country to use paper money widely, China was the first to experience this difficulty because the convertibility of its notes into metallic coin was often suspended. The result of these suspensions was the same as that which occurred later in other countries; an inconvertible currency usually prompted a sudden disappearance of high-quality coins from domestic circulation, as "bad money" drove out "good" in keeping with Gresham's Law.[33] Before the nineteenth century, the more pressing difficulty in most parts of the world was coping with the fluctuating relationship between official silver and gold coins. Under coinage systems made up of these "commodity monies," fluctuations in the market value of gold and silver or changes in the official value of gold or silver coins would often cause enormous disruption to the domestic monetary system. These fluctuations not only disrupted domestic accounting practices, they also frequently caused the sudden disappearance of one or the other coin from domestic circulation when the market prices strayed too far from the official mint price.

To cope with the lack of uniformity in domestic monetary systems (made worse by the presence of foreign currencies and various low-denomination monies), many states introduced abstract units of account

---

[31] Mackenzie (1953, 13, 48–58), Craig (1953, 253–54).

[32] Johnson (1995).

[33] von Glahn (1996). During one brief period from 1260 until the late 1270s, stable paper notes were used very extensively as the only legal means of exchange; the use of all coins was banned in trade, and paper notes were issued for very low denominations. By the late 1270s, however, confidence in the notes had collapsed.

with which people could value the various forms of money in circulation. These "nominal monies"—sometimes called "ghost" monies or "imaginary" monies—were designed to simplify economic transactions by providing a single accounting unit within each country's territory. But some felt that they only further contributed to the monetary heterogeneity by creating yet another monetary instrument that had to be used.[34] Moreover, in some European countries, two nominal monies coexisted, one based on a higher-denomination coin and the other based on a lower-denomination coin.[35] In the Ottoman Empire throughout the nineteenth century, different unofficial nominal monies were also used in different regions, cities, and even within the same city.[36] The same was true of China up until the 1930s.[37]

How Territorial Currencies Were Constructed

Only in the nineteenth century did territorially uniform and exclusive national currencies begin to emerge for the first time in world history. The construction of territorial currencies was accomplished only when state authorities addressed each of the three heterogeneous features of pre-nineteenth-century monetary systems just outlined. There was, in other words, nothing particularly "natural" about this monetary transformation. Instead, as Viviana Zelizer notes, it resulted from the "painstaking and deliberate activities of public authorities."[38] Territorial currencies were created at quite different speeds in different countries, and it was a gradual process in most countries, spread out over a number of decades. By 1914, some Western European countries, the United States, and Japan had largely completed the process. A number of other countries in Europe, Latin America, and the British Dominions (as well as colonized regions of Africa and Asia that will not be discussed until chapter 6) undertook many key reforms in this period, but they would not create a fully fledged territorial currency until the interwar years or later (as is described in chapters 7 and 9).

[34] This was, for example, the view of policymakers at the time of the French Revolution who abolished nominal monies in the country (Einaudi 1953).

[35] For example, Sweden in the seventeenth century (Heckscher and Rasmusson 1964, 34) or Denmark in the eighteenth century (Hansen 1983, 368) or Italian states in earlier centuries (Helfferich 1969 [1927], 41–42; Cipolla 1956, 49).

[36] Himadeh (1953, 24–25).

[37] Perlin (1994a, 135–46).

[38] Zelizer (1994, 205). When territorial currencies were created, Zelizer highlights that the homogeneous nature of the new national monetary system should not be overstated since money continued to be differentiated at the micro level through practices such as the earmarking of currency.

Standardizing Official Domestically issued Currency
Let me begin with the ways in which governments addressed the heterogeneity of official domestically issued currency. One of the most important activities of state authorities in this respect was to produce high-quality, uniform, and difficult-to-counterfeit coins and notes in mass quantities
for the first time. As is described in the next chapter, this was made possible only because of the application of new industrial equipment to the
production of coins and notes. In the next chapter, I also examine how
state officials reinforced the effects of this technological revolution by
launching much more concerted efforts to stamp out all counterfeit
money. The poor quality of coins and notes in circulation was also addressed by new initiatives to remove old, worn money on a regularized
basis.[39]

A second important activity involved the elimination of subnational
monetary standards and coinages in countries where they existed. Some
of the most dramatic reforms in this respect came in the second half of the
nineteenth century in countries where political changes created new centralized states. In Japan, for example, the leaders of the Meiji Restoration
in 1868 made the creation of a single monetary standard and coinage one
of their top economic priorities after assuming power. In Latin America,
Marichal shows that unified monetary standards often emerged in the
1880s and 1890s when states in that region had finally begun to consolidate power in a more centralized and cohesive way.[40] Similar homogeniz-
ing monetary reforms took place in the various new countries that
emerged out of political unification initiatives in this period. The new federal government created in Switzerland in 1848, for example, moved
within two years to substitute a new uniform monetary standard and coin
for various currencies of the cantons.[41] Shortly after political unification of
Italy, the new central government replaced the diverse coinages and standards of the various regions of Italy with a single uniform one. After creating their new country in 1867, Canadian politicians moved quickly to
abolish the distinct monetary standard that the province of Nova Scotia
had previously used.[42] In Germany, too, political unification in 1871 was
followed quickly by the consolidation of a single monetary standard and
coinage.[43]

A third key activity was the creation of large-scale, state-managed "fi-

[39] The British government, for example, began to remove old and worn coins in a regularized manner in the mid-1800s (Craig 1953, 311).
[40] Marichal (1997).
[41] Weber (1992).
[42] For Canada and Italy, see references in chapter 3.
[43] See James (1997).

duciary" coinages. As I have noted, fiduciary coins had existed before in history; low-denomination coins, in particular, usually had a value above their commodity value. But this value had rarely been stable because their supply had not been closely managed by the state and their convertibility into other forms of official money had not been guaranteed. In the nineteenth century, many countries transformed official higher-denomination coins into well-managed fiduciary coins whose official monetary value was guaranteed at a stable rate well above their metallic value. By 1914, these fiduciary coins dominated the coinage in many countries, and the old "full weight" gold and silver coins that had been so prominent had often disappeared entirely from circulation.[44]

This transformation in coinage was extremely important in reducing domestic monetary heterogeneity in every country where it took place. This was partly because the value of all coins now existed in a fixed relationship to each other over time. This change, in turn, reduced the need for abstract nominal monies, a development that was frequently encouraged by public authorities who adopted units of account that corresponded directly to real coins in circulation.[45] The supply of official coins in circulation was also now stabilized because there was much less risk that a large portion of the coinage would disappear when the market value of gold and silver altered.[46] Finally, states now had a strong incentive to eliminate unofficial money from domestic circulation because the management of a stable fiduciary coinage required the state to control the domestic coin supply more closely.

Britain pioneered the creation of a large-scale fiduciary coinage system when it adopted the gold standard in 1816, and it was the first country to experience these effects. To ensure that silver coins maintained a fixed value with respect to the new gold standard, the British government produced new fiduciary silver coins, and it assumed the role of stabilizing their value by controlling their supply and guaranteeing their convertibility into gold.[47] Britain's pioneering effort in creating a state-managed modern fiduciary coinage system was soon followed by other countries, with the same results in their domestic monetary systems. Marc Flan-

---

[44] For a good discussion of the creation of modern fiduciary coinages, see Cipolla (1956, ch.3). Some countries that had this modern coinage system still retained large numbers of "full weight" gold coins in circulation. See footnote 71.

[45] For the British case, see Craig (1953, 285).

[46] The risk of a disappearance of the coinage was not eliminated altogether, however, especially in places where the value of silver coins had not been diminished very much lower than their intrinsic value. When countries experienced a dramatic depreciation of their paper money, there could also still be a massive disappearance of coins, as noted later.

[47] See Redish (1990).

dreau correctly notes that countries did not need to adopt the gold standard in order to create a modern state-managed fiduciary silver coinage, as Britain had.[48] In practice, however, the adoption of the gold standard—or often a gold-exchange standard—was usually the moment when this kind of coinage was introduced for the first time. This was true for the United States (which created a fiduciary silver coinage in 1853) as well as many European countries such as Portugal (1854), Switzerland (1860), Italy (1862), France (1864), Belgium (1865), Germany (1873), and Austria-Hungary (1892).[49] Almost all Latin American and Asian countries lacked state-managed fiduciary silver coinages until they adopted gold-exchange standards in the late nineteenth and early twentieth centuries.[50] By the start of World War I, only a few independent countries, such as China, Ethiopia, the Ottoman Empire, and some countries in the Middle East and Latin America, did not yet have large-scale, state-managed fiduciary coinages.

Another kind of fiduciary money whose use grew rapidly during the nineteenth century, paper money, also required standardization.[51] Some states, such as Norway (1816) and Denmark (1818), had in fact given a note issue monopoly to a single bank very early on in the nineteenth century.[52] In most countries, however, the initial growth in the use of paper money led to a situation of considerable heterogeneity with multiple issuers, which states then addressed. As noted above, Japan and the United States presented quite extreme cases of note heterogeneity by the mid nineteenth century. In Japan, the new Meiji government began the process of note consolidation in the early 1870s. It moved quickly to replace the enormous number of notes issued by local lords with notes issued by the central government and by newly chartered banks. Then in 1882, a new central bank was created that issued notes three years later, notes that gradually assumed a monopoly position by 1905.[53] In the United States, the federal government finally took a decisive step to reduce the heterogeneity of U.S. notes in 1863 by pressuring all note-issuing banks to become "national banks" that issued a single standardized note. Although

---

[48] Flandreau (1996).

[49] See Conant (1969 [1927]). In many of these instances, countries initially remained formally on bimetallic standards by leaving the mint open to the free coinage of certain silver coins. When gold-silver ratios changed dramatically, however, they usually removed this option.

[50] See Rosenberg (1985). One exception was Puerto Rico in which the Spanish had created national fiduciary coin in 1895.

[51] For detailed histories of the standardization of note issues in the pre-1914 period, see Smith (1990), Goodhart (1988), Conant (1969 [1927]).

[52] Lindgren (1997).

[53] Takaki (1903), Boling (1988).

government-issued greenbacks as well as silver and gold certificates remained in circulation, the new national bank notes became the dominant note in circulation, and because their value was guaranteed across the whole country, they were rightly called by observers at the time a "national currency." In 1913, they began to be replaced by a new national note issued by the newly created Federal Reserve System, and these notes had become the exclusive note in circulation by the 1930s.[54]

In other countries, the note standardization process was less dramatic, but still significant. Some countries, such as Switzerland (1881), homogenized the note issue in the way that the United States had begun to do in 1863; they standardized the appearance and quality of the notes while permitting various private banks to continue to issue them. Others transferred the note issue from many competing private banks to a single central bank. The most famous example was England where the 1844 Bank Act gradually phased out the notes of various small "country" banks that had been issuing notes since the mid eighteenth century and promised the Bank of England a note monopoly. Some other examples included Belgium (1850), Portugal (1891), Germany (1875), Sweden (1897), Argentina (1890), Nicaragua (1911), Uruguay (1896), and Bolivia (1914). In other cases, such as Australia (1910) and Brazil (1898), the state itself took over the task of issuing notes from the private banks. Still other countries had initially granted banks a note monopoly in subnational zones or cities; in these instances, the creation of a single nationwide note involved replacing these subnational monopolies with a national one, as in Spain (1874) and France (1848).

In most of these instances, policymakers tried to keep their new standardized notes convertible into the national monetary standard, be it silver or gold. But when convertibility was suspended unexpectedly, considerable domestic monetary upheaval often resulted as good quality coins quickly disappeared. The creation of fiduciary coinages helped reduce this risk, but it did not eliminate it altogether since fiduciary silver or copper coins often still had considerable valuable metallic content in them. During the U.S. Civil War, for example, the dramatic depreciation of the paper currency prompted a massive disappearance of coins, as people began to hoard them, melt them down for their metallic content, and export them.

Not all independent countries created standardized note issues in the pre-1914 era. Countries such as China, Canada, New Zealand, South Africa, Italy, and many countries in Latin America did not make this move. In Ireland and Scotland, too, various private banks issued their own distinctive notes even after the decision was made to create a note

---

[54] Davis (1910) and De Kock (1939).

monopoly in England in 1844, despite the fact that the coinage of these
two regions had been assimilated with that of England for some time (in
1707 for Scotland and 1826 for Ireland).[55] Some countries that granted note
monopolies to private banks also did not end up with a note of standardized value across the country. In the Ottoman Empire, for example, the
Imperial Ottoman Bank was given a note monopoly in 1863, but its notes
did not circulate at par throughout the empire because they could only be
redeemed at its head office in Constantinople.[56] Similarly, in Iran, the
notes of the Imperial Bank of Persia, established as the sole bank of issue
in 1889, were only acceptable at the specific branch where they were issued. Given the difficulties of transportation and communication in the
country, and the fact that the value of coins fluctuated between towns, the
result was that several different subnational monetary zones existed in
practice.[57]

Another kind of fiduciary money—bank deposits—also became an increasingly important part of the money supply in many countries during
the nineteenth century. Interestingly, most governments showed much
more interest in regulating bank notes and coins than this form of money.
Despite this lack of attention, bank deposits emerged within the territorial
currency framework in countries that were consolidating this monetary
structure; that is, private banks denominated deposits in the new standardized national currency. The convertibility of bank deposits into other
forms of national money—much like that of privately issued notes—was
of course dependent on the stability of the specific bank where they were
held. During the last third of the century, central banks took an increasingly active role in defending the stability of private banks through
lender-of-last-resort activities, although some questioned the necessity
and desirability of these activities.[58] Monetary authorities also often facilitated the smooth transferability of bank deposits across the country by encouraging national networks of banks to be created and by establishing
nationwide payments and clearing systems when private banks themselves had not already created them.

Integrating Low-denomination Money and Removing Foreign Currencies
The creation of territorial currencies also involved the integration of low-
denomination money within the newly standardized official monetary
order and the removal of foreign currencies from domestic circulation. As

---

[55] Scottish copper coin remained in circulation for much of 1700s, however (Stewart
1971, 252).
[56] Himadeh (1953, 28).
[57] Jones (1986, 44).
[58] See, for example, Goodhart, Capie, and Schnadt (1994, 15).

noted in more detail in the next chapter, an important part of the former task involved the production of large quantities of high-quality, standardized "petty coins" whose value was fixed in a clear relationship to other official forms of money for the first time. Once these coins had been produced, public authorities also made more serious efforts to ban privately issued, low-denomination "local currencies."

Britain was the first country to make these moves. After ignoring the reform of low-denomination copper coins for most of the eighteenth century, the Royal Mint began using new industrial minting machinery to mass-produce high quality and homogeneous copper coins in 1821. These new coins quickly pushed out of circulation the various private tokens and counterfeits that had dominated low-denomination coinage. At the same time, the government's view of private tokens suddenly changed. During the eighteenth century, there had been no law against the issue of tokens that did not resemble official coin. Once the Mint was equipped to produce mass quantities of new copper coins, however, the government moved to outlaw the issue and circulation of these private tokens.[59]

Many countries around the world soon followed the British example. As Carothers and others have noted, the history of low-denomination coinage is less well documented than other aspects of monetary history.[60] But some examples of the spread of the introduction of industrial minting of low-denomination coins are outlined in the next chapter. A few examples can be cited here of how countries also moved to ban privately issued, low-denomination coin. In the United States, private low-denomination tokens had been widely used in the first half of the nineteenth century, but they were banned in 1862.[61] Private tokens also had been particularly widespread in mid-nineteenth-century Australia, but they were banned in 1860 as soon as adequate quantities of industrially produced British low-denomination bronze coin began to be imported.[62] Similarly, in Mexico, the government banned private tokens in 1889 after they had grown very rapidly in use over the previous decade, but the ban was not strictly enforced until 1905 when the government began for the first time to produce low-denomination copper and nickel coins in mass quantities.[63]

[59] Their issue and circulation were banned by an 1812 act of Parliament, but the act was not implemented until the mint's new coins were introduced (Craig 1953; House of Commons 1817).

[60] Carothers (1930).

[61] Bernard (1917). In a fascinating article, however, Timberlake (1987) notes how privately issued scrip was still used in quite widespread ways in more isolated mining and lumbering company towns in the United States, particularly in Appalachia, in the early decades of the twentieth century.

[62] Bank of New South Wales (1954).

[63] Pradeau (1958).

The removal of foreign currencies from domestic circulation was also a key task in the building of territorial currencies. Sometimes, foreign currencies disappeared from domestic circulation simply as a by-product of the initiatives just outlined. With the new standardization of coins and notes in circulation, it became more difficult for a foreign currency with different denominations and quality to enter the domestic circulation and be accepted.[64] As money increasingly assumed a fiduciary form, it was also less likely to be accepted abroad.[65] The value of fiduciary coins, for example, no longer depended on their intrinsic metallic value but instead on some knowledge of the trustworthiness of the government that issued them as well as the prospect that the holder could redeem these coins into gold or silver with that government. Foreign coin had also often been used to supplement an inadequate supply of domestically issued small denomination coinage. Once this supply was provided in a more stable manner with new fiduciary coinages, demand for foreign currencies dropped off. In the United States, for example, the introduction of an adequate supply of fiduciary silver coins in 1853 ended the circulation of foreign coins in major cities across the country very quickly.[66] Foreign coins also disappeared quickly from British circulation after the introduction of its new silver fiduciary coinage in 1816.

At the same time, public authorities actively pursued the removal of foreign currencies from circulation. Governments often discouraged the use of foreign currencies through the use of legal tender laws and rules about what currencies would be acceptable at public offices. The introduction of a fiduciary coinage often prompted governments to remove existing foreign coins from circulation because of the new need to manage the domestic coinage supply more closely. Andrew describes how the introduction of fiduciary coins around the world in the late nineteenth century led to an ever-decreasing range of circulation for the cosmopolitan Mexican dollar for this reason.[67] Some government initiatives to remove foreign coins were very extensive and time-consuming. One example comes from the United States in the late 1850s. Although foreign coins ceased to circulate in major U.S. cities after 1853, they continued to be common in rural areas. To rid the country of them, the government launched a four-year campaign between 1857 and 1861 in which citizens could exchange foreign coins for new copper coins the government had begun to produce.

[64] See for example Helfferich (1969 [1927], 49).

[65] This is not to say that fiduciary money would not be used abroad at all, as we shall see in subsequent chapters.

[66] Carothers (1930, ch.11)

[67] Andrew (1904).

This effort was very successful—people stood in lines with bags of old Spanish and Mexican coins for the exchange—and when it ended, the legal tender status of foreign coins was finally eliminated.[68] In Canada, too, all foreign silver coins were removed from domestic circulation in a massive operation in 1871 that cost close to $120,000 and involved more than sixty bank agencies and the posting of forty thousand circulars around the country.[69] Similarly, in Peru, a major coinage reform in the early 1860s encouraged the government to launch a three-year operation between 1864 and 1867 designed to remove debased Bolivian coins, which had been the main coin in domestic circulation since the 1830s (although the coins remained in use in southern Peru's remote altiplano until as late as 1920).[70]

Not all countries that created more standardized currencies welcomed the disappearance of foreign currencies from domestic circulation. In some European countries where the circulation of each other's silver coins had been common, governments became concerned when their new fiduciary coinages began to disrupt this practice. For reasons analyzed in chapter 6, they then created "monetary unions" that encouraged fiduciary coins of all member countries to continue to circulate in each other's territories. In countries that had adopted the gold standard, some governments also encouraged the circulation of foreign coins by granting legal tender status to selected foreign gold coins. After becoming an independent country, Canada, for example, made British sovereigns and U.S. "eagle" gold coins legal tender in its 1871 currency act. The practical importance of provisions such as this was usually negligible, however, since few gold coins were in circulation in Canada and most countries that were on the gold standard.[71] Although these latter provisions highlight how some policymakers saw countries on the gold standard as joined together in a kind of cosmopolitan monetary order, this was a misleading view. While all such countries embraced gold as a common standard, each country adopted different units of account in gold for their national currency. More important, as I have emphasized, the introduction of the gold-based monetary standard was usually the catalyst for countries to create much more consolidated, territorial fiduciary coinage systems for the first time and to exclude foreign coins from domestic circulation. (As we shall see in chapter 4, it also often encouraged government to create note mo-

---

[68] Carothers (1930, ch.11).

[69] Shortt (1986, 559), Weir (1903, 156, 160).

[70] Flatt (1994, 2:23), Jacobsen (1993, 160).

[71] For Canada, see Stokes (1939, 2). There were, however, a few exceptions of countries on the gold standard where substantial numbers of gold coins remained in circulation such as Portugal (Reis 2000), Germany, and Britain (e.g., Gesell 1934, 34).

nopolies.) Ironically, it was countries that were not on the gold standard in the late nineteenth and early twentieth centuries—such as China, Ethiopia, and some countries in the Middle East and Central America— where foreign coins continued to circulate most freely. The gold standard's cosmopolitan reputation was, thus, not very well deserved. Instead, it is better seen as the world's first "inter-national" monetary order because it joined together countries that had begun to consolidate territorial currencies for the first time in history.[72]

Conclusion

Territorial currencies are, thus, quite a recent historical phenomenon dating backing only to the nineteenth century. As we have seen, money was organized in different ways before that time. Foreign currencies circulated widely within domestic territories. Low-denomination money was disconnected from the official monetary system. Even the official domestically issued currency was quite heterogeneous. The creation of the first territorial currencies in the nineteenth century involved a transformation of each of these features of traditional monetary systems. As we have seen, the transformation was not a simple one. Instead, it involved extensive activities by political authorities. New efforts were made to produce and maintain good-quality, standardized notes and coins in circulation. Counterfeiting was attacked in a more rigorous manner. Subnational distinctive monetary standards and coinages were eliminated. For the first time, governments also created large-scale, state-managed fiduciary coinages. Note issues were standardized within the territory and nationwide bank networks, and payments and clearing systems were constructed where they did not exist. More serious attention was given to the production of standardized, low-denomination money that was linked to the official monetary system, and unofficial low-denomination, privately issued money was banned. In addition, foreign currencies often had to be physically withdrawn from domestic circulation in expensive and time-consuming operations.

As I mentioned briefly in the introduction, the timing of the construc-

---

[72] James (2001, 17) also makes this point. In gold standard countries where gold coins did not circulate, their central monetary authorities of course held gold as monetary reserve. But these reserves should not be seen to challenge the territoriality of domestic monetary systems any more than the establishment of foreign embassies challenges territoriality in the realm of political sovereignty. As Ruggie (1993) and others have noted, as soon as territorial spaces have been created, it is necessary to carve out "extraterritorial" realms to facilitate interaction between these spaces. In the monetary realm, the holding of foreign currency reserves by public monetary authorities can be seen as an example of this phenomenon.

tion of territorial currencies is important for recent debates in the field of international relations about the historical origins of territoriality. Specifically, it calls into question the idea that the Westphalian age of seventeenth-century Europe represented a sharp historical break that ushered in new practices of territoriality. Although the *principle* of monetary "territoriality" may have first been put forward in that age in Europe (although I have questioned even this point in the monetary case), its *practical application* in a concerted and successful fashion in the monetary realm did not come until the nineteenth century. This conclusion is one increasingly echoed by several other studies beyond the monetary realm as well.[73]

The argument that international relations scholars have overstated the significance of change in the Westphalian age has important contemporary implications. Many scholars describe challenges to territoriality in the current period—including contemporary monetary transformations—as ushering in a "post-Westphalian" world order. This phrase conjures up an image of a dramatic world order transformation of a kind that has not been seen in three hundred years. If that is its intended meaning,[74] the conclusions presented in this chapter and other recent scholarship suggest that the phrase is misleading. If territoriality has more recent historical origins, challenges to it today are less dramatic in long historical terms. In the monetary sector, this point needs to be made particularly strongly. For as I will argue in subsequent chapters, territorial currencies were not only constructed recently but they have also faced constant challenges throughout their short lives.

[73] Krasner (1993, 1999), Thompson (1994).
[74] See footnote 4 in the introduction.

2

Two Structural Preconditions
Nation-States and Industrial Technology

What explains the sudden creation of territorial currencies for the first time during the nineteenth century? The motivations that prompted monetary authorities to construct them will be discussed in the next chapters. Before examining these motivations I want to analyze two important structural developments that had to take place before these monetary structures could be successfully built. The first was the emergence of nation-states. A number of scholars have noted how this new kind of state was significant for the rise of territorial currencies in the nineteenth century. Building on their analyses, I argue that nation-states had unprecedented capabilities to regulate and influence the types of money used within the territories they governed, capabilities that were crucial for many of the tasks associated with creation of territorial currencies.

The second structural change was a technological one: the application of new industrial technologies to the production of money. The importance of industrial machinery in transforming the production of coins and notes has not received much attention in existing literature.[1] Histories of the key technological revolutions in the nature of money usually focus on the original invention of coins, then the first creation of paper money before turning to the development of electronic money today.[2] But if we are interested in the origin of territorial currencies, we must examine the emergence of "industrial" coins and notes in the nineteenth century.

The Importance of Nation-States

In the previous chapter, I noted the importance of the activities of public authorities in enabling territorial currencies to emerge. To conduct many of these activities successfully, authorities required a strong capacity to influence the people who lived in the territories they governed. This capac-

---

[1] For some important exceptions, to whose pioneering work I am indebted, see the works of Richard Doty cited in the bibliography, Redish (1990, 1995), and Perlin (1993, 254).

[2] For a recent example of this genre, see Weatherford (1997).

ity did not exist until the emergence of nation-states in the nineteenth century. My argument should not be mistaken as a restatement of the "state theory of money." This controversial theory, developed most fully in recent times by Knapp, asserts that money is whatever the state declares it to be.[3] One need not accept this theory to recognize the importance of state power in influencing the nature of money in history. Particularly important from our standpoint is that this power dramatically increased with the rise of nation-states in the nineteenth century. Indeed, even Ludwig von Mises, a very harsh critic of Knapp, makes this point.[4]

In what ways was the power of the nation-state significant for the creation of territorial currencies? A few well-known scholars—Anthony Giddens, Gianfranco Poggi, and Eric Hobsbawm—have commented in passing on the historical association between the emergence of nation-states and territorial currencies during the nineteenth century.[5] Of these writers, only Giddens has sought to explain how the emergence of the nation-state might have encouraged this monetary transformation. Giddens's analysis is limited by the fact that he seeks to explain only one feature of these new territorial currencies: their "fiduciary" nature. Still, his analysis provides us with a useful starting point. He argues that modern national currencies based on fiduciary forms of money could not emerge until the state could more effectively influence the forms of money used within the territory it governed. His reasoning is straightforward: fiduciary forms of money were much less likely to be accepted on a mass scale than "commodity" monies because their intrinsic value was less than their face value. In Giddens's analysis, this state capability emerged only when a more direct relationship between state and society was created for the first time with the rise of the nation-state.[6]

It is certainly true that the new direct link between state and society gave public authorities a much stronger ability to regulate the forms of money used by the population. The development of powerful nationwide policing structures for the first time in the nineteenth century enabled the state to enforce legal tender laws in a comprehensive fashion.[7] These laws could be used to force people to use whatever money the state declared to be valid.[8] The importance of legal tender laws in encouraging token money to be accepted, however, should not be overstated. They were often quite unimportant in countries where the use of token money

[3] Knapp (1924 [1905]).
[4] Von Mises (1953 [1924], 72–73).
[5] Giddens (1985, 155–58; 1990), Poggi (1978, 93), Hobsbawm (1992, 28).
[6] See also von Glahn (1996, 20).
[7] See for example Johnson (1995).
[8] See Weber (1968, 166–80).

evolved gradually and trust in state authorities was high.[9] In contexts where such trust had dramatically eroded, their strict application also usually induced considerable evasion.

Equally if not more important was the expansion of the state's role in the emerging national economy during the nineteenth century. As Knapp observed, states often tried to influence the money employed in their territory not through legal tender laws but simply through proclamations concerning which kinds of currency would be accepted at public offices and which would not.[10] These proclamations became much more effective in an age when the state was more involved in the daily economic life of the people it governed. This involvement came from developments such as the creation of nationally consolidated taxation systems, national infrastructure projects, nationwide military conscription, and the establishment of national networks of post offices, railway stations, and state-regulated banks.[11]

According to Giddens, nation-states also enabled modern fiduciary monetary systems to emerge because they were better able to cultivate the "trust" of the domestic population in the state's ability to manage money. After all, people did not use fiduciary money only because they were forced to, but also because they came to consider it a reliable form of money. Unlike "commodity money," however, trust in fiduciary money came not from its physical characteristics but rather from knowledge about the supplier.

Giddens suggests that trust in the state's ability to supply stable paper money was often cultivated by delegating the management of this money to a central bank run by "experts" from the merchant and banking communities, two groups that were dominant users of bank notes during the nineteenth century in many countries. More generally, it may also have been bolstered by the fact that the state was opened up to more representative forms of government with the arrival of the nationalist era.[12] Both

---

[9] Indeed, as Goodhart (1988, 22–23) notes, many governments did not make notes legal tender before World War I.

[10] Knapp (1924 [1905]). See also Weber (1968, 167).

[11] See for example Marichal (1997, 343), Von Mises (1953 [1924], 73).

[12] Interestingly, we shall see in chapters 4 and 7 that the prospect of the expansion of the electoral franchise beyond the upper and middle classes sometimes led elite policy-makers to worry about the stability of paper money. It is also interesting to note that, when initiatives to move to more representative government were blocked by elites, the middle class sometimes used the threat of withdrawing "trust" in fiduciary money as a political tool. An example came in Britain when the House of Lords rejected the 1832 reform bill to expand the electoral franchise. Placards appeared around London asking people to convert their Bank of England notes into gold as a way of increasing pressure for reform, a move that caused a serious drain on the Bank and encouraged the king to try to get the bill

Lindgren and Eggertsson also argue that the enhanced power and stability of the nation-state contributed to people's confidence in its ability to issue stable, well-accepted fiduciary currencies.[13]

In addition, the nation-state's greater capacity to prevent counterfeiting may have been very important in cultivating trust in a national fiduciary currency. Because the difference between the intrinsic value and face value of fiduciary money could be quite large, its increasingly widespread use encouraged counterfeiters. As I note below, industrial production techniques played a role in reducing large-scale counterfeiting of coins and notes. But isolated well-equipped individual counterfeiters could still cause considerable damage to the stability of a fiduciary monetary order in this new technological context. As with the enforcement of legal tender laws, this problem could be addressed more effectively once the policing role of the state expanded in a comprehensive fashion in the nineteenth century. In Britain, for example, Styles describes how Yorkshire counterfeiters in the eighteenth century benefited from their remoteness from active law enforcement. But with the arrival of regularized and more effective nationwide policing in the nineteenth century, counterfeiters in regions such as this were more effectively pursued.[14] Indeed, the need to prevent counterfeiting was often a key catalyst for the expansion of nationwide policing. In the United States, the creation of the Secret Service in 1865 was driven by the desire to protect the new national bank notes from counterfeiting, a task it performed very effectively.[15]

There is one final way that trust may have been cultivated by nation-states. The willingness of the population to "trust" the value of the new national fiduciary forms of money may also have been linked to emerging nationalist sentiments in each country. Giddens focuses on the importance of trust in the state that issued and managed fiduciary money, but trust in one's fellow citizens was also significant. When Bank of England notes were made inconvertible in 1797, for example, they were not made legal tender initially, but Coppetiers reminds us that they did not depreciate right away because thousands of merchants and bankers quickly signed voluntary agreements to continue to accept them at meetings held across the country.[16] This kind of interpersonal trust was obviously easier to generate and sustain if the people involved had come to see themselves as

---

passed. Although the tactic was effective, it also encouraged the government to soon make Bank of England notes legal tender for the first time (Acres 1931, 457–58).

[13] Lindgren (1997, 196–97), Eggertsson (1990, 242).
[14] Styles (1980). See also Cook (1993).
[15] Johnson (1995).
[16] Coppieters (1955, 37).

members of a common national community. In the case of Bank of England notes, this was certainly true; Rowlinson notes the solidarity of merchants and bankers "manifested itself throughout as loyalty to Britain."[17] This point should not be overstated. Appeals to patriotism have never been enough to sustain the value of a fiduciary currency for very long in adverse circumstances. But in combination with the other factors already mentioned, a sense of membership within the "imagined" community of the nation, to use Benedict Anderson's language, might have played a role in encouraging acceptance of the new "imagined" value of national fiduciary currencies.[18]

The greater capability of nation-states to influence and regulate the forms of money used by the inhabitants of its territory was important not just for the creation of modern large-scale fiduciary monies but also for other tasks that were involved in the creation of territorial currencies. We have already seen how the elimination of subnational monetary standards and money issues followed directly from the creation of powerful nation-states out of more decentralized political arrangements in Meiji Japan, late-nineteenth-century Latin America, and postunification Germany, Italy, and Switzerland. Tasks such as the banning of unofficial low-denomination money or the withdrawal of foreign coins also required a state with substantial direct power to regulate economic activities across the territory it governed.

The importance of the existence of modern nation-states for the consolidation of a territorial currency is also clear where this monetary reform was not carried out. This was certainly evident in China. As noted in the previous chapter, it had one of the most heterogeneous large-scale monetary orders in the nineteenth and early twentieth centuries. The weakness and lack of authority of China's central imperial state in this period was a key obstacle preventing China from creating a more homogeneous and nationally integrated monetary system. In the words of one American adviser at the turn of the century, the difficulty was "political as much as economic, arising chiefly from the lack of power in the central government to supersede the provincial coinage and currency systems."[19]

Boulton's Coinage Revolution

The emergence of powerful and centralized nation-states was not the only structural change that enabled territorial currencies to be consolidated for

---

[17] Rowlinson (1999, 62).

[18] Anderson (1983).

[19] Jencks quoted in Conant (1969 [1927], 601). See also Kahn (1926, 76), von Glahn (1996, 11).

the first time in the nineteenth century. A second development was the application of new industrial technologies to the production of money. The first application of industrial technology for this purpose came with respect to coins. The pioneer was the British industrialist Matthew Boulton, who is usually best known for his role (along with James Watt) in developing the steam engine. Between 1787 and 1797, Boulton perfected a new way of producing coins with steam-powered industrial technology that revolutionized the nature of coins and their place in the monetary system. Over the next two decades, he and his company sold the new coins—and even entire industrial mints—to regions around the world including Britain, Sierra Leone, Sumatra, Russia, France, the United States, Canada, Denmark, India, Mexico, and Brazil.[20] Those countries that did not receive Boulton's advice directly in this period soon introduced the new coining techniques themselves. By the late nineteenth century, there were few parts of the world that had not been affected by what Richard Doty calls Boulton's "coinage revolution."[21]

Today, it is easy to dismiss the importance of coins in the overall monetary order. But as we have seen, coins held a much more prominent position in monetary systems in the nineteenth century, and Boulton's technology had a major monetary impact. Indeed, Doty notes that the birth of what he calls "the modern coin" in this period was probably more important in its impact on monetary history than the invention of paper currency.[22] To appreciate its significance, we must first be reminded of how coins were previously made and how these manufacturing techniques influenced monetary systems. Techniques for manufacturing coins varied around the world before the nineteenth century. A fairly primitive process was that of manually hammering metal into coins. A more sophisticated technique—common by the seventeenth and eighteenth centuries in Europe—created "milled coins" that were produced by a screw press, which also allowed letters and grating to be placed on the edges of coins. In China, a third method was used involving multiple forging, instead of striking.[23]

All of these traditional manufacturing techniques contributed directly to the heterogeneity of official coinage before the nineteenth century. Their imprecision ensured that coins produced were usually not well standardized in their weight or in the designs placed on them. Coins were also easily worn with use, a problem that was rather serious in an era

---

[20] Doty (1986a, 1986b, 1987, 1991, 1994a, 1994b), Craig (1953, 264).
[21] Doty (1986a).
[22] Doty (1993).
[23] Perlin (1993, 255).

when old coins were not regularly withdrawn and recoinages were infrequent. These problems, coupled with the relatively simple design of official coins and the fact that the manufacturing of coin could be done with unsophisticated machinery that was easily hidden from authorities, prompted widespread counterfeiting.

The counterfeiting of preindustrial coinage also made the task of sustaining stable fiduciary coinages on a mass scale very difficult. As we have seen, stable fiduciary coinages required that the supply of fiduciary coins be closely controlled in order to maintain their fixed value. Before the nineteenth century, any effort to introduce large-scale fiduciary coins would tempt counterfeiters because of the considerable profits to be made. Large-scale counterfeiting would then mean that the state lost control of the supply of fiduciary coins and thus their value. Indeed, even after creating fiduciary coinage systems, many countries initially kept fiduciary coins quite close to their intrinsic value because of a fear of counterfeiters.[24]

The limitations of preindustrial coining also prevented public authorities from producing mass quantities of high-quality, low-denomination coins. Only with enormous time and expense could copper and bronze be worked in such a way with traditional techniques to produce very high-quality, low-denomination coins. Coining costs were particularly steep because the face value of these coins was very low. Indeed, copper coins would normally have to be produced at a loss in countries that were committed to keeping the metallic value of coin equal to its face value.[25] For these technological reasons, the task of making good-quality, low-denomination coins was one of the most vexing monetary problems facing governments before the nineteenth century. As we have seen, it discouraged many governments from making a serious effort to produce low-denomination coins altogether.

In some contexts, more serious efforts were made to produce low-denomination copper (e.g., the Mughal Empire) and bronze (e.g., Imperial China) coins because they were seen as a central part of the official monetary system. In Mughal India, very large quantities of copper coins were produced with traditional striking techniques by employing large numbers of skilled laborers in factory settings with well-organized production lines. Even more dramatic was the production of Chinese mints that,

---

[24] For Britain, see Craig (1953, 273–86). For France, see Redish (1991, 6). Many U.S. policymakers worried that their country's new fiduciary silver coins in 1853 would be massively counterfeited and would soon depreciate in value (Taxay 1966, 220; Carothers 1930, 127).

[25] Helfferich (1969 [1927], 46), Cipolla (1956, ch.3), Boeke (1953, 72), Elvin (1973, 147).

using multiple forging techniques, reached as many as 6 billion coins per year in the 1070s and 1080s.[26] The high costs of manufacturing in both instances, however, made this kind of large-scale production quite sporadic, leading to frequent shortages and considerable use of unofficial forms of low-denomination money.[27] Chinese coining technology also produced quite simple and crude coins. Mughal coins were higher quality, but this quality began to deteriorate as production expanded by the late 1600s.[28]

These various problems associated with traditional coin manufacturing techniques were overcome dramatically by Boulton's inventions. His new method of coin production involved striking coins in a steel collar with automatic steam-powered machinery (see figure 4). This method enabled coins to be produced in an identical fashion, thereby ensuring a more homogenous coinage in circulation. It also allowed coins to be designed in a more precise manner. Because of the use of steel collars, all Boulton's coins were perfectly round with the same diameter and their edging was perfectly perpendicular with a new kind of graining placed on it (a feature designed to prevent wear and tear). In addition, more precise artistic designs could be placed on the coins.

These various features also made counterfeiting a much more difficult task. Not only could individuals now more easily recognize counterfeits, but most counterfeiters now had greater difficulty replicating the official coin. Producing a convincing copy required the use of complex and noisy industrial machinery that was hard to hide from authorities. Because of its role in eliminating wide-scale counterfeiting, the use of industrial minting technology became a key precondition for the emergence of stable, state-managed fiduciary coinages. This connection was particularly clear in the U.K. case where the gold standard with this kind of fiduciary coinage system was introduced at the same time as Boulton refitted the Royal Mint. Redish also calls attention to its importance in other contexts such as France.[29]

The new steam-powered minting machinery also enabled very large quantities of coins to be produced at much lower cost. Already in 1787, Boulton noted that each one of the steam presses could produce sixty thousand coins per day.[30] By the turn of the century, it was clear that Boulton's mint at Soho could produce ten times the coins produced by the existing British Royal Mint in any given time period.[31] The scale of the coin

---

[26] von Glahn (1996, 48). See also Perlin (1993, 97–117, 155, 255).
[27] Elvin (1973), Perlin (1987, 1993), von Glahn (1996).
[28] Perlin (1987).
[29] Redish (1990, 1995).
[30] Pollard (1971, 31).
[31] Jenkinson (1880 [1805], 227).

COINING-PRESS IN THE ROYAL MINT OF LONDON.

Figure 4. Matthew Boulton's new coining press from 1836. Photograph courtesy of The British Museum. © The British Museum.

production that was now possible quickly forced Boulton to develop new ways to multiply the tools that were used to place the various designs on coins. Traditionally, each tool had been engraved by hand, but with such large-scale production these tools might not be identically made. A French inventor, who created a "reducing machine" that could mechanically reproduce an artist's original design for coins in different sizes and denominations, found a solution for Boulton.[32]

In enabling the mass production of high-quality coins at low cost, Boulton's industrial minting technology had a profound impact on low-denomination coins.[33] For the first time, his equipment made it economically and technologically possible to manufacture high-quality, low-denomination copper and bronze coins on a mass scale. As we shall see in the next chapter, the production of low-denomination copper coins had in fact been one of Boulton's most important initial goals in developing his new inventions.

---

[32] Pollard (1971).
[33] Doty (1986a), Perlin (1993, 254).

Because of Boulton's inventions, Britain was the first country to experience a dramatic transformation of its coinage. He was given a contract to refit the Royal Mint with his new machinery in 1805–10. When the ending of the Napoleonic wars finally provided the context for coinage reform after 1816, Boulton's machinery at the new Royal Mint was called on for the task. It performed this job admirably, transforming Britain's coinage overnight into a high-quality and homogeneous one in which counterfeits, private tokens, and foreign coins were rare.[34] Other countries that introduced Boulton's coins or coining techniques in the nineteenth century also experienced similar overnight transformations in the nature of the coinage systems. Indeed, their introduction quickly came to be seen as a necessary part of constructing a "modern," nationally homogeneous coinage system that could emulate the British model.

One example comes from Meiji Japan after 1868. As part of its efforts to reform the country's chaotic monetary system, the new government purchased a modern industrial mint in 1870–71 that had been used in Hong Kong, and it quickly helped to bring a much greater degree of homogeneity to Japan's coinage.[35] Another example comes from Siam soon after it opened up to trade with the West in 1855.[36] The country's monarch also saw the importation of a steam-powered industrial mint from Birmingham as one of the most important of his "modernizing" economic reforms. The traditional large-denomination money of Siam had been bullet-shaped silver coins, but the government's expert craftsmen could make only 2,400 per day in the early 1850s. When the opening of the country to foreign trade prompted a dramatic increase in the demand for money, this supply was suddenly extremely inadequate. The new mint was designed to address the money shortage, and it was capable of producing 100,000 coins per day. Because they were less bulky and much harder to counterfeit, the new flat coins it produced were also viewed as more appropriate for a more monetized economy. The government also used the new mint to produce low-denomination tin and copper coins to displace cowries, which had acted as the principal low-denomination money in Siam for centuries but were now criticized for being too cumbersome and having a fluctuating value vis-à-vis silver.[37]

Not all countries imported their new mints from abroad. In 1833, a U.S.

[34] Dyer and Gaspar (1992), Craig (1953, 268–73), Whiting (1971, 24).
[35] Hanashiro (1996), Imperial Mint (1923). The 1866 Tariff Convention signed with Western powers in fact required that Japan set up a modern mint by 1868.
[36] Another example in Asia at this time was Burma, which imported a Birmingham Mint in 1865 because of the desire of the local monarch to match, in the words of the Burmese Court Records, "the custom of other great and powerful states" (Robinson and Shaw 1980, 87).
[37] Thailand (1982, 18, 21), Le May (1924, 192–94; 1932, 68).

Mint official was sent to Europe to examine British and other modern minting technologies, and he returned from his trip to oversee the introduction of a new domestically produced, steam-powered mint in 1836.[38] This new mint finally gave the government the capacity for large-scale, high-quality coining; for example, the mint's coining capacity grew from 3 million coins per year in 1833 to 60 million by 1854. As a U.S. Congress report in 1856 noted, the importance of this technological change became especially clear in 1853 when the mint was called on to produce a massive amount of new small-denomination fiduciary silver coins.[39] A number of contemporaries also noted that it would make possible the massive withdrawal of foreign coins that then took place in the late 1850s.[40]

With its new technology, the United States also began to export mints. One of the early exports went to Peru in 1855. As in Siam, monetary transactions assumed a much greater role in Peru's economy after its "guano boom" opened up the country to foreign trade in the 1850s. At the time, Peru's monetary system, dominated by debased Bolivian coins, was chaotic, and policymakers favored a more reliable coinage that was convertible into foreign currencies at a stable rate. In this context, one of their first moves was to import a modern steam-powered mint from the United States in 1855. The mint was operational by 1857, and it enabled the government to pursue a massive monetary reform involving the introduction of a new decimal standard and the replacement of the Bolivian coins with new Peruvian ones in the 1860s. To meet the new demand for small change, the government also introduced new copper coins produced at the Philadelphia Mint (which itself had just begun production of a new copper coin a few years earlier in 1857).[41]

The way that Peru imported its copper coins highlights that even the monetary systems of those countries that did not construct a modern industrial mint were affected by the new coin manufacturing techniques. By the late nineteenth century, most countries without such a mint were contracting out their national coin production to industrial mints in leading industrial countries. Canada, for example, launched a series of major monetary reforms to introduce its own uniform national coinage between the 1850s and early 1870s, but it relied entirely on private Birmingham mints and the British Royal Mint to produce the new coinage (an arrange-

---

[38] Taxay (1966, chs. 8, 9, 12), and *Report by Franklin Peale of his visit to Europe, Philadelphia, June 17, 1835;* "Peale Correspondence," 1829–1886, Franklin Peale's Letters: 1829–1886, Box No.1 (NC-152, E-23); records of the Bureau of the Mint. U.S. Mint at Philadelphia, 1791–1936, Record Group 104; USNA.

[39] U.S. Congress (1856).

[40] See the U.S. Congress (1830, 14; 1834, 69).

[41] Flatt (1994 1:78, 2:42–48).

ment that lasted until 1907).[42] Many countries in Latin America also began in the nineteenth century to rely on the U.S. Mint to produce their coins.[43] When Greece created a more homogeneous coinage system in the late 1860s, it used the Paris mint to produce the new coinage in order to guarantee its quality and because it could not afford a new national mint.[44] Similarly, when Iran successfully introduced a new high-quality nickel coin in 1901 to replace the existing motley collection of debased official copper coin and unofficial cardboard tokens, the coins were produced at a European mint.[45]

The Transformation of Note Production

Industrial technology was just as important in helping to standardize domestic note issues. Its impact, however, was less immediately dramatic because paper currency was not used as extensively as coins in most countries at the time of the industrial revolution. In the few instances where notes were becoming very widespread at this time, however, many people quickly recognized its potential importance. Two of the most prominent and interesting instances involved England's experience with Bank of England notes during the "restriction" period when these notes were inconvertible (1797–1821), and France's experiment with assignats in the early 1790s.

In both instances, the sudden widespread use of paper notes produced a number of technological difficulties. The first was similar to one encountered in coin production: traditional preindustrial methods of producing notes were not very effective at manufacturing large quantities of standardized notes. The traditional printing method for notes in these two countries, as in many countries at this time, was to use a copper printing plate and a rolling press.[46] For notes to be standardized, the engravings in the copper printing plates had to be identical. This did not pose too many difficulties when the number of notes required was small. But when large-scale production was required, it did become problematic. In 1795, just before the Bank of England's massive expansion of its note issue, three men who could produce approximately two thousand notes per day printed the bank's notes. But by 1800, the required production of the new one- and two-pound notes alone was fifteen thousand notes per day. One response

---

[42] Haxby (1983), Helleiner (1999a).

[43] See Grigore (1972), Young (1925, 195).

[44] Einaudi (1997, 344–45).

[45] Jones (1986, 81–82).

[46] Mackenzie (1953). The other method in use in some places—such as fifteenth-century China and Tokugawa Japan—was surface printing, in which a block was inked and pressed on paper (Davies 1994, 182; Tsuen-Hsuin 1954, 98).

Figure 5. Bank of England one-pound note from 1803. Observe the poor quality of production. Photograph courtesy of The British Museum. © The British Museum.

of the bank was to hire additional people but the problems it faced were also technological.[47] Copper printing plates wore out quickly, sometimes after just several hundred prints, thus resulting in poor-quality notes. Without a mechanical way to duplicate plates, a team of engravers was constantly required to make new plates and these plates increasingly deviated from the prototype. The consequence was that the quality of note production dropped dramatically (see figure 5). The heterogeneity of the notes was compounded by the fact that the dates, numbers, and countersignatures on Bank of England notes were all hand written. Since one clerk could complete only about four hundred notes per day, by 1809 there were eighty-four people employed in this task and their writing was by no means standardized.

Similar problems were encountered a few years earlier in France with the production of the assignats.[48] Like Bank of England notes after 1797, the assignats were far from standardized. A key issue once again was the difficulty of creating a large number of identical copper printing plates. To overcome this problem, the French authorities experimented with creating a "master" engraving on a steel plate that was pressed into copper plates.

---

[47] Mackenzie (1953, 40), Harris (1967, 72–73). In 1175, as many as twelve hundred workers were employed in one note-making factory in China (Tsuen-Hsuin 1954, 98).

[48] Lafaurie (1981, 28–37).

But the results were still problematic—primarily because the amount of pressure applied on the copper plates was uneven—and the technique was dropped in 1793. As in England, the French government also had difficulties creating identical signatures. To reduce costs, they had already moved to print signatures in 1791 based on selected employees' writing, but these signatures became inconsistent when these individual employees left for other employment.

The lack of standardization among paper notes in both cases also encouraged very widespread counterfeiting. Counterfeiting of paper notes was always very tempting—more tempting than that of coins—given the low cost of production, and it was common in all cases of paper money use before industrial production techniques were introduced.[49] The technological difficulties involved in preventing counterfeiting of notes before the industrial era encouraged banks and policymakers to explore various means to eliminate the phenomenon. In Scotland where notes were widely used during the eighteenth century, counterfeiting was reduced by an efficient note clearinghouse system that returned notes quickly to the banks that had issued them.[50] In nineteenth-century China, counterfeiting was reduced somewhat through a "proof-slip" system in which notes were printed with an extra-wide right hand margin with words or phrases on it. The margin was then cut in half, with one half kept as reference with the value and date of its note recorded for verification in the future.[51] The most common tool to discourage counterfeiting in all instances, however, was the existence of tough legal sanctions, usually the death penalty.[52] These various strategies discouraged counterfeiting, especially in contexts where the note issue was small scale or restricted to a small geographical region or involved primarily high-denomination notes. But counterfeiting remained a key problem in all instances of widespread use.

It was particularly prevalent in the English and French cases. One reason was that notes with relatively simple designs were produced in such an unstandardized way.[53] Another was the fact that the technology for

[49] See Lindgren (1968, 406–7), Boling (1988, 5), Mackenzie (1953, 13); Tsuen-Hsuin (1954, 98–99).

[50] White (1984, 39).

[51] See Selgin (1992).

[52] Many preindustrial paper notes, such as Chinese notes in the Ming period and the assignats, carried a warning printed on them that forgery was punishable by death (Lafaurie 1981, 56; Committee 1993, 13). In the case of the assignats, punishments could be assigned against people who even just discredited the notes in conversation (Conant 1969 [1927], 43).

[53] Assignats experienced major counterfeiting almost as soon as they first appeared. Bank of England notes had always been counterfeited, but there was a "vast increase" in forged notes after 1797 as their quality dropped (despite efforts to improve anticounterfeiting devices on the notes such as watermarks). (Mackenzie 1953, 13, 38–48). Indeed, Harris

producing notes was easy to obtain. In England during the time of the Restriction, there were probably ten thousand copper engravers who were able to copy the Bank of England note.[54] In each instance, counterfeiting was also encouraged because low-denomination notes were suddenly introduced in a massive way among poorer people who had little experience handling security documents. Not surprisingly, most of those prosecuted for passing forged notes during the assignats episode in France and the Restriction period in England were poor, often illiterate people who may have had great difficulties telling a genuine note from a counterfeit one.[55]

The experiences with counterfeiting and the tough legal sanctions against it led to enormous disillusionment and distrust of paper money in England and France. In England, the Bank of England's crackdown on counterfeiting was so brutal that it led to a serious political backlash against the bank. More than three hundred people were sentenced to death between 1797–1817 for passing forged notes and many more were transported out of the country to Australia for life simply for possessing such notes.[56] Anger toward the bank was well symbolized by George Cruikshank's 1818 mock Bank of England note, which showed corpses hanging from a scaffold and the bank's Britannia devouring a live infant (see figure 6). The experience also led a widespread consensus in England that paper money—what some contemporaries called "filthy rags"—should not be used as a low-denomination, mass currency. As soon as it could in 1821, the bank stopped producing one and two pound notes and, even as late as 1891 during the Barings crisis, there was great reluctance to reintroduce low-denomination notes because of the fear of forgery.[57]

Another result of these unhappy episodes was an urgent search for a technological solution to counterfeiting. In England, Hewitt and Keyworth note that "from the public's point of view the campaign for a new note was almost a moral and philanthropic issue, a demand for social re-

---

(1967, 73) states that there was said at the time to be more variety among the official Bank of England notes than among the forgeries of them. Boling (1988, 5) notes that counterfeiting was very common in Tokugawa Japan for a similar reason. Hansatsu were mostly printed by wood blocks, a technique with uneven results and easy replication.

[54] Mackenzie (1953, 61).

[55] Harris (1967, 72), Mackenzie (1953, 48), Hewitt and Keyworth (1987, 33, 42), Wills (1981, 79, 112).

[56] Mackenzie (1953, 58–75). Many of these people were poor women who were often illiterate. For their very difficult circumstances, see Palk (1994). For anger toward the bank, see Great Britain (1818, 276, 434–35), Fetter (1965, 73). In France during the early 1790s, over thirteen hundred people were guillotined for counterfeiting assignats (Bower 1995, 59 fn6).

[57] Mackenzie (1953, 130).

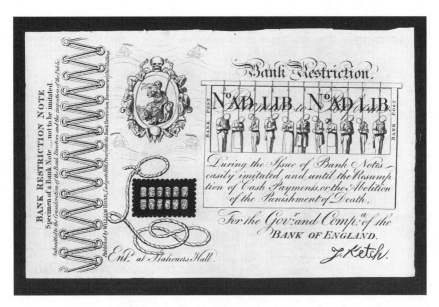

Figure 6. George Cruikshank's mock Bank of England note from 1818. In addition to the corpses and Britannia's devouring of a child, observe that the signature is by "J. Ketch," a nickname for the public hangman. Also note the ships in the background with banners labeled "transport," and the pound sign that resembles a hangman's noose. Photograph courtesy of The British Museum. © The British Museum.

form."[58] Soon after the restriction period began, the Bank of England offered a financial reward for suggestions that improved the quality of notes, and it received more than four hundred such suggestions in the next few years.[59] In response to these suggestions, Cook notes that the Bank of England had spent more than £200,000 by 1820 on more than one hundred projects trying to find a way to produce a "safe" note. The bank also held a formal competition in 1817–18 for inventors to come up with a way to improve note production, something the French government had also done in the 1790s during the assignats episode.[60] Out of these and other efforts, some interesting applications of new industrial technologies to the production of notes emerged.

One of the more important was the replacement of copper printing plates with steel plates. In Twyman's words, this resulted in "a far-reach-

---

[58] Hewitt and Keyworth (1987, 60).
[59] Mackenzie (1953, 49).
[60] Cook (1993, 38), Harris (1968).

ing improvement" in quality of printing because very fine engravings on steel plates could stand the wear of printing much better those on copper plates.[61] The invention of steel plate note production is usually attributed to a Philadelphia inventor, Jacob Perkins, who developed the technique in 1805 to prevent forgery. Perkins then went one step further and developed a mechanical technique—siderography—that allowed engraved steel plates to be copied in unlimited numbers. The idea had initially been proposed in the French competition, but he was the first to develop it into a workable technique for reducing forgery. By ensuring that every plate was identical, the process enabled standardized note production, eliminating the need for the team of engravers that the French government and Bank of England had required. Siderography was first used for printing notes in the United States, and by the end of the 1820s two to three hundred private banks used it in the United Kingdom. Interestingly, the Bank of England was unimpressed with Perkins's idea when it was submitted to its competition.[62]

There were other important innovations relating to the printing and engraving processes in this period. The introduction of a steam-powered, plate-printing press—first done at the Bank of Ireland in 1816—made printing more efficient. When it was introduced at the Bank of England in 1836, it was also accompanied by the introduction of a plate transfer press that created identical issues of notes for the first time. The invention of a machine that could print numbers and dates on notes automatically was also important. Its introduction (and the ending of the tradition of countersigning) in 1809 meant the Bank of England no longer needed its eighty-four employees who had done this task by hand and ensured that the notes were now more even and harder to alter in this respect. Two further innovations noted by MacKenzie were the "ruling machine" and the "rose engine," each of which allowed new kinds of detail to be engraved on printing plates in order to discourage counterfeiting. New England inventors created both in the early 1800s.[63] Counterfeiting was also discouraged by the use of compound-plate printing—a technique patented by William Congreve in 1821—which allowed two colors to be printed simultaneously.[64]

In the mid nineteenth century, one further innovation that had a profound impact on the printing process was the substitution of electrotyping and surface printing for the old system of plate engraving and printing.

---

[61] Twyman's (1970, 22).
[62] Mackenzie (1953, 33–34, 56–57), Harris (1968).
[63] Mackenzie (1953, 21, 31–34, 87–91).
[64] Greenland (1995).

This printing method was first proposed by Alfred Smee in 1841 after he had been appointed by the Bank of England to investigate ways to increase the security of its notes. Smee implemented the new technique when producing Bank of England notes in 1855 and it quickly began to be used elsewhere. In addition to reducing printing costs and increasing precision, this method ensured that ordinary copper engravers could no longer counterfeit notes.[65] Hewitt and Keyworth note that this change almost totally eradicated forgery in England.[66]

These various innovations played a major role in helping to consolidate the domestic note issue in countries around the world during the nineteenth century. They enabled a standardized note to be produced in large quantities and they helped to reduce counterfeiting. In some countries, local manufacturers simply studied and then emulated the new printing techniques used in England and the United States.[67] As in the case of coins, other countries contracted out the production of notes to modern facilities in the leading industrial countries. Indeed, companies such as the American Bank Note Company (United States) and Bradbury, Wilkinson, and Company (Britain) quickly became well known for producing notes for countries around the world.[68]

Conclusion

The rise of the nation-state and the invention of industrially manufactured money were thus both critical for the creation of territorial currencies. The importance of the nation-state was that it had a much greater capability to regulate and influence the types of money used within the territories it governed than previous kinds of political entities. This capability stemmed from such features as its policing powers, its larger economic role in the domestic economy, its centralized authority, and its ability to cultivate the "trust" of the domestic population in fiduciary money. Many of the activities described in the last chapter that were associated with the construction of territorial currencies relied on this capability. The industrialization of the production of coins and notes was also important in three ways. By enabling standardized, high-quality, difficult-to-counterfeit coins and notes to be produced in mass quantities for the first time, it improved the uniformity of the money in circulation. It allowed state-managed, large-scale fiduciary money systems to be created. And, finally, it

---

[65] Mackenzie (1953, 98–105), Harris (1969).
[66] Hewitt and Keyworth (1987, 156 fn6).
[67] See, for example, the Swedish case (Nathorst-Boos 1970, 91).
[68] Griffiths (1959), Nathorst-Boos (1970).

played a key role in enabling states to integrate low-denomination money into the official monetary system.

The existence of both a nation-state and "industrial" money had to be present for territorial currencies to emerge. When industrially produced money was introduced in contexts where a powerful nation-state did not yet exist, it often did not contribute very significantly to the territorialization of currency. In the United States before the mid 1860s, for example, counterfeiting of paper money remained pervasive despite technological improvements in bank note production because of the absence of effective nationwide policing. Indeed, the introduction of industrially produced money could even undermine the cohesion of some monetary systems when state authority was weak. A dramatic example comes from West Africa where copper "manillas" had traditionally been used as a key currency. At the end of the eighteenth century, Birmingham businesses began using industrial machinery to mass-produce these horseshoe-shaped copper pieces for use in trade with that region. The result was an inflation that undermined the relative stability and coherence of monetary orders in that region.[69] A similar set of events was experienced in western regions of North America where wampum beads were an important currency. These beads began to be mass-produced with industrial machinery during the nineteenth century by merchants involved in the fur trade, again causing a destabilizing inflation.[70] In neither case was there a powerful state to control the activities of these private money producers.

If both the existence of nation-states and "industrial money" were key preconditions for emergence of territorial currencies in the nineteenth century, they were by no means sufficient conditions. It is still necessary to explain why state policymakers actively chose to create such currencies in these new conditions. Before the nineteenth century, policymakers had not seen this project as a pressing task. Why did they suddenly pursue it with great seriousness and consistency in the nineteenth century? It is to this subject that we now turn.

[69] Vice (1983, 15), Onoh (1982, 15), Hogendorn and Johnson (1986, 3).
[70] Martien (1996).

3

Making Markets
Transaction Costs and Monetary Reform

Nineteenth- and early-twentieth-century policymakers had complex reasons to territorialize currencies. Not only did motivations vary considerably from country to country, but specific reforms were also often designed to serve several different objectives at the same time. I do not have the space to explain each relevant monetary reform in every country. Instead, I shall outline objectives that appeared in many contexts and that allow for a more generalized explanation to be developed. Four common sets of motivations reappeared in different contexts in this period. My argument is not that these four motivations were present in each country and each reform. Rather, these four sets of motivations help to explain the dominant reasons why policymakers introduced territorial currencies during this period.

I begin by examining the relationship between the territorialization of currencies and the construction of markets in the nineteenth and early twentieth centuries. Territorial currencies were often seen as a tool to reduce "transaction costs" in an age when markets were expanding rapidly. My argument is greatly indebted to the pioneering work of economic historian Douglass North. Although there are clear economic gains from trade, North has pointed out how participants can encounter large costs in making transactions with each other. These transaction costs are associated with activities such as the enforcement of contracts and property rights or the obtaining of accurate information about the various items being exchanged. For large-scale markets to emerge and flourish in the industrial age, North argues that transaction costs had to be reduced through institutional innovations that established clear property rights, standardized regulations of weights and measures, and mechanisms to enforce contracts.[1]

The creation of territorial currencies was another one of these institutional innovations that played a key role in reducing transaction costs during the nineteenth century. Unfortunately, neither North nor other

[1] North (1981, ch.12; 1985, 568).

"neoinstitutional" economic historians have analyzed the link between monetary reforms and the expansion of markets in the nineteenth century.[2] Instead, it has been a political scientist, David Woodruff, who has recently called attention to its importance. His recent book, *Money Unmade,* analyzes how the rise of barter and various "surrogate monies" in Russia during the 1990s played a major role in undermining an integrated market in the country. Drawing on this analysis, he suggests that more attention should be paid by economic historians to the ways in which the construction of territorial currencies historically have been associated with the goal of constructing spatially unified national markets. To make this point, he compares briefly the efforts of U.S. policymakers to consolidate a national bank note in 1863 with the failure of their Italian counterparts to do so throughout the nineteenth century. The successful consolidation of a national bank note in the former, he argues, reflected the strong commitment to a "national market-building project," a commitment that he argues was lacking in Italy among state officials and a regionally fragmented, export-oriented business elite.[3]

Although he does not attempt to develop this point in much detail, Woodruff's argument is fundamentally important. The construction of territorial currencies was indeed often closely tied to the goal of building spatially unified national markets. However, I believe that Woodruff's argument needs to be supplemented in two ways. The construction of national markets involved the extension of markets not just in a spatial sense, but also "vertically" to incorporate the poor more regularly within national market life. The desire to reduce currency-related transactions costs associated with this vertical dimension of national markets motivated some key territorializing monetary reforms in the nineteenth century. Yet an exclusive focus on the emergence of national markets does not fully explain how territorializing monetary reforms achieved the goal of reducing transaction costs. Peripheral countries, especially, sought to reduce transaction costs associated with international trade.

Constructing National Markets: The Spatial Dimension

As historians such as Fernand Braudel and Karl Polanyi have shown, the emergence of national markets was one of the most important economic

---

[2] North (1981, 36–37) mentions that new forms of money also were important in allowing large-scale markets to emerge, but the discussion is very brief. Some other "neoinstitutionalist" economists have devoted more attention to the importance of money in reducing transaction costs (e.g., Eggertsson 1990, 231–44). But I have not found any providing an analysis of the link between the rise of territorial currencies and the expansion of markets in the nineteenth century.

[3] Quote from Woodruff (1999, 210).

developments of the nineteenth century.[4] The vast bulk of economic life before the nineteenth century was highly localized. Where long-distance trade was extensive before the nineteenth century, it did not integrate economic activity within the territory of a state into a coherent national market. The emergence of national markets was closely associated with the rise and spread of industrial technologies such as the railway and the telegraph, which undermined the pervasive localism of the pre-nineteenth-century era. National markets did not, however, emerge spontaneously with the industrial age. As neoinstitutionalist economists remind us, their creation had to be facilitated by the active efforts of state authorities to reduce transaction costs.

A crucial task in this respect was the building of a territorial currency. Without a uniform currency across the country, those engaged in new nationwide commercial transactions encountered considerable costs in exchanging currencies and assessing their relative worth. In addition, as cross-national commerce accelerated, diverse forms of currency used across the country increasingly intermingled, raising the transaction costs of doing business everywhere within the country. No wonder then that business groups and state officials seeking to promote the emergence of national markets became proponents of territorial currencies.

The U.S. example of this phenomenon in the mid nineteenth century chosen by Woodruff is a good one. As we saw in chapter 1, an enormous number of paper notes issued by private banks in various states circulated in the country before 1863. Most of the notes were not readily accepted outside of the local region in which the issuing bank was located without some discount. As nationwide commerce grew dramatically after 1840, this situation created increasingly large transaction costs for businesses. Those merchants who were operating nationally had to traverse various subnational bank note zones in the course of their regular business. In the words of one senator in 1863, "The different states were as to their bank notes so many foreign nations each refusing the paper of the other, except at continually varying rates of discount. Frequently there was a greater loss on paper taken or sent from an eastern to a western State than on English bank notes converted into Austrian money in Vienna."[5] With the expanded scale of commerce, notes also circulated more widely and even localized businesses found the valuing of various discounted notes in circulation an increasingly cumbersome task. As one observer at the time noted, "Those who were engaged in business—from the largest merchant to the keeper of a corner grocery—had to keep on his desk a Bank Note

---

[4] Braudel (1985b), Polanyi (1944).
[5] Sherman quoted in Davis (1910, 15).

Detector almost as large as a Family Bible, and had to be constantly getting new editions of it, in order to know what notes were counterfeit, what genuine, and as regarded even the genuine, to know what were worth par, and what rates of discount the others might be taken."[6] Not surprisingly, when the government created a uniform national bank note in 1863, one important goal—although not the only one, as we shall see—was to eliminate these enormous transaction costs.[7]

The connection between monetary reform and spatial transaction costs was also prominent in countries where policymakers were actively trying to create a national market in a top-down fashion. Soon after the Meiji Restoration, Japanese policymakers chose for this reason in 1872 to abolish the notes issued by local lords that were a dominant currency in most parts of the country. In addition to their heterogeneous character, the notes had circulated primarily only in their area of issue, and their values were related to each other only by confusing exchange rates.[8] German policymakers at the time of unification also saw monetary reform as a way to foster intra-German commerce. As far back as the early 1810s in Germany, merchants and travelers had complained about the transaction costs associated with the decentralized monetary order of German states.[9] Various monetary treaties gradually reduced these costs, but they remained considerable at the time of unification. In introducing a new uniform gold-based monetary standard at unification, Bismarck deliberately made a clean break from the various silver standards in use before unification in order to foster national economic coherence. In Nugent's words, "The biggest attraction of the gold standard was its usefulness as a spur to national unification."[10] The creation of a German central bank with monopoly note issue was also driven partly by this goal. Not only would a uniform note reduce domestic transaction costs, but the central bank could also provide a nationwide payments system and clearing house for the new country's banks.[11]

Monetary reforms at the time of Italian unification provide a further example. Although Woodruff cites Italy as a case where there was little interest in the creation of a national market, this was not entirely the case. Many Italian nationalists supported the drive for unification in order to create a larger national-scale market that was nowhere near existence at

---

[6] Rose (1869, 9).

[7] Sharkey (1959, 225), Davis (1910, 12–13), Johnson (1995).

[8] Takaki (1903, 32).

[9] Holtfrerich (1989, 216), Price (1949, 12–19, 34, 56).

[10] Nugent (1968, 119, see also 63–64).

[11] Goodhart, Capie, and Schnadt (1994, 9), Goodhart (1988, 106), Knauerhase (1974, 25–27).

the time.[12] Although they failed to create a unified bank note in the nineteenth century, Italian policymakers did create a common coin and standard in Italy in 1862 partly to serve this goal. As railways began to be built, nationalist leaders became aware of the inconveniences created by provincial coins and units of account. In the words of a parliamentary committee at the time: "These inconveniences are aggravated, and become so much the more felt, in consequence of those more powerful means of communication by which the interests and the peoples are more bound together—On the line from Milan to Ancona, you pass across four monetary zones; those, namely, of Lombardy, Parma, Modena, and the Romagnas; each of which has its coinage, its numerations, unknown on the other side of the frontier, which for any other purpose is already forgotten."[13]

We also see similar concerns in Latin America in the late nineteenth century in the context of the integrated national markets that began to emerge during the export booms of the time. In Argentina, large-scale foreign investment and the building of railways began opening up the interior of the country for increased trade after the late 1870s. A leading bank complained to the finance minister in 1878 about the way the country's chaotic currency created large transaction costs for inland merchants hoping to buy products from the Atlantic coast. Indeed, merchants had to exchange money several times in the course of this trade. Once political conditions had changed after 1880, a national standard was finally introduced to replace the situation in which the unit of account differed between provinces and even between cities in some cases.[14]

The emergence of national-scale markets also sometimes provided the prompt for state authorities to end the use of unofficial monetary standards within previously remote regions of the territories they governed. In France, many rural regions had long used unofficial accounting units such as écus or pistoles, and the authorities paid little attention. These units had caused no trouble when the regions existed in conditions of "autarchy," but in the late nineteenth century these regions were beginning to be incorporated within the wider national markets and official coins were coming into increasing use. In this context, the unofficial standards began to create what Eugen Weber calls "dire confusion" and the government was prompted to ban their use.[15]

A final example of the link between spatial transaction costs and terri-

---

[12] Clough (1964, 19).
[13] Government of Italy (1868 [1862], 304).
[14] Ford (1962, 93), Williams (1920, 31–34).
[15] Quote from Weber (1976, 34). See also Clout (1977, 470).

torializing monetary reforms comes from the British decision to create the gold standard with fiduciary silver coinage in 1816. As I argue below, the main prompt for the reform was the desire to address the inadequate nature of the country's low-denomination silver coinage. But the reform was also partly linked to the emergence of a national market by Charles Jenkinson whose well-known 1805 work, *Treatise on the Coins of the Realm*, provided the main theoretical justification for the reform. In the work, he compared Britain's monetary situation to that of other highly commercial city-states in the past, such as Amsterdam and Genoa. He recalled how they had created abstract "bank money" as a way of coping with transaction costs in their very heterogeneous domestic monetary systems. As noted in chapter 1, leading merchants in these cities had been encouraged to hold accounts at a public bank that were denominated in this fictitious bank money, and all large-scale trade was conducted via credits and debits to these accounts. Jenkinson noted how Britain's rapidly expanding commerce was now creating a similar need for a single standard to reduce transaction costs, but he argued that the country required a different solution because it was the first country to have a national-scale market. In Britain, he noted that "the business of commerce is not confined to one or a few cities or towns, but is spread over a large extent of territory, in every part of which trade and manufacturers are in great activity."[16] In this context, he argued, it made more sense to create single standard that was based on a real coin available to all people throughout the country instead of an abstract standard available only to the leading merchants in one city. Jenkinson saw the gold standard with its fiduciary silver coinage as the solution.

Constructing National Markets: The "Vertical" Dimension
Woodruff is thus correct to call our attention to the link between the emergence of spatially unified national markets and the territorialization of currencies in the nineteenth century. But the construction of national markets was not just a spatial process. It was also a "vertical" one involving the incorporation of the poor within the new national market in a comprehensive way for the first time. Before the nineteenth century, the poor often existed in a relatively isolated economic realm from the wealthy. While the latter were involved and affected by the world of high commerce and long-distance trade, the economic life of the poor consisted primarily of activity within localized, largely self-sufficient rural economies. In the nineteenth century, this began to change as the industrial revolution incorporated the poor increasingly into a national market economy in many countries. Relatively self-reliant peasants relying on subsistence

[16] Jenkinson (1880 [1805], 138).

agriculture became wage laborers. Everyday items that had been obtained by barter or in small, localized rural markets were now purchased with official coins in a larger national market context.

In this context, three features of pre-nineteenth-century monetary systems became increasingly problematic. The first was the uneven supply and heterogeneous quality of low-denomination money. Money was now a much more central element in the lives of the poor as well as in the lives of those who interacted economically with the poor on a regular basis. In every place where this economic transformation took place, there was a massive increase in the demand for low-denomination money for wage payments and retail trade. When the supply of this money was not reliable or the quality of it was uneven, it caused enormous transaction costs for those now dependent on a very large number of operations involving low-denomination payments.[17]

The second was the uncertain nature of the relationship between low-denomination money and higher denomination officially sanctioned money. As noted in chapter 1, low- and high-denomination forms of money had really served two relatively autonomous kinds of economies in the preindustrial world; the former were used mostly in very localized, often rural contexts, while the latter were used in large-scale and long-distance trade. Without a strong connection between these two economies, the variable exchange rate or uncertain "convertibility" between these two forms of money did not pose much of a problem. But when these two distinct economic realms were increasingly interconnected in the industrial age, problems were created. The everyday livelihood of the poor depended on purchases of products from large-scale national markets, and they required a "convertible" form of money to make these purchases. The poor were also paid wages by employers who derived their income from participation in this larger economy. More generally, rising incomes in the industrial age also ensured that the poor increasingly used higher-denomination forms of money.

Third, as the poor came to use official higher-denomination money more in their everyday lives, its heterogeneous features were viewed as increasingly problematic. As we shall see below, because so many of the poor were illiterate or without access to relevant information, policymakers became particularly concerned about the ability of this social class to distinguish between the quality of various privately issued bank notes. The standardization of currency within the country often came to be seen as a measure that protected the poor and helped them to adjust to a more monetized economy.

---

[17] These phenomena were also apparent in preindustrial societies that became highly commercialized (Perlin 1987, 1994).

The desire to overcome transaction costs associated with these three features of preindustrial monetary systems provided an important stimulus for many of the reforms that created territorial currencies. We can see this first with respect to the efforts to produce a more stable supply of official low-denomination money. As the first country to experience the industrial revolution, the British case is illustrative. We have already seen how the country's low-denomination copper coinage during the eighteenth century was extremely heterogeneous, consisting of poor quality official coins, counterfeits, and various private tokens. When the industrial revolution took off, frustration with the condition of low-denomination money grew dramatically. This frustration was particularly acute in regions such as Birmingham where the industrial revolution was producing a new large laboring class that depended on wages and retail transactions in low-denomination money for its livelihood. To fill the growing demand for low-denomination coins, many privately issued tokens and counterfeits began to appear there in the late eighteenth century.[18] Although these forms of money filled a need, they also had many costs for laborers; the use of counterfeits cheated laborers directly, while the private tokens were often inconvertible outside of a very specific context. Merchants who dealt with the poor also found the growing tokens and counterfeits cumbersome. Not surprisingly, many petitions soon circulated and public meetings were held in these regions to demand a more stable supply of new official copper coins and to complain about the way in which counterfeits and tokens often disadvantaged the poor.[19]

Interestingly, Matthew Boulton was particularly prominent in demanding this reform. Like many other industrialists, he had direct experience with the problems that the widespread shortage of low-denomination money was causing for retail transactions and the payment of wages. His personal experience acted as the prompt—in addition to some profit motives[20]—to develop his new coining press, and he appealed to the government to use his new machinery to produce more adequate official, low-denomination money. He even became involved in producing private tokens as a way of encouraging the government to act. In Doty's words, "He held the earnest conviction that the provision of good minor coins in large volume was of singular social value to the public at large" and especially for the poor.[21]

---

[18] Doty (1986a, 34), Craig (1953, 248–54), Mathias (1979, 191–200).

[19] Dickinson (1937, 138–39), Mathias (1979, 200–201).

[20] Margolis (1988) notes that Boulton and Watt had acquired shares in many Cornish copper mines (in return for selling them steam engines) that needed an outlet for their copper, especially when prices were very low in the late 1780s. He argues that Boulton thus had an incentive to see the mines do well by encouraging copper coining.

[21] Doty (1994a, 23). See also Doty (1986b, 124), Dickinson (1937, 135–39).

These demands of Boulton and others initially fell on deaf ears. Throughout the eighteenth century, the government had largely ignored the problems caused by inadequate low-denomination coinage. English monarchs had traditionally seen the coinage of copper, in Davis's words, as "beneath their dignity."[22] Many in the Royal Mint held a similar view, with one official noting in 1751 that "copper coins with us are properly not money, but a kind of tokens" for the poor and another stating in 1782 that producing them was "not considered as properly belonging to the Mint."[23] Members of Parliament, made up primarily of wealthy merchants and landowners, also did not share the interest of industrialists, retail merchants, and laborers in reforming the copper coin.[24]

The changing political situation ushered in by the French Revolution and the costly Napoleonic wars finally encouraged reform. As Harling notes, these political developments encouraged serious challenges to the legitimacy of traditional elites in Britain, and they responded by suddenly showing a much greater interest in economic reforms that could be portrayed as serving the general interest.[25] Although Harling does not mention it, the issue of reforming low-denomination money fit well into this project of legitimating elite political authority. The issue of the state's neglect of the production of copper coin was one that had encouraged open challenges of the elite's legitimacy. Many private issues of copper tokens carried inscriptions attacking the government, including republican messages during this era. One industrialist, John Wilkinson, went so far as to place his own image on the token coin he issued in 1788 (see figure 7). In this context, creating a more adequate quantity of a new official copper coin, with the king's portrait on it, made political sense.[26]

Concerns about transaction costs for low-denomination payments also prompted a ban on privately issued low-denomination "tokens" in 1812 (a ban that was then implemented fully once the mint's new coins were produced). In the 1810–12 period, an enormous quantity of private tokens appeared in some parts of the country, often produced by copper mining companies disposing of surplus stock that had emerged with a sudden

---

[22] Davis (1895, xiv). See also Mathias (1979, 191).

[23] Quoted in Craig (1953, 250). See also Whiting (1971, 13), Peck (1970, 204), Clain-Stefanelli (1985, 34).

[24] Whiting (1971, 21), Mathias (1979, 195).

[25] Harling (1996); see also Colley (1996, ch.4).

[26] The king himself examined and approved the design of the new copper coin issued in 1821 (Mint 7/73, PRO). In his 1805 treatise that advocated this reform among others, Jenkinson—himself from a well-established family and very much a member of the establishment (Gash 1984)—reminded the king of how successful coinage reforms in the past had helped solidify political support for the monarch from the people (Jenkinson 1880 [1805], 111).

Figure 7. Industrialist John Wilkinson's private token with his own image, 1788. Photograph courtesy of The British Museum. © The British Museum.

decline in the copper price. Because of their overabundance, these tokens often could not be redeemed at full value and complaints to Parliament were soon made. Some petitions expressed concerned about the impact on the poor who received wages in these tokens but could only spend them at a discount that could range as high as 50 percent.[27] Others noted the inconveniences for businesses that dealt with the poor, such as this petition from London retailers in 1813: "In those extensive concerns that have deal-

---

[27] Great Britain (1817, 1314), Bell (1964, xv), Davis (1969, xxxiii).

ings with the poorer classes of the community; namely, those of Brewers, Distillers and others, the injury sustained is beyond calculation. In some of these establishments, numerous person are constantly engaged in collecting and packing up Copper, and in several instances even horses and carts are employed for the purpose of conveying it home."[28]

The British case shows well how the project of reforming low-denomination money was closely tied to a desire to reduce transaction costs encountered in low-denomination payments in the context of industrialization. In more peripheral countries, the incorporation of the poor within a national market usually took place in the context of intensified economic interactions with richer, industrialized countries, rather than through indigenous industrialization. Once again, however, this economic transformation often acted as the catalyst for reforms of low-denomination money. In the last chapter, we saw how both Siam and Peru suddenly reformed their low-denomination money when expanding trade with industrial powers in the mid-1850s produced demand for a better quality, low-denomination money. Mexico also presents an interesting example. Beginning in the 1880s, the proliferation of plantations and mines serving export markets suddenly resulted in a dramatic shortage of low-denomination money throughout the country. The shortage was initially addressed by private tokens, mostly issued by mine and plantation owners. But because these tokens could usually only be redeemed at a company store where prices were often artificially high, there was often enormous resentment among workers who were paid in these tokens. This resentment boiled over into some violent demonstrations and "serious outbreaks occurred in various parts of the country."[29] The government responded by banning the issue of private tokens in 1889, although this ban was not initially well enforced, and the tokens did not begin to disappear until the government finally began to supply large quantities of good-quality, low-denomination copper and nickel coins after 1905. Interestingly, the political importance of the issue was made clear after the 1911–1917 revolution when the new 1917 constitution included a provision declaring that all wages must be paid in legal tender.[30]

Concerns for the transaction costs faced by the poor and those who transacted with them were important not just in prompting reforms of copper coinage and private tokens. They were also central in encouraging countries to introduce the gold standard with a fiduciary silver coinage system. A number of scholars have noted that the United Kingdom, the

---

[28] Wholesale et al. (1814, 2).
[29] Pradeau (1958, 571–72). See also Leslie and Pradeau (1972).
[30] Pradeau (1958, 572), Long (1969).

United States, and many continental European countries that undertook this monetary reform during the nineteenth century were prompted much less by theoretical arguments than by a practical desire to address the problem of the low-denomination silver coin at the time. Faced with sudden shortages of good-quality, low-denomination silver coins when their country's currency was made inconvertible (the British case after 1797) or when market gold-silver price ratios changed dramatically (the U.S. and continental European cases in the 1850s), policymakers saw the creation of a gold standard with fiduciary silver currency as a way of preventing low-denomination silver money from disappearing from circulation. In Carother's words, the monetary reform was driven "primarily due to the impelling need for a stable and convenient small change currency."[31]

This explanation is convincing, but it raises the question of why this strategy was not pursued before the nineteenth century when states also faced similar shortages of low-denomination silver coins. In earlier eras, policymakers had responded by simply adjusting the official value of silver coins, or doing a general recoinage.[32] The choice to create a fiduciary coin was a new one. We have already noted one answer: that industrial technology and the rise of the nation-states made the supply of large-scale, state-managed fiduciary coinages possible for the first time. Equally important, however, was a demand-side change. The maintenance of a stable, lower-denomination silver coinage became a more pressing need in the nineteenth century because the poor now relied heavily on these coins in their everyday life in the industrial age. The instabilities associated with "full-weight" bimetallic coinages had become increasingly costly to the mass of the population as they became involved in a more market-based economic life that was associated with industrialization. As one member of the U.S. House of Representatives put it in demanding a fiduciary coinage in 1853, the shortage of silver coins "does not injure your Wall Street brokers, who deal by thousands; they are making a profit by it; but it is a serious injury to the laboring millions of the country, who deal in small sums."[33]

Given these new economic circumstances, it is not surprising that there were widespread popular protests in the countries mentioned when good-quality silver coins suddenly disappeared from domestic circulation in the nineteenth century.[34] The decision to create a fiduciary silver

---

[31] Carothers (1930, 137). See also Redish (1990, 1991, 1995), Fetter (1965, 61), Martin (1973).

[32] Redish (1991, 5).

[33] C. L. Durham quoted in *Congressional Globe*, Feb. 1, 1853, p.191.

[34] For Britain, see Great Britain (1816b, 239), Fetter (1965, 65). For the United States and continental Europe, see Carothers (1930), Willis (1901), Martin (1973).

coinage in these countries was often a direct response to these demands, rather than a reflection of new theoretical support for the gold standard. Indeed, supporters of the reform often made clear that they saw the measure as only a temporary expedient, since they were opposed in principle to the idea of a fiduciary coinage, seeing it as a debased coinage.[35] The fact that the introduction of the gold standard was often linked to this concern about transaction costs relating to low-denomination money helps to explain what Gallarotti has referred to as the unplanned nature of the emergence of the international gold standard.[36] Since a key goal in joining the gold standard was this inward-looking one, policymakers often had little sense that they were also creating what came later to be seen as an organized "international economic regime."

There is one final way that concerns for transaction costs involving the poor played a role encouraging territorializing monetary reforms. The creation of a state-regulated uniform bank note was sometimes driven by worries about the ability of the poor to distinguish between diverse privately issued notes in an era when they were forced to use notes more and more in their daily lives.[37] Because of their illiteracy or limited access to information, the poor were assumed to have less ability to evaluate both the quality of a note and the bank that issued it. It was also argued that the creation of a uniform note might benefit the poor by making the detection of counterfeiting easier. These arguments played a role—although not the decisive one—in encouraging English policymakers to grant a monopoly note issue to the Bank of England in 1844. When small country banks had collapsed in earlier financial crises, such as that in 1825, many poor people in country towns lost much of their savings held in notes issued by these banks. It was, in the words of one member of the House of Lords, a "scene of complicated misery, and distress" that especially affected "the lower orders of the community."[38] For this reason, supporters of the 1844 act argued that restricting country bank notes was a matter of social justice. The prime minister also noted that the rural poor usually did not have a choice of banks and should not have to accept the costs of the poor management of the local bank whose notes they were forced to accept.[39]

---

[35] For the U.S. case in 1853, see Carothers (1930, 126), Willem (1959, 18), Taxay (1966, 220), Martin (1973, 826–27); *Congressional Globe*, Feb. 1, 1853, appendix, 191–92. For European countries, see Carothers (1930, 136), Willis (1901). To highlight the temporary nature of the move, governments often left mints open for silver coinage in principle, creating a "limping" gold standard. But then when prices moved the other way in the late 1860s and early 1870s, and there was a risk of a large reentry of silver into domestic circulation for countries that kept open free coinage, most governments closed this option.

[36] Gallaroti (1995).

[37] For this general point, see Smith (1990, 176), Von Mises (1953 [1924], 398).

[38] The Marquis of Lansdown in Great Britain (1826, 133).

[39] Andreades (1966, 287–88).

Supporters of the decision to create a uniform national bank note in the United States in 1863 also sometimes cited their desire to protect the poor. Privately issued notes at the time were not always backed fully by their issuers and holders of the notes could suffer losses when they tried to redeem them. Sophisticated merchants could usually protect themselves from losses by using bank note detectors or simply through their greater familiarity with the various notes.[40] But others were often less fortunate; as one contemporary observer noted, these losses "have fallen mainly on the poorer classes."[41] One of the objectives behind the 1863 move was thus to create, in the words of U.S. treasury secretary Chase, a "safe currency for the masses" by ensuring that the new uniform national note could only be issued by banks that backed them with government bonds. As he argued, the new currency was needed "so that labor should not be cheated of its rewards."[42]

Even in cases where a fully standardized note was not created, special concern was often given to the poor. In Canada, a system of multiple private notes persisted until the 1930s, but the government chose in 1870 to monopolize low-denomination notes. A key reason was concern for the impact of bank failures on the poor.[43] As one politician put it, "The larger notes were in the hands of merchants who were better able to take care of themselves" and thus the government "had adopted a mixed scheme in which they regarded the safety of the poorer classes as the first concern."[44] In Mexico, where there was strong resistance to the creation of single national note, the government moved in 1897 to encourage a single note issuer in each state of the country on similar grounds. In McCaleb's words, the finance minister "was against the absolute and unrestricted liberty of banks. The ignorance of the masses as to values and the want of confidence in banks outside the cities demanded that banking development should be closely controlled."[45] In other countries, low-denomination notes were simply banned for the same reason of protecting the poor.[46]

The concerns of elite policymakers about the abilities of the poor to distinguish "good" notes from "bad" were not always compassionate ones. They were also self-interested: the rich felt they needed to be protected from the poor's "irrational" behavior. Policymakers believed that the poor

[40] Rockoff (1991, 93).
[41] Quoted in Davis (1910, 16).
[42] Quotes in Davis (1910, 89, 91).
[43] Shortt (1986, 575–79, 612).
[44] George Cartier in Government of Canada (1870, 801).
[45] McCaleb (1920, 97).
[46] Chile's free banking law of 1860, for example, outlawed notes below 20 pesos value (Subercaseaux 1922, 75).

were more likely to panic unnecessarily in response to rumors of a bank's difficulties because of their lack of knowledge. If they dumped a bank's notes unnecessarily, this might produce an insolvent bank. One of the advocates of the Canadian decision to monopolize low-denomination notes, for example, noted: "My reason for recommending that the Government should assume the one and two dollar notes was that these notes were generally in the hands of poor and ignorant people who created "runs" on the banks on the slightest alarm."[47] Similarly, in England, Coppieters describes the thinking that encouraged the restriction of the country bank notes: "Being usually *ignorant* and sometimes illiterate, they [the holders of small notes] reacted collectively and often violently to public rumours. Being *poor* they were hit immediately by the loss of a note and reacted at once."[48]

The Issue of International Transaction Costs
The construction of national markets in the nineteenth century did not involve just the bolstering of the internal economic coherence of a country. Many economic nationalists also associated it with the creation of a more distinct boundary between the domestic and international economy, one that could be used to foster greater national economic self-reliance. Monetary reform was often seen by these figures as a key tool to achieve this goal. In particular, they called for the creation of inconvertible national fiduciary currencies to discourage cross-border commerce by *increasing* international transaction costs.

This was, for example, an argument put forward by the well-known American economic nationalist Henry Carey. During the U.S. Civil War, he strongly endorsed the issue of an inconvertible currency, arguing that it would discourage imports and act as a monetary reinforcement of the country's protectionist trade policy.[49] In Canada, economic nationalist Isaac Buchanan echoed this argument with his "national currency" movement. During the 1870s and early 1880s, his supporters lobbied the Canadian government to create an inconvertible national currency as a way of discouraging imports, promoting domestic industry, and reducing the country's dependence on foreign loans.[50] Perhaps the most interesting economic nationalist thinker was Johann Fichte, who wrote a book in 1800 titled *The Closed Commercial State*. In this book, he advocated not just an in-

---

[47] Weir (1903, 160).
[48] Coppieters (1955, 62). See also Smith (1990, 188).
[49] Sharkey (1959).
[50] "Proposal of a National Currency Reform League for Canada," October 28, 1879, Manuscript Group 24 D14, v.108 file 070979, CNA.

convertible national fiduciary currency, but also the use of exchange controls to promote economic self-sufficiency. Fichte argued that, in contrast to "world money" such as gold or silver, an inconvertible national fiduciary currency made out of paper (or even leather) would allow the state to make these exchange controls effective because domestic citizens would not have currency that was acceptable to foreigners in the international economy. As he put it, "All the possibility of world trade depends upon the possession of means of exchange that are accepted throughout the world and upon our ability to accept such means of exchange."[51]

These thinkers identified some important reasons why policymakers might choose to create territorial currencies. Such a currency, if made inconvertible, could *increase* international transaction costs both by creating an exchange rate risk between the domestic and international economy and by strengthening the ability of the state to enforce controls on cross-border flows of money. Both of these results could serve the goal of fostering a more distinct and autonomous national economy. Indeed, as we shall see in chapter 9, many policymakers who created territorial currencies in poorer countries after World War II cited these reasons as important rationales for the monetary reforms they launched.

In the liberal era before the First World War, however, this kind of thinking had very little influence on policymaking. In Canada, Buchanan's movement was able to prompt the government to lower the specie reserve backing for its note and increase the note issue in 1880, but the country's elite was resolutely opposed to an inconvertible currency.[52] In the United States, when the currency was made inconvertible during the Civil War and some inconvertible "greenbacks" were issued by the state, the main motivation was the pressure of war finance rather than the realization of ideas like those put forward by Carey. Indeed, most experiences of inconvertible currencies during the nineteenth century were temporary ones linked to an experience of war or revolution. Even policymakers in those countries that had inconvertible currencies for most of the nineteenth century—such as Austria-Hungary or Russia—would have preferred convertible money.[53] There was, in other words, little support in policymaking circles for these kinds of policies whose deliberate aim was to foster national economic self-reliance. This was an era of growing international economic integration when policymakers were inclined to see their efforts to construct national markets as going hand in hand with the goal of strengthening economic links with the outside world.

Interestingly, in the monetary realm, the goals of national consolidation

---

[51] Quoted in Heilperin (1960, 92).
[52] Shortt (1986, 712).
[53] Conant (1969 [1927], ch. 9–10)

and international economic integration were often complementary in a very concrete manner. As we saw in the first part of this chapter, the introduction of the gold standard with a fiduciary silver coinage in many countries was driven primarily by the inward-looking goal of consolidating the domestic monetary system. But it also received support from more internationalist groups seeking to reduce transaction costs in their trade and investment with Britain and other countries that had already introduced gold standards. To many of these groups, the importance of the gold standard had little to do with the creation of a fiduciary silver coinage and much more to do with minimizing international transaction costs.[54] Indeed, this dual advantage of the gold standard—reducing transaction costs both within and between countries—helps to explain its considerable popularity in an age when national and international markets were growing at the same time.

In poorer countries during the late nineteenth and early twentieth centuries, it is worth noting that the rationale for adopting a gold-based monetary standard was often primarily the "extroverted" one of fostering trade and investment links with rich "gold standard" countries. Within countries on the silver standard, for example, domestic societal interests seeking to attract international investment worried that the rapid depreciation of silver vis-à-vis gold in this period would undermine the confidence of foreign investors.[55] Importers shared their concern because the depreciating exchange rate posed problems for them too.[56] Also pushing for the reform were foreigners from "core" countries with strong economic links to specific poorer countries. Across much of Latin America, U.S. policymakers played a key role after 1900 in pressing local politicians to introduce gold exchange standards.[57] In the Middle East, various European powers also pressed governments in the late nineteenth century to stabilize local currencies on a gold basis.[58] When we examine the policies of colonial powers in chapter 8, we will also see the decisive role they played in this period in placing colonies on the gold exchange standards in order to facilitate their trade and investment.

[54] For this view in Germany, see Holtfrerich (1989), Zucker (1975, 64–66), Knapp (1924 [1905], 277–79). See also this view in Denmark (Bendixen 1967, 95–96). There was, of course, a debate throughout the nineteenth century among internationalist groups about whether a bimetallic international monetary standard might be preferable to the international gold standard. This was a key issue for discussion at international monetary conferences in 1878, 1881, and 1892.

[55] Bordo and Rockoff (1996).

[56] Conant (1969 [1927], 486). By contrast, many exporters were strongly opposed to the gold standard since they benefited from the depreciating silver-based currency. See the opposition of coffee exporters in Central America (Bulmer-Thomas 1987, 28–29).

[57] Rosenberg (1985, 1999).

[58] Issawi (1982, 177).

Although gold-based standards were often adopted for this outward-looking reason in poorer countries, the move still had the side effect of helping to build a more consolidated domestic monetary order. It did this partly by ushering in a fiduciary coinage system with all of the effects we have seen in chapter 1. In order to gain greater control over the supply of coins, governments were also now encouraged to remove foreign coins and unofficial domestic monies.[59] To maintain a gold-based standard, it was also often deemed necessary to create a monopoly note issue for reasons described in the next chapter.

At the same time, however, policymakers' "extroverted" orientation often was apparent in the partial nature of domestic monetary consolidation. When Siam introduced a gold exchange standard in 1902, the internal spatial coherence of the country's monetary system remained weak, with foreign coins used in various regions until the 1920s.[60] Similarly, when Nicaragua adopted a gold exchange standard with U.S. help in 1912, the eastern part of the country, which was quite disconnected economically, took a long time to adopt the new currency.[61] Some countries that introduced the gold-based monetary standards also did not create a perfectly functioning fiduciary coinage system, thus neglecting one of the most important internal benefits of this monetary order. For example, when Mexico introduced the gold standard in 1905 to encourage trade and investment with gold countries, the governing elite left in domestic circulation the full-weight Mexican silver peso with free coinage because of this coin's longstanding status as an international currency. This proved to be a costly decision. Although the coin was assigned a fixed subsidiary value, an increase in the world silver price in 1905–7 prompted the silver pesos to disappear from domestic circulation because their metallic value became greater than the face value assigned to them. The government was unable to replace the lost coins with new ones quickly enough and the resulting shortage of silver coins caused enormous economic disruption to the poorer classes who relied heavily on the use of these coins. Indeed, this monetary disruption has been described as one of the catalysts for the Mexican revolution that began in 1911.[62]

---

[59] In Siam the introduction of a gold exchange standard in 1902 prompted the government to remove large quantities of the traditional silver bullet money that was still in circulation. Similarly, when Costa Rica joined the gold standard in 1896, it withdrew all the old foreign coins that had long plagued its monetary system (Young 1925, 197–99).

[60] Similarly, even after Peru adopted a gold exchange standard in the 1897–1900 period, the country's remote southern altiplano region retained a distinctive monetary system based on debased Bolivian coins as the main currency until as late as 1920 (Jacobsen 1993, 160).

[61] Young (1925, ch. 12).

[62] McCaleb (1920, 149–50, 160, 195–97), Rosenberg (1985, 189).

Conclusion

A first motivation for territorializing currencies in the nineteenth century, then, was to reduce domestic—and to some extent international—currency-related transaction costs. In developing this argument, I am not trying to present an overly functional explanation of the link between territorializing reforms and market development. In all the examples cited above, monetary reforms grew out of concrete political demands by specific groups. As we have seen, the demands often came from the very societal groups who were experiencing the inadequacies of the old monetary order most directly as markets developed. In other countries, reforms were promoted by state elites who sought to facilitate rapid economic development by cultivating international economic links and/or constructing a national-scale economy in a top-down fashion.

The goal of reducing transaction costs was not endorsed by everyone and monetary reform initiatives often produced highly contested political struggles for this reason. In some cases, opposition came from groups who had benefited economically from the large transaction costs of the preterritorial currency order. These often included private bankers who made considerable profits from the monetary heterogeneity that preceded territorializing reforms. Another important source of opposition arose from groups that did not favor the goal of facilitating the emergence of new markets either at the domestic or international level. We have already noted economic nationalists who opposed the goal of international economic integration. There were also groups who sought to defend economic localism in the face of emerging national markets. A good example comes from China where poor regions often resisted the efforts of the central government to ban local currencies issued in iron, lead, or even pottery for this reason. These currencies acted as a form of protectionism for local markets; because they were very difficult to convert into official currency, nonlocal merchants who earned them were encouraged to spend them locally.[63] In each country, the trajectory of monetary reform thus reflected the relative power and balance of political forces opposed to and supportive of reforms. As we shall see in the next chapters, there were also many other reasons unrelated to transaction costs for either opposing or supporting initiatives to create territorial currencies.

---

[63] Pomeranz and Topic (1999, 15–16). Similarly, in Canada, merchants in communities alongside the newly built transcontinental railways in the 1880s continued to issue local token currencies as a way of encouraging customers to return and prevent railway settlements from taking away their business (Tannahill 1967).

4

Multiple Macroeconomic and Fiscal Motivations

In this chapter, I examine two motivations for creating territorial currencies in the nineteenth and early twentieth centuries that have received much more attention than those related to transaction costs. The first was control of the domestic money supply in order to influence national macroeconomic conditions. It is widely recognized that this goal played a particularly important role in encouraging the standardization of note issues in the nineteenth century. I argue that there were three different ways in which the link between note standardization and national macroeconomic goals was conceived in the nineteenth and early twentieth centuries. Specifically, the views of "classical liberals" on the question have received more attention than those of "liberal nationalists" and "macroeconomic activists."

I also examine fiscal motivations that encouraged policymakers to territorialize currencies during this period. A number of scholars have argued that territorial currencies were created primarily to satisfy the growing fiscal needs of the state. By monopolizing the issue of money within the territories they governed, states could maximize their seigniorage gains. I think that the importance of this motivation is sometimes overstated. Moreover, the focus on seigniorage gains has steered attention away from another important fiscal motivation for creating territorial currencies: that of reducing transaction costs faced by the public sector in operating new modern systems of taxation, budgeting, and accounting in a heterogeneous monetary context.

Macroeconomic Motivations

An important reason for creating territorial currencies was to acquire a greater degree of control over the domestic money supply in order to influence national macroeconomic conditions. If a state-regulated homogeneous and exclusive form of money could be established within a country, the domestic money supply could be more easily controlled. The goal of creating a monopoly issuer of money in order to regulate its supply for macroeconomic reasons was not a new one.[1] But it had new urgency in the nineteenth century. One reason was that paper notes were becoming increasingly important within the domestic monetary systems of many countries. As their use grew, their influence on national macroeconomic conditions raised concerns among policymakers everywhere. Paper notes, a fiduciary form of money, seemed to require more purposeful supply control than did the metallic coins that had dominated most monetary systems before the nineteenth century.

Also important was the increasingly pervasive use of money in the industrial age. In a highly monetized economy, policymakers were forced to recognize the greater importance of the national money supply to the economic well-being of the country. Indeed, examining the role of national money supply became a key preoccupation of political economy as it became an increasingly established and "scientific" discipline in the nineteenth century. The changed political climate reinforced this new scientific interest in national macroeconomics. In an age of rising nationalism and popular sovereignty, the issuing of money was no longer seen to serve only the monarch but also the people and their economic welfare.

Classical Economic Liberalism and Monopoly Note Issues
The link between the standardization of bank notes and the desire to control the domestic money supply for macroeconomic purposes in the nineteenth century has received considerable attention from historians. But existing literature often overlooks the fact that there were three different ways in which the issue was thought about in this period. Let us begin with the approach that has received most attention: the "classical liberal" one that became particularly prominent in England at the time of the 1844 Bank Act.

We have already seen how the decision to create a note monopoly in England was driven by some concerns relating to transaction costs faced by the poor. The more important motivation for the decision, however, was the desire to manage the domestic money supply in a way that simulated the automatic macroeconomic adjustment mechanisms of the gold standard. This motivation is very clear when we examine the content of the 1844 Bank Act. In addition to enabling the bank to acquire a note monopoly over time, it also strictly regulated the issuing of its notes, requiring that they be backed 100 percent by gold reserves. The significance of the 1844 Bank Act was felt well beyond England. The power of Britain in this period and the Bank of England's prestige ensured that the act served

---

[1] von Glahn (1996) notes that Chinese ancient thought advocated that the state should have monopoly over money supply in order to regulate its quantity to maintain price stability and satisfy the needs of producers and consumers.

as a model for other countries to follow, as we will see in subsequent chapters. Given its importance, we need to examine the political sources of the classical liberal motivation for monopolizing the bank note in more detail.

To begin with, it is important to recognize the central role played by Prime Minister Robert Peel in the drafting of the 1844 Act. As Fetter notes, the act "was in the full sense of the name 'Peel's Act'."[2] In response to financial crises in 1825, 1837, and 1839, two parliamentary committees examined the need for bank reform in 1832 and 1840–41. But because no consensus had emerged from them, Peel was able to play a decisive role in shaping the course of monetary reform. Monetary issues had interested him as far back as 1819 when he had authored the bill that restored the convertibility of the Bank of England's notes into gold. He had been attracted to the gold standard because it represented a monetary system in which the money supply was governed by automatic market principles. Like other "liberal Tories," Peel was skeptical of government intervention in the monetary system and he was a follower of "bullionist" monetary thinking.[3] Bullionists supported the quantity theory of money that held that changes in the money supply could not affect the real economy. They also embraced the price-specie flow model that David Hume had initially developed to explain how a country's money supply would fluctuate automatically under the gold standard to correct external imbalances and reestablish international equilibrium.[4]

In the first half of the nineteenth century, English bullionists faced a difficulty. Although Hume's model assumed most domestic money to be gold coins, bank notes issued by the Bank of England and country banks were becoming a dominant form of money in the country. The bullionists' key objective became to ensure that the supply of these notes changed in accordance with the requirements of the gold standard. At the time of 1819 act, the issue received little attention because there was not yet a consensus that the note issue influenced the exchange rate. But it could no longer be ignored after the financial crises in the 1820s and 1830s were blamed on country banks that were said to be expanding their note issue more than the country's gold reserves warranted. This explanation of these financial crises rested on a belief—that came to be called the "currency school" position—that the note issue in England as a whole must be adjusted in direct correspondence with the rise and fall of its gold reserves. This would most easily be done by centralizing the note issue in

---

[2] Fetter (1965, 183). See also Horsefield (1953).
[3] Hilton (1979).
[4] See Eichengreen (1985).

the hands of a single institution such as the Bank of England.[5] Peel was a strong supporter of this "currency school" solution to the problem of financial crises after the early 1830s. In the early 1840s, he decided to take the initiative to implement its recommendations.

He made clear, however, that he was driven to propose the 1844 Bank Act not just by economic theory, but also by political conditions at the time. The late 1830s and early 1840s were a time of great social and political unrest in Britain with the powerful Chartist movement demanding the extension of the electoral franchise to the working class. As Ramsay notes, Peel himself believed the country was on the verge of a revolution.[6] As an economic liberal, he was very critical of those Chartists who had encouraged popular expectations of how the government might intervene in the economy to address issues of social justice, and he sought to insulate the state from such expectations.[7] In the monetary sphere, he was particularly worried by the prominence of demands for an end to the gold standard. One of the key leaders of the Chartist movement, Thomas Attwood, had been the leading opponent of the 1819 act and an advocate of a managed inconvertible currency over the previous three decades. His ideas and those of his "Birmingham school" (described below) commanded little respect among economists, but Peel believed (wrongly, as we will see) that the "vast majority" in the country supported them.[8] Peel's initiative to introduce the 1844 Bank Act was explicitly designed to reduce expectations of the state's role in money management and insulate this management from popular politics. It did this by ensuring that the bank managed the note issue in an automatic, nondiscretionary manner in keeping with the 100 percent reserve principle.[9]

Peel's desire to insulate monetary management from popular political pressures also led him to reject proposals—initially put forward by David Ricardo in 1816—to remove the note issue from the Bank of England altogether and give it to a government body that would be responsible to parliament. Peel himself was distrustful of the bank's discretionary power (as

---

[5] See Smith (1990 [1936], ch.2). It is important to note that the currency school view did not necessarily lead to support for a note monopoly for a single institution. It should have been possible to assign each country bank a specific fixed fiduciary issue. This is in fact the approach that Peel took with respect to banks in Scotland and Ireland. Some contemporaries suggested it as an approach for England too, but it received little attention at the time.

[6] Ramsay (1928, 228).

[7] Harling (1996, 228).

[8] Peel quoted in Hilton (1979, 596).

[9] Fetter (1965, 177–80, 185–86). For Peel's fear of the Birmingham school, see also Great Britain (1844, 726–30).

he had been in 1819)[10], and he was keen to make the point that the issuing of notes was one of the sovereign powers of government.[11] But he was persuaded that the independence of the note issue from politicians would be more easily guaranteed if the bank retained this privilege.

In order to simulate the automatic adjustment mechanisms of the gold standard, Peel had created a note monopoly that established a tool for centralized national monetary management. Some classical economic liberals worried about this strategy. They opposed the establishment of a note monopoly on the grounds that the note issue would likely be abused and that it was not compatible with the liberal commitment to free markets. The views of these "free bankers" and their political influence will be discussed in chapter 6. This perspective has also reemerged as a prominent liberal critique of territorial currencies in the current age, as we shall see in chapter 10.[12]

One further comment must be made about the 1844 Bank Act. A key limitation of the act was that it failed to address the growing role of bank deposits in the money supply. If the goal had been to gain complete control over the money supply, the 1844 Act should have outlined some way to influence the creation of bank deposits. In fact, the act did nothing of the sort because members of the currency school did not believe that bank deposits affected the total circulation of money.[13] This oversight would soon be corrected, and by the interwar period the influencing of bank deposit creation was seen as a central task for central banks everywhere, as we shall see in chapter 7.

Liberal Nationalism
Policymakers in many other countries (and colonial authorities as we shall see in chapter 8) also created monopoly note issues as part of their efforts to join or maintain gold-based monetary standards in the nineteenth and early twentieth centuries. Some had the same macroeconomic objectives as Peel, but many did not. While sharing the liberal goal of maintaining the convertibility of the currency into gold, some policymakers' underlying macroeconomic objectives were much more nationalist. Instead of trying to minimize the state's discretionary macroeconomic influence in the economy, they sought to bolster it in order to achieve national goals. I refer to this as a "liberal nationalist" position.

[10] Hilton (1977, 1979).
[11] Parker (1899, 136).
[12] The "currency school" also faced opposition from another group of economic liberals—the "banking school"—who agreed that a note monopoly should be created, but argued primarily that the bank should be given more flexibility in the management of the note issue during crises (Fetter 1965, 187–92).
[13] Smith (1990 [1936], 78–79, 89).

Some governments created central banks with a note monopoly to enable them to maintain the gold convertibility of their currency but in a way that *protected* the country from the automatic adjustment mechanisms of the gold standard. By concentrating the gold reserves in a central bank, monetary authorities could manage and ration them in a way that provided some insulation from international economic shocks. A central bank with influence over the banking system would also be able to paper over trade balances by attracting short-term capital flows from abroad by adjusting its interest rate. The central bank could also conduct open market operations in foreign exchange markets designed to maintain gold convertibility while protecting the domestic economy from the effects of interest rate changes. In these ways, national monetary policy would not be a tool that reinforced the self-regulating nature of international markets as Peel had wished. Instead, in Polanyi's words, it would create "what amounted to veritable artificial weather conditions," insulating the nation from the vagaries of changing trade patterns and flows of capital. In these contexts, the establishment of a central bank was really what Polanyi calls a form of "monetary protectionism."[14]

In the late nineteenth and early twentieth centuries, many established and leading central banks in Europe had already begun to engage in these "protectionist" monetary practices.[15] In countries where they did not yet exist, central banks with monopoly note issues were often created in this period in order to emulate their foreign counterparts. The creation of the Federal Reserve in 1913 provides a good example. A key catalyst for its creation was the major financial crisis in 1907 that had produced domestic financial panic and pressure on the dollar. Although the United States had the largest gold reserves in the world at the time, because these were scattered around the country in private banks, no public authority was able to mobilize them to protect the dollar or stabilize domestic markets. The creation of the Federal Reserve transformed this situation by centralizing the gold reserves of the country in the Federal Reserve banks. Supporters hoped that the Fed would also be able to manage the exchange rate more effectively through discount rate changes or open market operations in foreign exchange markets. They argued that the Fed would, in Lawrence Broz's words, "create in the United States the institutions of discretionary control, which allowed European monetary authorities to insure gold convertibility in the face of temporary foreign drains."[16] At the same time, the Fed was also empowered to foster deeper and broader domestic financial markets that could help lessen the dependence of U.S. merchants on Lon-

---

[14] Polanyi (1944, 205, 202).
[15] See Broz (1997, ch.3).
[16] Ibid., 151–52.

don financial markets and encourage a greater international use of the dollar. Before the Fed's creation, most U.S. foreign trade was financed through London, which increased the exposure of the country to British monetary conditions and benefited the British banking community.[17]

In addition to strengthening a country's power vis-à-vis the international economy, central banks with monopoly note issues were also created by liberal nationalists as a means of strengthening the state's ability to intervene in the domestic macroeconomy. We can see this motivation in Japan's decision to create a central bank with a monopoly note issue in 1882. The decision was driven partly by the liberal goal of making it easier for Japan to establish the convertibility of its currency. But at the same time, the monetary reform was designed to enable the state to intervene in the domestic economy to promote rapid industrial development. The architect of the 1882 reforms, Matsukata, made clear that he thought the nationalist ideas of Frederick List were more relevant to Japan at the time than the ideas of classical liberals such as Adam Smith.[18] Indeed, Holtfrerich and Iwami speculate that he modeled the new central bank after the Belgian National Bank because the Belgium government exerted strong control over that bank.[19] In his mind, the promotion of industrialization required a macroeconomic context in which the money supply did not constrain growth.[20]

Matsukata had in fact been the architect of a deflation after the overissue of private and government notes in the late 1870s, but by 1882 he was very concerned about monetary stringency. In particular, he worried that the shortage of money domestically was exacerbated by the fact that there was no real national money market or central lender of last resort. In these conditions, private banks held more specie than they needed to, and money did not flow internally to regions that needed it most within the country. Matsukata believed that the private banks were acting like isolated feudal lords, not sharing their capital with each other and engaging in little nationwide cooperation.[21] He hoped that a new central bank could address these problems by centralizing reserve holdings, acting as a lender of last resort, and directing money to regions of the country where it was most needed. As he put it:

[17] Ibid., Kemmerer (1971, 21).
[18] Reischauer (1986, 84).
[19] Holtfrerich and Iwami (1999).
[20] Matsukata (1899). In the pre-Meiji period, local governments had often expanded the supply of locally issued notes in order to promote economic growth, and this experience continued to influence the thought of Meiji policymakers (Nishikawa and Saito 1985; Takaki 1903, 14).
[21] Shinjo (1962, 42–43).

The monetary circulation of a community may fitly be compared to the circulation of blood in a human body. . . . Now the Central Bank is to the financial system of a country, what the heart is to the system of blood circulation in a human body; the one is just as indispensable as the other. To regulate the circulation of the currency of a country, to call it in to a place where it is wanting, and to send it out from a place where there is a surplus, thus to keep even and steady the constant flow of the currency,— this is the office of the Central Bank in a country.[22]

Macroeconomic Activism

The third perspective on the question of how a standardized note issue might serve the national macroeconomic goals of a country was a more radical one. Its advocates rejected the classical liberal premise that money had neutral effects on the macroeconomy, arguing that its active management could strongly influence employment and production levels. These "macroeconomic activists" advocated inconvertible national currencies that were managed with a primarily domestic goal of maximizing national economic growth and employment. Because nineteenth-century macroeconomic activists did not have direct influence on policy, their views have received less attention from historians. But for our purposes, they are important because they anticipated influential opinions in the twentieth century.

The most well-developed argument of this kind was put forward by Thomas Attwood in Britain, a middle-class banker from Birmingham we encountered above as a lead opponent of Peel in both 1819 and 1844.[23] Attwood believed generally in free markets, but during a depression or period of high unemployment, he felt that the government could provide "some kind of artificial stimulus" to production by expanding the money supply or depreciating the currency.[24] In contrast to classical liberals, he argued that unemployment or low levels of national income *could* have a monetary origin because some prices did not adjust to clear markets as flexibly as classical liberals assumed. Attwood went further to argue that the government could also stimulate a depressed economy through deficit spending and he developed what appeared to be a primitive concept of the Keynesian multiplier. To pursue these activist domestically oriented macroeconomic policies, he insisted that it was necessary to have an inconvertible currency. As he put it in 1826, only an inconvertible paper note is "self-existent, self-dependent, liable to no foreign actions, entirely

---

[22] Quoted ibid., 43.
[23] For his ideas, see Hawtrey (1928, ch.4), Moss (1981), Fetter (1964), Checkland (1948), Briggs (1948).
[24] Attwood (1964 [1816], 44).

under our own control; contracting, expanding, or remaining fixed, according as the wants and exigencies of the community may require."[25]

Attwood's ideas and those of his "Birmingham school" of political economy had a rather modern tone in their endorsement of discretionary national macroeconomic planning. He argued that through wise monetary management, as well as an active fiscal policy, a country should be able to rid itself of boom and bust cycles. This kind of ambitious planning was especially necessary, he believed, because his country had become the first in history in which money was so central to social existence. As he put it in 1826, "No precedent exists in history like England at this period. . . . *Here* the *division of labour* has become extreme. . . . *Money* becomes thus the very *life blood* of the political system; and its ample and healthy supply is just as necessary to our political body, as blood itself is to animal life."[26]

Economic nationalists in other countries echoed Attwood's ideas during the nineteenth century. In the United States, advocates of the issue of greenbacks during the U.S. Civil War made the case that this inconvertible government-issued currency could promote the economic growth of the nation.[27] In Canada, a parallel "beaverback" movement emerged in the 1870s making a similar argument. As its leader, Isaac Buchanan (who we already encountered in the last chapter), put it, money "should be something capable of being expanded permanently to the extent which the wisdom of Parliament sees to be required for the full employment of the people, and the development of the productive resources of the country."[28] In many Latin American countries, there were also advocates of inconvertible currencies who insisted that this monetary structure could insulate their countries macroeconomically from external influences and constraints.[29] The most radical advocate of national monetary planning was Johann Fichte, who was discussed briefly in the last chapter as a supporter of inconvertible currencies as a tool to promote national economic self-sufficiency. He also saw this form of money as a mechanism for national macroeconomic control. While Attwood and others generally favored free markets, Fichte advocated a much more interventionist state that provided for the economic needs of its people, guaranteeing work and regulating wages and prices. He argued that an inconvertible cur-

[25] Attwood (1964 [1826], 34).

[26] Ibid., 37–38.

[27] See Unger (1964), Sharkey (1959). Carey, however, was a supporter of "free banking" within the nation (Nugent 1968).

[28] "Proposal of a National Currency Reform League for Canada," October 28, 1879, Manuscript Group 24 D14, v.108 file 070979, CNA.

[29] Martín Aceña and Reis (2000), Fetter (1931).

rency would allow the state to better control domestic price levels and through exchange controls insulate itself macroeconomically from the world economy.

As noted in the last chapter, advocates of inconvertible currencies had little direct influence on policymaking in the nineteenth century. Even Attwood's relatively sophisticated critique of classical liberalism was not taken seriously in mainstream policymaking circles. As Lionel Robbins put it, advocates of inconvertible money in Britain were seen as "lunatics or enemies of society," although the possibility that they would gain popular support did worry the elite as we have seen.[30] Given that the ideas of macroeconomic activists would become very influential during the twentieth century, why did they have so little impact during the nineteenth century? Some prominent monetary historians have suggested that the narrowness of the electoral franchise played a key role. Without political pressure from the masses, governments could endure the domestic economic fluctuations—such as unemployment and decreased wages and prices—that accompanied a fixed exchange rate. When the electoral franchise widened in the early twentieth century, these domestic fluctuations became politically unacceptable and governments turned to more domestically oriented, activist monetary policy.[31]

This view has considerable merit. Support for inconvertible, activist monetary management was often strongest among the less wealthy during the nineteenth century. In Canada, for example, Buchanan's movement had "very considerable success among the masses" by the end of the 1870s.[32] Similarly, the "greenback" movement in the United States found strong support among farmers and labor.[33] Fichte, too, associated his call for a managed national currency with the values of popular sovereignty that had emerged from the French Revolution. Indeed, as Hayes points out, Fichte's work drew heavily on, and was in many ways an apology for, the experience of the inconvertible assignats in place during the early years of the revolution.[34]

But Attwood's experience suggests that this point should not be overstated. Attwood spent much of his political life attempting to expand the electoral franchise precisely because he believed that the masses would be more inclined to favor his monetary ideas. Interestingly, however, his allies in the movement for political reform often opposed his monetary pro-

---

[30] Quoted in Fetter (1965, 237).
[31] See Reis (1995, 13), Eichengreen (1992).
[32] Shortt (1986, 712).
[33] Sharkey (1959), Nugent (1968, 24).
[34] Hayes (1931, 263–64).

posals. In 1830, for example, he took a lead role in organizing the Birmingham Political Union of Middle and Lower Classes, which soon brought about the 1832 reform act giving the vote to middle class men. But the alliance he created between middle and lower classes carried a price: leaders of the lower classes insisted that he not mention his currency ideas until after the Reform Bill was passed. As an MP representing Birmingham, he then became a leading figure in the Chartist movement, which pressed for the extension of the electoral franchise to the working class. But just after presenting its petition with over 1 million signatures to Parliament in 1839, he learned that leading members of the Chartist movement had signed a placard publicly rejecting his monetary ideas, a move that devastated him and prompted his withdrawal from public life.[35]

Why was there such opposition to macroeconomic activism among other political reformers? Many of the leading political radicals of the time—most prominently, William Cobbett—were deeply opposed to the idea of inconvertible money. Their opposition stemmed partly from England's experience of an inconvertible currency during the Napoleonic wars when they had witnessed the poor quality of Bank of England notes—the "filthy rags"—and widespread counterfeiting. Drawing on that period, they also believed that an inconvertible currency would give private bankers, and especially the Bank of England, too much power.[36] Most importantly, however, they associated inconvertible money with inflationary conditions that could be very harmful to the poor.[37] Particularly prominent in their minds was the French experience with assignats in the 1790s that had culminated in hyperinflation. That experience, combined with others in the United States and elsewhere, soured many political radicals in Britain and other countries on the idea of a managed, inconvertible paper money for generations to come.[38]

Attwood felt these fears were ungrounded. He argued that his proposal would not give power to the Bank of England because his notes would be issued by a government agency that was responsible to Parliament. He was also opposed to inflation and felt that inconvertible money need not be associated with it. The assignats, he argued, had been issued by a "tyrannical government" whereas his proposed currency would "be sanctioned by the British Parliament, which is, in fact, the British nation."[39] To be sure that an

---

[35] Fetter (1964), Moss (1980, 287).

[36] Fetter (1965, 69–71), Harling (1996, 94).

[37] Moss (1980, 287)

[38] This was true, for example, of the first major political economist in the United States, Daniel Raymond, who in most other aspects shared similar views as Fichte, Carey, and Buchanan (Neill, 1897, 35, 40–41).

[39] Quoted in Moss (1981, 31). A similar argument had been made by early advocates of the assignats when comparing them to notes that John Law had developed in France ear-

activist monetary policy was not inflationary, he even suggested that each county in the country be required to issue regular reports to the government about the price of wheat and agricultural wages. Despite these arguments, his political allies remained wary of his monetary ideas. Attwood's experience shows that activist, domestically oriented monetary planning was precluded not just by electoral exclusion. Some high-profile experiences with inconvertible money haunted nineteenth-century activists and policymakers and gave strength to the liberal advocacy of convertible currencies and disciplined monetary policy.

Fiscal Motivations

By providing states with a tool to control the country's money supply, the construction of territorial currencies enabled policymakers to address the macroeconomic needs of the people they governed in a more direct manner. At the same time, the construction of territorial currencies also gave states a more efficient tool for extracting resources from citizens by maximizing seigniorage revenue. Seigniorage is usually defined as the sum of money accruing to the issuer of money that is derived from the difference between the cost of producing money and its nominal value.[40] When monetary systems were made up primarily of metallic coins before the nineteenth century, seigniorage was usually taken in one of two ways. The minter of coins could openly earn a profit by adding an extra "seigniorage" charge (above the normal mint charge that offset the cost of minting). Alternatively, it could be taken in a more hidden manner by debasing the coin through a reduction of its weight or its "fineness" (by increasing the proportion of nonprecious alloy). If the public detected this surreptitious strategy, its effectiveness would be undermined, as people would either not accept the coins or accept them only at a discount.

Before the nineteenth century, there is little question that seigniorage goals were central to the state's involvement in the monetary system. In the era before the rise of the modern nation state, borrowing was often difficult and taxation systems were underdeveloped. In this context, control of the coinage was often a very important source of revenue for governments.[41] One would expect such fiscal goals also to have played a role in encouraging the creation of territorial currencies in the nineteenth century. The various reforms we have been examining, after all, had the potential to expand greatly seigniorage revenue. States often created a mo-

---

lier in the eighteenth century: "Paper money under a despotism is dangerous; it favors corruption; but in a nation constitutionally governed . . . that danger no longer exists" (M. Matrineau quoted in White 1933, 3–4).

 [40] See for example Cohen (1998, 39).

 [41] See Bonney (1995, 466–72) in the European context.

nopoly issuer of money in their territory, thereby maximizing the seigniorage to be gained by that issuer within that political space. We have also seen how the territorialization of money involved the creation of fiduciary coins, which produced more seigniorage benefits for the issuer. The growing use of paper notes in the nineteenth century also created new opportunities for seigniorage (although when these notes were backed 100 percent by metallic or foreign currency reserves, the seigniorage stemmed only from any interest earned on these reserves). Finally, as bank deposits became more important, governments could earn seigniorage indirectly by borrowing from a national central bank, which then created new deposits in private banks. When this created inflation, it could also produce further indirect fiscal benefits for the state if it devalued government debt (in cases where the debt was issued at an interest rate that did not anticipate the inflation).[42]

Seigniorage Goals

But to what extent were the various monetary reforms associated with the creation of territorial currencies in the nineteenth century actually linked to fiscal concerns of the state? Some scholars argue that these concerns were the most important ones. This view is most prevalent among many economic liberals who are skeptical of politicians' goals in the economy.[43] But others such as Giddens, who argues that modern national currencies emerged from the state's need to finance modern warfare, share this view.[44] More generally, Goodhart notes that there is a long tradition of "chartalist" thinking, which argues that sovereign states have sought to monopolize money creation primarily because of their own fiscal needs.[45]

When these kinds of arguments attribute the territorialization of currencies exclusively to fiscal motivations, they are clearly overstated. We have already seen how nineteenth-century monetary reforms were also driven by concerns relating to transaction costs and macroeconomic objectives, and we shall see in the next chapter that concerns about national identities were also important. Some analysts point out, however, that we should not neglect the importance of the pre-nineteenth-century history as a backdrop for these reforms. White makes this case with respect to the 1844 decision to grant a note monopoly to the Bank of England.[46] Although the goal of maximizing seigniorage did not drive this decision, he argues that special privileges given to the bank in the late seventeenth and

---

[42] As income taxes became more common in the twentieth century, inflation could also generate indirect fiscal benefits if it produced income tax "bracket creep."

[43] See White (1984), Smith (1990 [1936]), Dowd (1992), Glasner (1989).

[44] Giddens (1990). See also Dodd (1994, 32–33).

[45] Goodhart (1998).

[46] White (1984).

eighteenth centuries for fiscal reasons influenced the outcome of the debate in the 1840s enormously. There is no doubt that the bank's initial establishment in 1694 was approved in return for a loan to the reigning monarch and that further loans accompanied renewals of its charter in its early years. White argues that the special privileges given to the bank undermined the stability of alternative private issuers of money in ways that encouraged policymakers later to support a monopoly note issue for the bank. By contrast, in Scotland where fiscally driven government intervention did not exist, he notes that a system of equally sized competitive note issuers flourished and was popular. White's argument has merit, but I note in the next chapter that the case that a system of "free banking" would emerge naturally and flourish without difficulties in the absence of state intervention is a controversial one.

Returning to the question of the direct role of seigniorage concerns in driving nineteenth-century territorializing reforms, there is no question that seigniorage concerns did encourage some of them. Fiscal pressures associated with modern warfare did, for example, prompt some governments to consolidate the note issue under state control in order to increase seigniorage gains. The decision to create a national bank note during the U.S. Civil War is one of the best-known examples. In the previous chapter, we have seen how this decision was driven partly by the desire to decrease transaction costs. But without a fiscal motivation, it is unlikely that the measure would have passed Congress.[47] Since the notes were still issued by private banks, they did not provide direct seigniorage revenue to the federal state. Instead, revenue stemmed from the fact that the notes had to be backed partially by government bonds. This measure was partly justified on the grounds that the bonds could be sold to redeem notes if the bank went bankrupt, but it was also designed to generate revenue for the federal state during the Civil War.

Fiscal pressures associated with the handling of domestic conflict also drove efforts to unify the note issue in other countries. In France, the government's decision in 1848 to grant the Bank of France a note monopoly was driven by its need for extra financial resources to fight domestic insurgents.[48] In Japan, the government's decision to issue a countrywide note right after the Meiji Restoration in 1868 also stemmed from the fact that the new government needed revenue to fight internal military challenges to its rule.[49]

Fiscal pressures facing states during the nineteenth century also derived from costs associated with the pursuit of "late development" strate-

---

[47] Sharkey (1959, 226).
[48] Smith (1990 [1936], 33).
[49] Takaki (1903, 9–17).

gies, such as large public works projects and the building of a modern bureaucracy. In Canada, the government's decision to monopolize low-denomination notes in 1870 was driven not just by the concern for the poor
noted in the last chapter but also by the desire for revenue at a time when
its budget was severely strained by these kind of costs. The government
would have preferred to monopolize the whole note issue, but encountered enormous opposition from private banks.[50] The Australian government's decision in 1909 to replace British coin with a new national coin
was also driven by this motivation. Two years previously, it had asked
Britain to share the seigniorage profits the latter earned from the circulation of British coins in Australia. Britain's refusal to do so acted as a key
prompt for the introduction of the new national currency.[51] The next year,
a new Labour government also established a note issue monopoly under
the Treasury, partly as a means of capturing seigniorage profits that had
previously gone to the private banks.[52]

In general, though, there are fewer examples than one might expect
where fiscal motivations were clearly outlined by policymakers as a rationale for their reforms. One reason may simply be that policymakers
were wary of admitting this rationale for reforms. The seigniorage gained
from a monopoly note issue was, after all, strongly attacked in many
countries as a "forced loan."[53] Because private sector issuers of notes often
supported these attacks, some governments tried to counter this criticism
by noting that those issuers were already earning profits from the note
issue, profits that should instead be going to "the people."[54] The seigniorage earned from the creation of fiduciary coins was also a sensitive issue.
In many countries, there was initially considerable opposition to the introduction of fiduciary coins on the grounds that they represented a debasement of the coinage. Nearly twenty years after the creation of a fiduciary
silver coinage in the United States, for example, congressmen were still
complaining about the "untruthful coinage" that had been created.[55] In
cases where the seigniorage benefits of the creation of fiduciary coins
were acknowledged, policymakers were usually quick to point out that
these were not the motivation for the reform.[56]

[50] Government of Canada (1870, 216, 253–54), Shortt (1986, 560).

[51] Hargreaves (1972, 141), Loynes (1974, 11), Hopkins (1970, 122).

[52] Plumptre (1940, 86). The desire to maximize seigniorage also played a key role in encouraging note monopolies to be established in other late developing countries such as
Sweden (Schuler 1992) and Spain (Goodhart, Capie, and Schnadt 1994, 164).

[53] See for example Government of Canada (1870, 251, 262)

[54] See Hincks (1873, 9), Plumptre (1940, 86), Nathorst-Boos (1970, 90).

[55] Quote from *Congressional Globe*, Jan. 9, 1872, 324.

[56] See for example Pepoli (1862, 302).

Another reason that fiscal motivations did not always figure prominently may have been that some territorializing monetary reforms did not alter seigniorage revenue as much as one might expect. Even before the creation of a note monopoly, many governments imposed a tax on private issuers of notes according to the average amount of their circulation.[57] If the tax had been set at a high level, the monopolization of the note issue under state control did not necessarily generate much more revenue to the state.

A final reason may be that the significance of seigniorage within the overall context of public revenue began to decline for many states during the nineteenth century. As already noted, seigniorage is particularly important in contexts where both borrowing and taxation are difficult. One of these contexts is wartime. But even in peacetime, these conditions were very common for most states before the nineteenth century because financial markets were underdeveloped and taxation systems were poorly organized. As modern nation-states began to emerge during the nineteenth century, however, governments' capacity to borrow and tax increased dramatically. Thus, at the very moment that seigniorage benefits could be maximized, governments' peacetime needs for this source of revenue were diminishing. For many modern states, the more significant issue was reducing the transaction costs associated with the operation of a modern fiscal bureaucracy, an issue to which we now turn.

The Fiscal Transaction Costs of Government

The link between the state's fiscal needs and the creation of territorial currencies should not be seen only in the context of the goal of maximizing seigniorage. Equally, if not more, important for modern nation-states were concerns about what we might call the "fiscal transaction costs" of modern government. In the previous chapter, we saw how governments created territorial currencies partly in order to reduce currency-related transaction costs faced by the private sector. But they also sought to minimize these costs for their own operations as part of efforts to increase the efficiency of modern public systems of taxation, budgeting, and accounting.

The goal of reducing fiscal transaction costs had often prompted monetary reforms in the past. Well before the nineteenth century, the introduction of money itself in different regions of the world had often been driven by the desire of public authorities to have a more convenient means of raising taxes and conducting their fiscal operations. Operating a large-scale public fiscal system via payments "in kind" is, after all, highly ineffi-

---

[57] This was true, for example, in England before 1844, and Italy during the late nineteenth century (Toniolo 1990).

cient. In the nineteenth century, however, concerns about fiscal transaction costs grew dramatically. In their exhaustive history of the fiscal practices of governments, Webber and Wildavsky note how the nineteenth century was a period of dramatic fiscal reforms.[58] Governments began for the first time to centralize their capacity to collect taxes and spend money in keeping with modern forms of fiscal planning and budgeting. This more rational and centralized fiscal administration was capable of mobilizing and distributing resources on a much more efficient, predictable, and large-scale basis.

But for this new centralized fiscal machinery to operate smoothly, the transaction costs associated with extracting and deploying resources for the state in a heterogeneous national monetary system needed to be minimized. Distinct monetary standards that existed in different parts of the territory often greatly complicated efforts to collect taxes and develop spending plans on a standardized basis. The motley collection of foreign coins that dominated many domestic monetary systems also greatly complicated the collection and assessment of taxes because these coins each had their own distinct and changing values vis-à-vis the official monetary standard. Particularly troublesome was pervasive use among the poor of uneven, poor-quality, low-denomination forms of money. The transaction costs involved in assigning a value to, and even physically collecting, these forms of money for revenue purposes were often enormous.

The creation of a more homogeneous and exclusive national currency in the nineteenth century was often driven by a desire to overcome these kinds of fiscal transaction costs. In Italy, for example, the finance minister noted that the task of unifying the coinage and standard of the country in 1862 was crucial for integrating not just Italy's markets but also "our financial administration." With the payment of the military being one of the first countrywide fiscal functions, it is not coincidental that he highlighted the transaction costs encountered in that area. The use of different coins in each province, he argued, caused problems for not just for consumers but "above all among our poor soldiers, who, being compelled frequently to change their abode, are more than others obliged to sustain the effects of such a state of things."[59]

Concerns about fiscal transaction costs drove the adoption of a common monetary standard in Canada soon after the creation of that country in 1867. Policymakers worried about the complications caused by the Nova Scotian monetary standard, which was different than that used in the other provinces. As the finance minister John Rose noted, the separate standard created "great inconvenience" for commerce as well as for "col-

---

[58] Webber and Wildavsky (1986)
[59] Quotes from Pepoli (1862, 302, 300).

lection on internal revenue."[60] Indeed, even in advance of the currency assimilation, the government began to collect taxes in Nova Scotia in Canadian currency to ease its difficulties.[61]

Two more examples come from cases we have already examined. In early Meiji Japan, the central government banned locally issued notes partly because government revenue received in them created considerable complexities for government fiscal operations. These notes usually could not be spent outside the region of issue, and they had confusing exchange rates between them, a factor that greatly complicated the central government's ability to estimate its income accurately.[62] The second example involved the creation of the national bank note in the United States in 1863. In addition to other motivations outlined already, the U.S. treasury secretary supported this move on the grounds that it would reduce fiscal transaction costs. Since the collapse of the Second Bank of the United States in the 1840s, the federal government had conducted its receipts and payments only in coins and specie because state bank notes were not always reliable or current in all parts of the country. By creating a new national bank note, the government would now have a paper currency that it could receive and pay out at par across the whole country.[63] In addition, the new national banks created by the legislation could act as depositors for government funds, a function that had been restricted to government offices since 1846.

The connection between the introduction of a modern fiscal system and currency reform was also evident in many states in the periphery of the world economy that were threatened by foreign domination. Nationalist reformers in these regions often hoped to create modern bureaucracies that could exercise control over their territories and mobilize revenue to build a strong military and national economy. Part of this task was seen to involve the creation of a more homogeneous currency that could reduce fiscal transaction costs of government. In the Ottoman Empire during the late nineteenth century, for example, reformers called unsuccessfully for the "rationalization of the currency" as part of their effort to strengthen the empire's ability to conduct efficient taxation, budgeting, and accountancy.[64] The same was true in Korea in the years just preceding Japan's conquest of that country in the early twentieth century.[65]

[60] Government of Canada (1967, 357–58).
[61] Government of Canada (1967, 411).
[62] Takaki (1903, 30).
[63] Letter from Secretary Chase to Hon. S. Stooper of the House of Representatives, Jan. 2, 1864; Entry 16, Committee of Congress (Letters Sent to); Records of Secretary of the Treasury, Record Group 56; USNA. See also Conant (1969 [1927], 341, 355–56).
[64] Quote from Lewis (1961, 176).
[65] Han (1970, 420), Duus (1995, 162–68).

In the late nineteenth century, some governments in peripheral countries also had concerns about how currency-related *international* transaction costs influenced their fiscal situation. In the previous chapter, we saw how the depreciation of silver vis-à-vis gold in this period caused considerable transaction costs for merchants involved in commerce between rich countries on gold standards and poorer countries on silver standards. As was noted, the desire to eliminate those costs acted as a prompt for the latter to join the gold-based monetary standard. It was not just private merchants, however, that were frustrated by fluctuations in the silver-gold exchange rate. So too were governments with large gold-denominated external loans to repay. Across much of Latin America in the late nineteenth century, a key motivation for governments supporting the adoption of a gold-based standard was to avoid the costly impact of silver's depreciation on their budgets.[66]

Conclusion

In this chapter, we have explored two more sets of reasons why policymakers created territorial currencies in the nineteenth and early twentieth centuries. Both macroeconomic and fiscal motivations have been widely recognized as important, but these motivations were sometimes more complicated than existing scholarship has noted. On the macroeconomic front, there were in fact three distinct ways in which control over the domestic money supply via a note monopoly was linked to national macroeconomic objectives. As we shall see, these three strands will reappear throughout the twentieth century and continue to exert a decisive impact on the evolution of territorial currencies in different ways. On the fiscal front, the desire to maximize seigniorage did encourage some monetary reforms, a point widely recognized in existing literature. But I have suggested that its importance should not be overstated and that the desire to reduce fiscal transaction costs was often equally if not more significant.

As noted in the conclusion of the last chapter, the creation of territorial currencies was often a highly contested political process. Before ending this chapter, it is worth noting that some of the opposition to the new territorial currencies came from groups who rejected these national macroeconomic and fiscal goals. In the macroeconomic realm, we have already noted the opposition of "free bankers" whose views will be discussed in more detail in chapter 6. Another source of opposition came from groups committed to subnational forms of macroeconomic management. In Mexico during the late nineteenth century, for example, opposition to the creation of a central bank with a nationwide monopoly note issue stemmed

[66] Bulmer-Thomas (1987, 28–29; 1994), Kemmerer (1916, 474).

partly from groups who believed that distinct monopoly issuers in each state would be better able to respond to conditions in the various isolated regions of the country.[67] Similarly, peasants in Peru's remote altiplano resisted the efforts of the central government to withdraw debased Bolivian coins because this distinct currency served as an important countercyclical macroeconomic tool for them. In depressions, the value of this coin would depreciate, thereby ensuring a higher price was paid to wool producers, while in boom times, it would appreciate resulting in a lower price being paid.[68]

Resistance to the creation of territorial currencies also had fiscal origins in many instances. As noted already, private banks were often very reluctant to abandon profits they earned from the notes they issued. So too were subnational authorities. In Japan, local lords put up strong resistance to the creation of the national note in 1868–69 because it would undermine the seigniorage revenue they earned from their own notes. There was even an attempted assassination of the person who had initially proposed the idea and the army had to be used to enforce the note's acceptance and circulation.[69] In Germany, considerable opposition to the centralization of the coinage and note issue in the 1870s stemmed from the old feudal elite and subnational authorities who often relied heavily on seigniorage revenue.[70] Not all subnational authorities even shared the desire to standardize the national currency as a means of increasing the efficiency of government operations. In the previous chapter, we saw how some private sector groups could make profits from a heterogeneous domestic monetary system. The same was true of some subnational governments. In China, for example, many local government officials preferred the existing monetary heterogeneity because they made profits not just from their own coin and notes issues, but also from collecting central government taxes in diverse currencies with fluctuating exchange rates. Although they had to forward tax revenue to a higher level of government in a fixed amount of silver, they often collected the revenue in copper, and they were able to manipulate the local copper-silver exchange rate in ways that made this operation very profitable.[71]

---

[67] McCaleb (1920, 96–97, 110).
[68] Jacobsen (1993, 161).
[69] Takaki (1903, 18).
[70] Holtfrereich (1989, 217–18), James (1997, 14–15, 31).
[71] Pomeranz (1993, 44–52).

5

National Identities and Territorial Currencies

In many different countries, policymakers had another reason to construct territorial currencies: the desire to strengthen national identities. As Benedict Anderson has noted, national identities are a specific form of political identity in which individuals feel that they are linked as members of an "imagined community" that is sovereign, limited to a particular territory, and bound by a kind of "horizontal comradeship."[1] The idea of nationhood flourished for the first time on a widespread scale during the nineteenth century, the same era that territorial currencies were first created in many parts of the world. Policymakers who wanted to foster this new sense of political identity sometimes saw the creation of territorial currencies as a useful tool for this task. In some cases, territorial currencies were used to strengthen a "top-down" nation building project in which state officials sought to cultivate a set of common nationalist beliefs and culture. In instances where a national identity was already present, the demand for territorial currencies often stemmed from a belief that this monetary structure could reflect and reinforce this identity in important ways.

The connection that policymakers drew between national identities and territorial currencies has been remarkably understudied in contemporary academic literature. In the large and rapidly growing literature on the history of nationalism and national identities, currency structures are rarely mentioned. If we turn to the shelves of books on the history of money and currencies, the significance of territorial currencies to national identities is sometimes acknowledged, but usually just in passing before attention is focused on more economic issues. Even recent important writing on the sociology and culture of currencies has neglected the issue.[2] The lack of attention to the subject in academic literature is particularly surprising given the prominence that it is receiving in public discussion at the moment, particularly in Europe. Opponents of the European Union's common currency project often argue that the abandonment of national currencies will "dilute" their national identity.[3] Researchers have also found that attitudes of some

---

[1] Anderson (1983).
[2] See Dodd (1994), Zelizer (1994), Parry and Bloch (1989).

Europeans toward the euro are influenced by their concerns about its implications for national identities.[4] In this chapter, I show four distinct ways that the creation of territorial currencies was connected to the project of nation building by nineteenth- and early-twentieth-century policymakers.

The Imagery and Naming of Territorial Currencies

Perhaps the most obvious way that territorial currencies were seen to foster national identities was through the imagery emblazoned on them. Anyone who has visited currency museums cannot help but notice the nationalist imagery that was increasingly placed on most countries' coins and notes during the nineteenth and early twentieth centuries. Strangely, however, these images and their purposes have not attracted the attention of scholars of nationalism who have examined nationalist imagery on objects such as flags, stamps, and statues.[5] Even Eric Hobsbawm's important essay on the mass production of nationalist tradition in the late nineteenth century ignores this topic, despite his brief acknowledgment that money is the "most universal form of public imagery."[6]

Policymakers engaged in nation building during the nineteenth and early twentieth centuries did not neglect the potential importance of imagery on money. It had long been recognized by the powerful. Well before the nationalist age, monarchs and emperors around the world sought to advertise their power and authority by implanting their seal or portrait on forms of money they issued. They also recognized that the influence of this imagery among their subjects would be greatest if their money circulated as widely as possible throughout the territory they governed. A similar recognition lay behind some territorializing monetary reforms in the nineteenth and early twentieth centuries. In this period, however, the imagery and the uses to which it was put began to change.

Let us begin with the imagery itself. The first signs of a significant shift in images on money to reflect nationalist ideas and identities can be found in the late eighteenth and early nineteenth centuries in the context of the political revolutions in France and the Americas. In France, the revolutionary government replaced Latin wording with inscriptions written in French and also covered its coins and the paper assignats with allegorical images of the French people, of the rights of man, and of liberty, equality, and fraternity that had been chosen in a public competition rather than by

---

[3] Quotation from the British politician, Mr. Heathcoate-Amory, in *The Financial Times,* May 28, 1994.

[4] Meier and Kirchler (1998).

[5] For brief exceptions in numismatic literature, see Doty (1989), Hewitt (1994), Swanson (1995). See also Gilbert (1998), McGinley (1993).

[6] Hobsbawm (1983, 281).

Figure 8. French fifty-sols coin from 1793 with allegorical female figures, one representing Justice and the other "Droits de l'homme." Photograph courtesy of The British Museum. © The British Museum.

the monarch (see figure 8).[7] Similarly, in the newly independent United States, the Congress, declaring it a "monarchical" practice, refused to put an image of President Washington on its coins and instead substituted a figure of "Liberty."[8] This kind of imagery was also common on the coins of the newly independent republics of Latin America. The importance attached to these images by political leaders was made clear by Morelos's comments in Mexico in 1814: "This nation has been made to venerate royalty and our citizens uncover their heads each time they see the effigy of the king on the coinage. . . . If we don't permit any other form of money except the one we have devised . . . we will obtain our Liberty."[9]

---

[7] Porteous (1969, 230–31), Lafaurie (1981).

[8] Taxay (1966, 31, 57–61), Carothers (1930, 54, 61).

[9] Quoted in Pradeau (1962, 16). See Doty (1989) for imagery on Latin American coins.

It was not until in the last third of the nineteenth century, however, that most independent governments across the world began a more systematic and organized campaign to place nationalist imagery on their money. According to Hobsbawm, nationalist imagery on flags and stamps in this period was driven by the desire of public authorities to devise new methods of maintaining legitimacy in the face of domestic challenges to their rule. He explains how governments across the world in this era launched extensive initiatives to cultivate the allegiance of citizens by instilling in them a sense of collective identity centered around nationalist images of a common past and culture.[10] Although Hobsbawm does not mention it, elaborate iconography on money, especially bank notes, played a major role in these initiatives, and governments were aided by advances in the technology of printing that permitted strikingly detailed imagery to be placed on paper currency for the first time.[11]

The types of imagery in this period were quite similar from country to country. Indeed, often the same bank note companies and artists were involved in the design of many countries' notes and coins, thus contributing to the uniformity of the practice (though not, of course, of the specific images). Japan's bank notes, for example, were transformed in 1872 from a traditional Japanese style to a Western style based on the U.S. model for the simple reason that they were initially engraved and printed by the Continental Bank Note Company of New York, the same company that had engraved the U.S. national bank notes of 1863 (see figure 9).[12] Particularly common images were historical scenes, reminding and teaching citizens of key events, personalities, and landmarks in the nation's history. Also prominent were portrayals of the everyday life of national citizens as well as of the economic progress of the nation. Landscapes were also common, perhaps not surprisingly since, as Simon Schama reminds us, such images were instrumental in the construction of national identities in most countries.[13] The images of the nation also went beyond these common motifs in interesting ways in some instances. Insecure Canada, for example, covered one note with an image of an allegorical figure pointing to the country's place on a map of the world, as if to remind recent immigrants where on the globe their new country could be found (see figure 10).[14]

To what extent did a concern with the power of this symbolism actually

[10] Hobsbawm (1983).
[11] For this importance of technological change in printing (although excluding a discussion of money), see Anderson (1991).
[12] Boling (1988).
[13] Schama (1993). For accounts of the imagery on national currencies in various countries during the nineteenth and early twentieth centuries, see Hewitt (1994).
[14] Gilbert (1998).

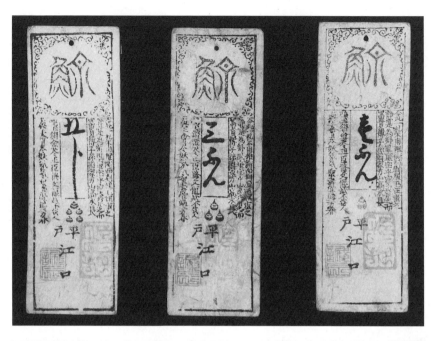

Figure 9. Hansatsu notes from pre-Meiji Japan and Japanese 1872 banknote printed by Continental Bank Note Company of New York. Photograph courtesy of The British Museum. © The British Museum.

drive monetary reforms that resulted in territorial currencies? An episode where it did play some role was the creation of the national bank note in the United States in 1863. In previous chapters, we have seen how fiscal and transaction costs drove this monetary reform. At the same time, supporters of the reform also made it clear that they hoped the new notes

Figure 10. One-dollar Dominion of Canada note from 1870. National Currency Collection, Bank of Canada, photography James Zagon, Ottawa.

could be used in a symbolic way to enhance a "a sentiment of nationality," a pressing goal given the civil war that was raging.[15] To this end, the new notes were emblazoned with detailed vignettes of personalities (e.g., Columbus, Franklin, Washington), events (e.g., the signing of the Declaration of Independence, the Battle of Lexington, the pilgrim's landing, the baptism of Pocahontas, the surrender of General Burgoyne) and symbols (the flag, the eagle, the Capitol) that were seen as seminal to the history and image of the nation (see figure 11).[16] The symbolic shift here was dramatic. The notes issued by private banks before 1863 had also been elaborately decorated, but the images had been overwhelmingly of very localized landmarks, personalities, and historical events, and were designed to enhance the trustworthiness of the note in a primarily local context.[17] Now, the secretary of the treasury insisted that the designs on the notes be "National in their character."[18]

Why was imagery on money seen to be so significant to the project of nation building? Here is the explanation given by the chief clerk in the U.S. Treasury who first advocated the use of the new imagery on the 1863 bank notes described above:

[15] Senator John Sherman quoted in Davis (1910, 80). As Swanson (1995) notes, the Confederacy had in fact emblazoned its new notes with nationalist images a few months earlier.

[16] Friedberg (1962).

[17] Angus (1974, 35), Doty (1995).

[18] Secretary Chase, "To Artists, Engineers and Others" undated; Press Copies of Official and Miscellaneous Letters Sent, 1862–1912, Vol.1 of 326; Records of the Bureau of Engraving and Printing, Record Group 318; USNA. Although this document is undated, its placement in the archives suggests that it was written in early March 1863.

Figure 11. Five-hundred-dollar U.S. National Bank note from 1863 with image of the surrender of General Burgoyne. Photograph courtesy of The Smithsonian Institution, NCC, Douglas Mudd. Reproduction rights retained by The Smithsonian Institution.

> A series properly selected, with their subject titles imprinted on the notes, would tend to teach the masses the prominent periods in our country's history. The laboring man who should receive every Saturday night, a copy of the 'Surrender of Burgoyne' for his weekly wages, would soon inquire who General Burgoyne was, and to whom he surrendered. This curiosity would be aroused and he would learn the facts from a fellow laborer or from his employer. The same would be true of other National pictures, and in time many would be taught leading incidents in our country's history, so that they would soon be familiar to those who would never read them in books, teaching them history and imbuing them with a National feeling.[19]

In this passage, the chief clerk identified two central points about the potential power of nationalist imagery on money in constructing a collective national identity. First, images on money were guaranteed a much larger audience than images carried by other media because of the pervasiveness of the use of money with the rise of national markets. The U.S. clerk suggested that the images on money may have been particularly effective in conveying messages to poor and illiterate citizens. In contexts where the infrastructural reach of the state was weak, transport and com-

---

[19] Letter from S. M. Clark to Secretary Chase, March 28, 1863, Press Copies of Official and Miscellaneous Letters Sent, 1862–1912, Vol.1 of 346; Records of the Bureau of Engraving and Printing, Record Group 318, USNA. Clark's example of General Burgoyne's image turned out to be a poor one since this image ended up being placed on the $500 note, a note that laborers could not be expected to receive in their weekly wages at the time.

munications were difficult, and illiteracy was high, imagery on money often provided a state with among the only means to convey symbolic messages to vast numbers of such citizens.[20]

Second, images on money may also have been particularly important because they were encountered so regularly in the context of daily routines. As Fernand Braudel puts it in discussing world economic history between the fifteenth and eighteenth centuries, money was one of the basic "structures of everyday life."[21] With the spread of markets, it became even more so in the nineteenth century. The U.S. clerk argued that this gave particular force to the imagery on it, providing a frequent reminder to people that they were members of what nationalists considered to be a common, homogeneous community. Like statues and flags, currencies could thus act as ever-present reinforcement of what Michael Billig calls "banal nationalism"; that is, the collection of ideological habits of practice and belief that reproduce nations as nations at an everyday level.[22] Indeed, national currencies may have acted as much more effective purveyors of nationalist messages than flags or anthems. As Virginia Hewitt observes, coins and bank notes are "among the most mass-produced objects in the world, painstakingly designed for millions of people to use." As she notes, they thus offer "an unparalleled opportunity for officially-sanctioned propaganda, to colour the recipient's view."[23]

The desire to exploit the power of imagery on money played a role in encouraging not just uniform bank notes to be created, but also a uniform coinage. A good example comes from Italy in 1862, soon after the unification of the country. The minister responsible for proposing the creation of a new uniform coin for the country noted the many economic benefits of the move, but he also stated that the symbolic political benefit "dominates all others."[24] Making a similar point as the U.S. clerk, he told the Chamber of Deputies: "Money, while it circulates in the hands of all as a sign and equivalent of every kind of value, is likewise the most popular, the most constant and most universal monument that can represent the unity of the nation. It is for this reason that the emancipated peoples look with suspicion upon the old coins, which connect themselves in their thoughts with

---

[20] Doty (1989) makes a similar point in the context of nineteenth-century Latin America. See also Swanson (1995) for the case of the United States. Anderson (1991) also highlights the importance of printed images in an age of widespread illiteracy (although not on money).

[21] Braudel (1985a).

[22] Billig (1995, 41–42) himself briefly mentions the potential role of currencies in this respect.

[23] Hewitt (1994, 11).

[24] Pepoli (1862, 300).

the humiliations and the slaveries that they have endured, and with one voice ask for a coinage bearing the effigy of the unifying king." The new unified coinage, a parliamentary committee also noted, would be an "emblem and pledge of the stability of the new order of things thus cancelling any vestige, any claim of an irrevocable past."[25] Interestingly, in Germany, nationalist policymakers were more cautious in their use of imagery when creating new uniform gold and silver coins in 1871 after unification. While one side of the coins carried the imperial eagle of the new Empire, the other still retained the portrait of specific subnational authorities or the coat of arms of free cities (see figure 12). In James's words, this concession "helped to ensure popular acceptance of a reform that might otherwise have been quite traumatic."[26]

Before finishing this discussion of the symbolic use of territorial currencies, one further point needs to be made about the symbolic uses of money during the nineteenth century. In a number of countries, the names given to coins and currencies reinforced the nationalist images engraved on them. In 1795, for example, the revolutionary government in France abandoned the age-old practice of naming its currency after an indicator of weight—the "livre"—and adopted the new name of the "franc." The choice was partly meant to restore confidence in the currency after the inflationary experience of the assignats; the franc had been a very stable French coin issued back the fourteenth century.[27] But the name also provided a reminder of the deep history of the nation and highlighted the kind of "free" community being imagined after the revolution.

The British soon followed suit in the 1816 coinage reform. Colley notes how the British were often in competition with the French in this period to find ways of expressing their distinctive national identity.[28] Although she does not mention it, the choice of the name *sovereign* for the new gold coin at the centerpiece of reform is a good example of this phenomenon. As in the French case, this name evoked the history of the country; a coin by the same name had first been issued in 1489. This earlier coin was not widely remembered, but it was likely known by the Master of the Mint, Wellesley Pole, who was deeply interested in numismatic history and who even established the first numismatic museum in the country.[29] At the same time, the name highlighted the different kind of national identity that existed in Britain. While the French emphasized their nation's freedom, a "cult of the

---

[25] Quotes from ibid., 300; Government of Italy (1862, 304).
[26] James (1997, 9).
[27] Moens (1991, 133).
[28] Colley (1992, 229–30).
[29] Dyer (1999, 42), Dyer and Gaspar (1992, 472–79).

Figure 12. Five-mark coin issued by Hamburg in 1876. Photograph courtesy of The British Museum. © The British Museum.

monarchy" became a central way in which nationalism was expressed in Britain in this period.[30] Pole was also committed to designing coins in a more interesting manner than past practice, and the imagery chosen for the coin reinforced the contrast with France.[31] In addition to the monarch's head on one side, the other carried an image of St. George on horseback

---

[30] Quote from Colley (1992, 225).

[31] For Pole's interest in the design of coins, see Craig (1953, 294). In 1817, he even announced that all new designs for coins would be chosen from a competition open to artists across the country for the first time.

slaying the dragon (see figure 13). As *The Gentlemen's Magazine* argued at the time, the image symbolized the "genius and valour of Britain triumphing over the Demon of anarchy and Despotism."[32] The importance of these comparisons to France may also have been heightened because a key goal of the 1816 monetary reform that introduced the new sovereign and fiduciary silver coins was to force out of domestic circulation the underweight French silver coins that had been entering Britain in the previous few years. The influx of this "French trash," as Pole called it, had been a development that Fetter describes as particularly "galling to British pride."[33]

Many other countries renamed their coins and currencies in nationalist ways in the years before the First World War. Particularly common were names that evoked historical memories. Among the more interesting were the names chosen by many Latin American governments for their currencies when they underwent dramatic monetary reforms in the late nineteenth and early twentieth centuries. Panama named its new currency after the explorer Balboa in 1904, while El Salvador in 1892 and Costa Rica in 1896 replaced their pesos with "colons" in honor of the four hundredth anniversary of Christopher Columbus's arrival in the Americas. Many others chose famous liberators from the time of independence such as Bolivar (Venezuela and Bolivia), Sucre (Ecuador), and Cordoba (Nicaragua).[34] The growth of national numismatic societies and interest in national numismatic history in the nineteenth century highlighted a further way in which national currencies came to symbolize a connection between the deep past of the nation and its present.[35]

Territorial Currencies as a Medium of National Communication

Territorial currencies were seen to foster national identities not just in these symbolic ways. In a more concrete sense, some policymakers hoped that territorial currencies would cultivate a national consciousness by fostering economic communication and interaction among the members of the nation. The goal of reducing domestic currency-related transaction costs, in other words, was seen to serve not just the economic goal of building a national market but also the political goal of fostering a collective identity. As one American supporter of a single national bank note ar-

---

[32] *The Gentleman's Magazine* 88, part II (1818), 368. I am indebted to Kevin Clancy at the Royal Mint for this quotation and reference.

[33] Pole quotation from Great Britain (1816b, 1021) and second quotation is Fetter's (1965, 65).

[34] Grigore (1972, 34), Young (1925, 65, 151, 193–94).

[35] See Adelson (1958, 55–56), Carson (1986).

Figure 13. British 1820 sovereign with image of St. George slaying the dragon. Photograph courtesy of The British Museum. © The British Museum.

gued in 1861: "Every citizen . . . who is supplied with such a currency—a currency which will be equal to gold through every foot of our territory, and everywhere of the same value, with which he can travel from Oregon to Florida and from Maine to New Mexico, would feel and realize, every time he handled or looked at such a bill bearing the national mark, that the union of these states is verily a personal benefit and blessing to all."[36]

Nineteenth-century analysts often drew a parallel between money and

[36] Potter (1877, 5).

language because both acted as a basic medium of social communication within the nation.[37] An Italian parliamentary commission examining the need to unify the currency of the new country noted in 1862 how use of diverse local coins and units of account was preventing unity in "economic language."[38] Little wonder then that the creation of a territorial currency was sometimes seen alongside that of a standardized national language as a crucial step in helping inhabitants of a national territory feel that they were a part of the same national community. As one Canadian politician advocating the abolition of Nova Scotia's separate monetary standard in 1871 put it, the experience of using a common Canadian currency "would make the people of the Dominion feel more like one people."[39]

These nineteenth-century policymakers were hinting at a point later developed in detail by the scholar Karl Deutsch. He argued that national identities emerged only once a people could begin to communicate more effectively and over a wide range of subjects. In his list of channels of social communication that could bolster the "communicative efficiency" within the nation, he briefly mentions the example of the role of a common currency.[40] Historian Eugen Weber also cites the growing use of a national currency among the rural poor of France as one part of a broader transformation that changed "peasants into Frenchman" in the late nineteenth century. In his words, the new standardized national currency became "a universal language that all understood and all now wanted to speak."[41]

Although these authors do not explore in detail the ways that territorial currencies may have fostered national identities, the link might have been an important one in nineteenth-century societies where "the individual is more and more tied into the economy of exchanges."[42] The reforms of low-denomination money, in particular, may have encouraged a closer sense of identification with the nation among the poor, as they experienced the concrete benefits that the new monetary arrangements brought and the associated sense of membership in the national society. Gabriel Ardant, for example, described how the creation of egalitarian taxation structures in the nineteenth century contributed to a sense of national consciousness and belonging in the same ways. Territorial currencies may have represented a second example of what he calls the financial "infra-

[37] See Shell (1982).
[38] Government of Italy (1862, 307).
[39] Mr. Magill in Dominion of Canada Parliament (1871, 304).
[40] Quote from Deutsch (1966, 98). He mentions common currencies on p. 50.
[41] Quote from Weber (1976, 40); see also xii, 32–34.
[42] Quote from Ardant (1975, 227).

structure of national feeling" that emerged in that era.[43] Indeed, as we have seen, initial efforts to reform low-denomination money in countries such as Britain emerged only once elite policymakers had been forced to see the poor as citizens in the wake of the French Revolution.

Money, Trust, and the "Spiritual Unity" of the Nation

Some advocates of standardized state-issued national bank notes argued that their existence might bolster national identities in another concrete manner. While metallic forms of money had intrinsic value, these policy-makers pointed out that the value of a paper currency was dependent on the trustworthiness of the institution that issued it or guaranteed its value. When this institution was a state, some argued that this new dependence might encourage a closer identification with the state among the users of the currency. Like it or not, inhabitants of a country would be forced to recognize that the value and use of their money was now dependent on their relationship with the state.

Once again, we can turn to the creation of the U.S. national bank note in 1863 for arguments of this kind. In this case, the state did not issue the new bank notes, but the notes all had to be backed by government bonds. For this reason, supporters of the new currency argued that the self-inter-est of the citizen would now be tied up with that of the central govern-ment to a greater degree. As Senator Sherman argued, the new uniform currency would make "every stockholder, every mechanic, every laborer who holds one of these notes . . . interested in the Government." He con-tinued: "If we are dependent on the United States for a currency and a medium of exchange, we shall have a broader and more generous nation-ality."[44] Similarly, the treasury secretary hoped the new currency would encourage "the stimulation of the patriotism of the people which would arise from their closer touch with national affairs in consequence of their direct interest in government securities brought about by the popular dis-tribution of the loans."[45]

This kind of argument was also particularly common among national-ist advocates of inconvertible currencies. Even though they had little di-rect influence on policy in the nineteenth century, it is interesting to exam-ine their views. One thinker who deserves special mention in this context was Adam Muller, a conservative Prussian who acquired considerable in-fluence as a nationalist critic of liberal economics in Metternich's Austria as well as in Europe as a whole in the early nineteenth century. He be-

---

[43] Ibid., 229.
[44] Quotes from Johnson (1995, 176, 172).
[45] Quoted in Davis (1910, 106).

lieved, in Erich Roll's words, that "the state's duty is to awaken national pride, the feeling of 'oneness' with the national state in the economic sphere."[46] He favored inconvertible national currencies on the grounds that they would strengthen the allegiance of citizens to the nation. Roll explains that Muller thought metallic money was too "cosmopolitan," a feature that ensured that it "destroys the links which should tie each individual indissolubly to his own national state." By contrast, inconvertible paper currencies were "patriotic" because they "tied men closely into the state."[47] In Muller's own words, a national currency that was inconvertible would act as an expression of the "inner spiritual unity" of the nation.[48]

Other advocates of inconvertible money in the nineteenth century made a similar point. In Britain, Attwood argued that an inconvertible currency was beneficial not just because it created a tool for activist macroeconomic management but also because it would cultivate patriotism, particularly in the context of a foreign invasion. He argued that when a country had a convertible paper currency, foreign invasions usually induced citizens to dump the currency in favor of gold. No such panic would be produced with an inconvertible currency, he believed, because it would ensure that "every man's interest would be bound up in that of his country."[49] Similarly, one Canadian member of Parliament who advocated an inconvertible national currency told the country's House of Commons in 1882: "If a man has $1,000 in paper money, the value of which exists only in the country of its creation, while it may not be worth ten cents outside that country, he has an incentive to support its institutions, in addition to his patriotism, because he knows if the country goes down his money will be valueless. But the man with a $1,000 of gold in the bank, which he knows will be taken in any part of the world, can readily withdraw it and leave his country if it should get into difficulty; he is not obliged to fight its battles."[50]

In the nineteenth-century context, these arguments that an inconvertible paper currency could foster national identities were not entirely convincing. Recall the experience of the assignats in France. At the time of the initial issue of assignats, the finance committee of the French Assembly had made the similar argument that "it will bind the interests of the citizens to the public good."[51] But the currency was quickly produced in excessive amounts to meet government financial needs and the result was a

---

[46] Roll (1939, 223).
[47] Quotes from ibid., 224, Bell (1953, 307). These are not direct quotes from Muller.
[48] Quoted in Pribam (1983, 212).
[49] Attwood (1964 [1826], 32).
[50] Mr. Wallace quoted in O'Hanly (1882, 12).
[51] Quoted in White (1933, 3).

highly destabilizing hyperinflation. Far from cultivating a sense of national loyalty and national "spiritual unity," the assignats soon produced a very different sentiment: deep popular discontent and alienation from the state. This discontent was particularly strong among the poor who bore the brunt of the upheaval. The revolutionary government initially sought to deflect blame for the monetary chaos on foreign speculators, but by 1795, they were forced to abolish the assignats and introduce a new convertible currency, the franc.[52] The relationship between national paper currencies and national identities was thus likely a much more conditional one than Muller had suggested: if the former were not managed in a trustworthy and relatively stable fashion, they were unlikely to foster the latter.

Territorial Currencies and National Sovereignty

Some nineteenth-century policymakers drew one final connection between territorial currencies and national identities. As noted already, nations are imagined as "sovereign" political communities. Some of those who supported the creation of a territorial currency did so on the grounds that it would strengthen national identities by bolstering national sovereignty. The link between the issuing of money and sovereignty dates back well before the nineteenth century. In chapter 1, we noted how the issuing of a currency was long seen as a prerogative of ruling authorities and an essential attribute of their sovereignty in many parts of the world. Hayek suggests that this long-standing practice was related to the fact that coins were seen as "symbols of might, like the flag, through which the ruler asserted his authority."[53] Glasner argues that it was also related to fiscal concerns. Before powers of taxation were well developed, he notes that governments had to be very wary of private mints because their ability to generate large revenue could be used to finance domestic political uprisings. Control over mints was thus crucial to maintaining power. Glasner argues that even when taxation systems became more sophisticated the link between sovereignty and the issuing of currency remained crucial because of the financial needs of the state during wartime. Governments recognized that seigniorage could act as a critical "revenue of last resort" during wartime.[54]

Whatever the exact historical origins of the link between sovereignty and the issue of currency, the association remained in the nineteenth century. But it was also transformed in two important ways. To begin with,

---

[52] See White (1933).
[53] Hayek (1990, 29). See also Bagehot ([1868] 1978, 59–61).
[54] Glasner (1989, ch.2).

sovereignty in the monetary realm came to be more closely associated in a practical sense with the maintenance of a territorial currency. Scholars of sovereignty note how its expression in specific state practices has changed considerably in each historical era, and how the emergence of the nation-state in the nineteenth century marked a particularly important historical break in which state practices associated with sovereignty were transformed.[55] The new practices that emerged from the experiences of powerful nation-states often became "models" for other countries to emulate in their efforts to create modern sovereign nation-states.[56] In the words of John Meyer, the models represented a kind of "world culture" that had influence in countries across the globe.[57] This pattern was certainly evident in the monetary realm. Before the nineteenth century, Cohen notes how "the sovereign right of coinage was hardly ever interpreted in exclusively territorial terms. Few states expected—even, in principle, claimed—a monopoly for their own coins within their own frontiers."[58] Once many powerful states had created territorial currencies, however, these monetary structures increasingly came to be seen as a "model" for how modern sovereign nation-states should organize their monetary systems. For example, the circulation of foreign coins domestically, which had been a practice long accepted as normal, now came to be seen as something incompatible with modern nationhood. By the late 1860s, Canadian monetary specialists were describing the continued circulation of foreign coins as something about which they were "ashamed."[59]

The direct emulation of the practices of powerful states was particularly evident in Meiji Japan where policymakers looked to Western countries for models of how to organize their monetary system as part of their dramatic initiative to create a modern sovereign nation-state. As its 1871 Coinage Act stated, the goal of its initial coinage reforms was "to adopt a system of coinage which shall be in consonance with the best usages of the nations of the world."[60] Indeed, the modern Western-style mint they imported in 1870–71 became a leading symbol of modernizing values more generally in Japan at this time.[61] Their construction of a central bank with a monopoly note issue in the early 1880s was also partly driven by a desire to emulate the best practices of Western nations. The finance minister had traveled through Europe in the late 1870s making a detailed study of the

[55] See for example Krasner (1999), Biersteker and Weber (1996).
[56] Anderson (1983).
[57] Meyer (1987). See also Meyer et al. (1997).
[58] Cohen (1998, 28). See also Cipolla (1956, 14).
[59] Sandham (1869, 9).
[60] Quoted in Matsukata (1899, 6).
[61] Hanashiro (1996), Imperial Mint (1923).

best practices of European central banks and settled on the Belgian central bank as a model for Japan to emulate, as described in the previous chapter.[62]

The second transformation in the link between sovereignty and the issue of currency emerged out of a change in the concept of sovereignty itself. Instead of being something belonging to a monarch, sovereignty was increasingly associated with the nation or "the people" in the nationalist age. Many of those committed to this new sense of "popular sovereignty" came to see a territorial currency as an important tool that could help contribute to its realization. Such a currency could "belong" to the nation and be managed in a way that served its economic needs. Indeed, we saw in the last chapter how some nationalists, such as Matsukata in Japan and Attwood in Britain, depicted the relationship between a territorial currency and the nation as similar to that of blood in the human body.[63]

The people who made the connection between popular sovereignty and territorial currencies were usually critics of classical economic liberalism. They included figures such as Johann Fichte and Isaac Buchanan whose macroeconomic views were outlined in the previous chapter. Here, I want simply to sketch how they saw this monetary reform as enabling not just a new kind of national macroeconomic policy but also a new nationalist political identity based on popular sovereignty. Buchanan's writings make this point particularly clearly. He and his supporters argued that the state, rather than private banks, should be the institution issuing notes in Canada because money was linked to sovereignty.[64] They did not have in mind the privileges of a monarch, but rather the needs of the people. In Buchanan's words, money should be "a thing of or belonging to a country, not of or belonging to the world." While an inconvertible national paper currency fit this description, a currency based on a universal form of money such as gold was seen by Buchanan as "disloyal" and "unpatriotic" because it would serve only an "alien" class "whose boast is that money capital owns no allegiance to country."[65]

The fact that these thinkers were critics of economic liberalism was important in encouraging them to recognize this potential link between territorial currencies and new national identities. Because they felt money

---

[62] Reischauer (1986, 83).

[63] Earlier European thinkers such as Thomas Hobbes and William Petty also used this image (Monroe 1923, 276; Bonney 1995, 468; Jackson 1996, 11–12). In the fifteenth century, a Vietnamese ruler also referred to money as the "pulse" of the people (Woodside 1997, 261).

[64] See Wright (1885, 31).

[65] "Nothing Could be More Practically Disloyal, Unpatriotic, and UnChristian Than the Hard Money Legislation of England," January 1880, Manuscript Group 24, D14, Vol. 108, 070994, CNA.

could be actively managed to achieve national goals, it was natural that they would see popular sovereignty as requiring a territorial currency that the nation could manage. Although this view would become very influential in the twentieth century, we have seen already how it had little direct influence on policymaking in the nineteenth century. Most policymakers accepted the economic liberal argument that money should not be actively managed. For them, the notion that a commitment to popular sovereignty would require the creation of an independent territorial currency was not as natural an idea.

Conclusion

I have attempted to show in this chapter that the territorializing of currencies in the nineteenth and early twentieth centuries was clearly linked in some instances to the goal of bolstering national identities. Indeed, this link was multifaceted. At the level of iconography and naming, policymakers recognized that exclusive and standardized coins and notes might provide an effective vehicle for their project of constructing a sense of collective tradition and memory. By reducing transaction costs within the nation, a territorial currency was also seen to be like a national language; it would bring citizens together by facilitating "communication" among them. Because trust plays such a large role in the use and acceptance of modern forms of money, territorial currencies were viewed as something that might encourage identification with the nation-state at a deeper psychological level. And finally, territorial currencies were increasingly associated with national sovereignty.

Did territorial currencies actually play a role in bolstering national identities in one or all of these four ways in the nineteenth and early twentieth centuries? This question is beyond the scope of this book. As noted at the start of this chapter, it is also a question that has been largely ignored in existing academic writing. This neglect is hard to explain, but it may be related partly to the fact that historians of money tend to be economic historians who are inclined to view money primarily as an economic phenomenon. A study of the relationship between territorial currencies and national identities, however, requires an examination of money also as a sociological and cultural phenomenon. As one observant monetary economist recently noted about the importance of the symbolic value of national currencies: "Economics does not help us understand this matter, but it should not, for that reason, be ignored."[66]

But historians of nationalism have also almost entirely ignored the study of national currencies. This partly reflects the relative neglect of the

[66] Laidler (1991, 87).

economic dimensions of nationalism among historians. It may also be related to the influence of two famous sociologists of money, George Simmel and Karl Marx. Although coming from quite different ideological perspectives, both thinkers developed a similar and influential view of the impact of modern money on social identities. Each argued that the pervasive use of money in modern societies had the effect of transforming traditional social and personal ties into ones characterized by impersonal and instrumental economic calculations. Money's ability to assign value in a standardized way to diverse items was seen to dissolve the concrete relationships of traditional societies and replace them with abstract and impersonal social relations. For this reason, Marx referred to money as a kind of "radical leveler" that "does away with all distinctions" associated with traditional social relations.[67] Likewise, Simmel wrote of the "colorlessness" of money, its "uncompromising objectivity," and its indifference to "particular interests, origins, or relations," features that derived from its ability to "become a denominator for all values."[68] For our purposes, what is interesting about this perspective is that it steers analytical attention away from the potential links between territorial currencies and national identities. If modern money undermines social context and tradition, how could it be linked to the sense of collectivity and common history that underlie national identities? Similarly, if modern money promoted rationality, how could it cultivate the kind of emotional attachments to the nation on which national identities rest?

In the last few years, Marx's and Simmel's approach to the study of the link between modern money and social identities has begun to be subject to considerable critique. Through detailed historical work, Viviana Zelizer in particular has shown how their approach neglects the ways in which money has always been profoundly embedded in various localized cultural and social structures and thus invested with very diverse kinds of social meaning. She has demonstrated this point by examining the pervasive practice of earmarking modern currencies and the creation of special forms of localized currency in the United States during the very nineteenth historical period that Marx and Simmel were analyzing.[69]

In this chapter, I have shown that Zelizer's important point is relevant not just at the microlevel of earmarked and localized forms of money but also at the macrolevel of territorial currencies. The project to create territorial currencies was, after all, seen by many nationalists as something that could help strengthen a new kind of national identity. Far from displaying

---

[67] Marx (1974, 132).
[68] Simmel ([1900] 1978, 377, 373, 128, 440).
[69] Zelizer (1994). See also recent work by anthropologists such as Lambek (2001).

"uncompromising objectivity" or doing "away with all distinctions," territorial currencies in the nineteenth century were often invested with social meaning that was intricately connected to the intensely political project of constructing unique and distinct national identities. In other words, the very thing that Marx and Simmel thought destroyed traditional collective identities was being used to weave a new kind of national identity. Indeed, by doing away "with all distinctions" through its "leveling" and "communistic" characteristics, money may have been ideally suited to promote this new community that was "imagined" as a kind of horizontal comradeship.

Part 2
The Contestation and Spread of Territorial Currencies

6

Two Nineteenth-Century Challenges
Currency Unions and Free Banking

In the first section of this book, I outlined the reasons why territorial currencies first emerged in the nineteenth and early twentieth centuries. I now turn to two themes: the spread of the territorial currency model to other regions of the world in the twentieth century, and the contested nature of this monetary structure throughout the nineteenth and twentieth centuries. I have already noted at various places how many groups opposed the adoption of territorial currencies before World War I. People with a vested interest in preserving heterogeneous monetary orders drove much of this opposition. Some opponents, however, had more principled reasons for objecting to the creation of territorial currencies. I have noted briefly, for example, how some opponents sought to preserve economic localism. I have reserved to this chapter, however, a discussion of the two groups who offered the most prominent principled sources of opposition to territorial currencies in the nineteenth century.

The first were "free bankers" who objected to monopoly issuers of currency within a country on the grounds that this was incompatible with economic liberalism. They worried that monopoly issuers would abuse their dominant monetary position, and they preferred to leave the management of money to the free market. The free banking movement had some success in encouraging countries to reject the creation of monopoly note issuers in the nineteenth century. At the same time, their influence in these cases should not be overstated because this outcome often reflected the influence of groups with different goals.

The second prominent principled opponents of territorial currencies were advocates of international "monetary unions." They were driven partly by a desire to reduce international transaction costs, and partly by a variety of political goals described in the second half of this chapter. Like free bankers, they generated considerable interest in their ideas. During the 1860s and 1870s, many countries in Europe joined regional monetary unions that encouraged the domestic circulation of each other's currencies. In 1867, serious political negotiations were even undertaken to explore the creation of a world monetary union, although these negotiations ultimately failed. A key reason for this failure was the higher priority given at the time to nationalist goals we have examined in previous chapters. I also seek to explain the failure of regional monetary union in North America in this period, a case that has received little academic attention to date.

The Influence of the Free Banking Movement

There were many countries that did not create a standardized note issue in the nineteenth century. One reason was the influence of a "free banking" school within liberal economic circles. As we saw in chapter 4, many classical economic liberals during the nineteenth century advocated note monopolies, but "free bankers" challenged this recommendation. A note monopoly, they argued, was contrary to the ideas of free competition that economic liberalism stood for. They preferred to see a decentralized banking system in which various private banks issued notes—backed by their own gold reserves—on a competitive basis free from most regulations.[1] Indeed, they could cite prominent liberals such as Adam Smith and David Hume in support of this recommendation.

To make their case, they directly challenged the rationale developed by classical economic liberals for a note monopoly.[2] Recall that there had been both a macroeconomic and a microeconomic rationale for note monopolies in classical liberal circles. At the macroeconomic level, the "currency school" had argued that a note monopoly would enable the country's currency to be managed according to the automatic principles of the gold standard. Supporters of this school had been particularly concerned that competitive private note issuers were tempted to overissue notes during economic booms. Free bankers replied, however, that the tendency for overissue was in fact much greater in a system with a monopoly issuer that faced no competitive checks. Also worrying to them was the fact that monopoly issuers often had a close relationship to the state that had financial reasons to encourage excessive note creation. By contrast, in a system of free banking, they argued, the supply of currency would be constrained by competition. To support this argument, they pointed to Scotland, which had had a system of unregulated competitive note issue for more than a hundred years before 1845 (when stiff regulations were introduced, as noted below). Throughout this period, Scottish banks had made their notes inconvertible only during the Napoleonic wars, when

---

[1] A few free bankers even argued against a government monopoly of the coin, stating that free competition among private mints would prevent debasement (White 1984, 63, 85–86; Hodgskin 1966, 190–95).

[2] Good descriptions of these arguments can be found in White (1984) and Smith (1990).

they suspended payments to prevent people in England from draining their reserves. A key reason for this exemplary record, free bankers argued, was the existence of competition. Any bank that overissued would quickly find its notes discounted within an efficient note clearinghouse system the banks had created among themselves. The result was that the supply of currency never exceeded demand.

As we saw in chapter 3, liberal supporters of a note monopoly also sought to eliminate microeconomic inefficiencies associated with a heterogeneous note issue. Without a standardized national bank note, they argued, not only were individuals (especially the poor) exposed to the risk of loss if a specific private issuer failed, but counterfeiting was encouraged and notes were not always equally acceptable across the spatial territory of the country. Again, free bankers argued that these microeconomic problems were overstated. In Scotland, the risk of financial loss had been minimal because private banks were disciplined by the note exchange clearinghouse system to act in a responsible manner. The note exchange system had also ensured that private notes were equally acceptable across the whole country and that counterfeiting was not much of problem because each bank's notes were returned quickly to it.

More generally, supporters of free banking argued that their cause had acquired a bad name in many countries not because of its internal imperfections but because governments had rarely given free banking a chance to flourish. In England where the instability of private country banks had been widely criticized, free bankers argued that this instability was caused by the heavy restrictions imposed by the government on the banks' freedom of action. A rule restricting banks' partnerships to six meant they were usually poorly capitalized. They were also unable to establish an efficient nationwide exchange of notes because of a law prohibiting them from having branches in London.

To the extent that microeconomic problems did arise in systems of competitive notes in other countries, free bankers also argued that they could be addressed through limited government regulation. Adam Smith, for example, had suggested that multiple note issues should be restricted to higher-denomination money in order to minimize the transaction costs encountered in small, everyday payments.[3] Note holders could also be protected from bank failures by forcing banks to deposit funds with the government that could be drawn on to redeem note holders in the event of a collapse.[4] Governments could also force bankers to make their notes re-

---

[3] Smith (1976, 343).
[4] This approach was adopted in New York State in the 1838–63 "free banking" period, and in Canada after 1890.

deemable at offices across the whole country as a way of minimizing spatial transaction costs.[5]

These various arguments in favor of free banking were disputed at the time and remain controversial today.[6] For the purposes of this book, what is significant is not their accuracy but their influence on policymaking. Free banking had considerable political support in policymaking circles in many countries, especially during the highpoint of economic liberalism in the 1850s and 1860s. But often this support was not enough to prevent the creation of note monopolies. Because of its importance in influencing nineteenth-century monetary thought, the English case provides a particularly interesting example.[7] Although many English economic liberals expressed admiration for the Scottish system of free banking, most still backed the move to give the Bank of England a note monopoly in 1844. Frank Fetter argues that free bankers chose not to challenge the 1844 Bank Act because of their fear that a debate among liberals might give strength to their opponents, namely Attwood and his Birmingham school.[8] Lawrence White also suggests that the free banking movement was dealt a setback by the death of their leader, Henry Parnell, in 1842. In addition, he argues that the country bankers and joint stock bankers, who might have been expected to support free banking, were co-opted by specific provisions of the 1844 act. Although the act set out the goal of giving the bank a note monopoly, it did so only gradually, freezing the note issue of existing banks at the 1844 level and removing it altogether only if they merged with other banks.[9]

Interestingly, Peel did not extend the Bank of England's note monopoly to Scotland in 1844. Instead, he allowed its private banks to continue issuing their distinctive notes, but imposed strict regulations on them (and Irish bank note issuers), which effectively ended "free banking." To ensure that their operations conformed to the intentions of the 1844 Bank Act, Scottish banks were told in 1845 that they could increase their note issue beyond existing levels only if the notes were covered 100 percent by gold. Peel had made clear his preference for a single note issue across all of Britain, but bowed to the political reality that this would be strongly

---

[5] In Canada in 1890, a few years after the country's first nationwide railway was complete, the government required all private note issuers to establish redemption offices for their notes in major cities across the country. This move ensured that all notes circulated across the whole country without a discount for the first time (Conant 1969 [1927], 465).

[6] See for example Capie and Wood (1991), Goodhart (1988).

[7] For the German, French, and Belgian cases, see Smith (1990, ch. 4), James (1997, 14–15).

[8] Fetter (1965, 212–14).

[9] White (1984, 78).

opposed by the Scottish banks as well as by Scottish nationalists.[10] English politicians had learned in 1825 the extent to which nationalist sentiments in Scotland could be mobilized in defense of its independent note issues. At that time, an initiative from London to restrict low-denomination Scottish bank notes had generated passionate Scottish opposition, which some analysts see as the origins of modern Scottish nationalism. Sir Walter Scott led this protest and defended the independent bank notes on many grounds, including the belief that they contributed to Scotland's national identity.[11]

In other countries, the arguments of free bankers were more successful than they had been in England in preventing or postponing the monopolization of the note issue. In Chile, a free banking law introduced in 1860 had been promoted actively by a French free banking enthusiast, Juan Gustavo Courcelle Seneuil, who had arrived in the country in 1855 and soon became an adviser to the finance minister.[12] Free banking ideology also played a role in Italy in preventing the creation of a monopoly note issue after unification.[13] Free bankers were also prominent in the successful efforts to prevent a full note monopoly from being created in Canada after the formation of the country.[14]

In each of these countries, however, free bankers were not the only ones arguing against the creation of a monopoly note issue. Private banks that did not want to give up their profitable note issue as well as regionalist interests who opposed the consolidation of central state power often joined the free bankers.[15] Also significant in Italy and Chile was the support of groups who believed that multiple note issuers might increase the money supply.[16] Similarly, in Canada, groups from the west of the country supported a competitive note issue because they thought it would expand credit and create a more elastic supply of currency that could match their changing seasonal needs for money.[17] These latter examples are interesting because they suggest that free banking was often supported for a reason that economic liberals would be reluctant to endorse: the belief that banking unconstrained by regulation could stimulate the economy by leading to a rapid expansion of credit and the money supply. This position

[10] Saville (1996, 361–63), Clapham (1966, 186–87, 465).
[11] For the argument that this marked the origin of modern Scottish nationalism, see Scott (1981 [1826], viii).
[12] Subercaseaux (1922, 71, 75).
[13] Whyte (1930, 117), Toniolo (1990, 56–58), Sannucci (1989, 255–56).
[14] Government of Canada (1870, 244, 257–58; 1975, 558).
[15] Toniolo (1990, 56–58), Shortt (1986, 560).
[16] Sannucci (1989, 255–56), Rodriguez (2000, 175–76).
[17] Shortt (1986, 560), Government of Canada (1975, 563, 569).

also found support in the United States, where Henry Carey, an economic nationalist and supporter of an inconvertible currency, became one of the most prominent advocates of free banking.[18]

Nineteenth-Century Currency Unions

The other prominent principled source of opposition to territorial currencies during the nineteenth century came from advocates of international currency unions. The most ambitious proposal of this kind was put forward in the 1850s and 1860s. This was a period when international economic integration was intensifying dramatically with the expansion of railways, the telegraph, and steamships. It was also a time when enthusiasm for international free trade and economic liberalism reached its highpoint in the nineteenth century. In this context, it was not surprising that the idea of creating a world monetary union would emerge as a prominent proposal.

The Proposal for a World Monetary Union

The idea first attracted attention at the International Exhibition at London's Crystal Place in 1851 where people had experienced difficulties comparing prices of items from different countries. Throughout the 1850s and early 1860s, it was actively promoted in places such as the International Statistics Congresses in 1853, 1855, 1859, and 1863, alongside proposals to standardize weights and measures on a worldwide basis. It was also soon endorsed by prominent liberal economists, such as Jevons, Bagehot, Mill, and Chevalier, as well as by internationally oriented business groups such as the English Chamber of Commerce and the New York State Chamber of Commerce.

In addition, the idea attracted the attention of politicians in many countries, and in 1867 a major international conference was held in Paris to discuss it. Delegates from the United States, Russia, the Ottoman Empire, and all European countries attended. Many governments that did not send delegates, such as those in China, Canada, Japan, and many South American countries, also expressed support for the idea.[19] At the conference, delegates were not allowed to bind their countries to any decision, but they did reach unanimous agreement (with the exception of Netherlands) on the following recommendations to their own governments. Instead of creating a single international currency, they encouraged countries joining the union to adopt two principal measures. First, all countries

---

[18] See Unger (1964, 50–52).
[19] See Russell (1898), Royal Commission (1868), Perlman (1993), Nugent (1968, 69). For Canada's and Japan's interest, see Helleiner (forthcoming), Shinjo (1962).

would be required to adopt the gold standard with the gold five French franc acting as the common unit of account. Second, all countries should create national gold coins with the same gold content as the twenty-five French franc gold coin. These coins would then become legal tender in all other member countries; in Britain and the United States, for example, these internationally circulating coins would be equivalent to one British pound or five U.S. dollars. To implement these two proposals, various countries would need to adjust the gold content of their currencies; in the British and U.S. cases, the gold content would be reduced slightly, by 0.9 percent and 3.8 percent respectively. The new gold coins would maintain their distinct national names and still have national emblems on them, but countries would be encouraged to add inscriptions to these coins that read "coin of the union" and indicated the relationship between their value and the French five-franc piece.

Supporters of these recommendations argued that they would facilitate worldwide commerce by reducing international transaction costs. Because foreign prices would be easier to understand and compare, businesses would be encouraged to become more involved in international trade and finance. Debtor countries might also find it easier to borrow and pay debts when the money of creditor and debtor countries was easier to compare. Similarly, the costs of remitting money across borders would be reduced since this could now be done using coins instead of bills of exchange on which brokerage expenses had to be paid. Travelers, too, would not need to make as much use of money changers if they carried the new universal coins.[20]

Despite these benefits, some argued that the proposals did not go far enough. One complaint was that the conference did not make lower-denomination coins, such as British pence, American cents, and French centimes, comparable.[21] In fact, the conference had examined the question of unifying these coins but had decided that "the interests, habits, and prejudices of the people are too strong against it."[22] This decision meant that the difficulty of comparing prices at the 1851 exhibition would still not be entirely solved. Another complaint was most travelers did not carry coins, but rather currency notes that would still need to be converted by money changers.[23] The prominent English financial journalist, Walter Bagehot, also argued that the conference should have created a common unit of ac-

[20] For a good summary of these various arguments in favor of the proposals, see Royal Commission (1868, vii–viii, 314). See also Russell (1898, 85–92).

[21] Bagehot ([1868] 1978, 83–84), U.S. Government (1868, 312–13).

[22] International Conference (1868, 51).

[23] Royal Commission (1868, 76). The idea of creating a uniform bank note attracted almost no attention at the time, although Einaudi (2000, 295) notes one exception.

count, abolishing the expressions "pound," "franc," and "dollars." In his words, "Any person reading a newspaper from any country should see the same figures and have an instant feeling in his mind of what they meant." A new universal unit could act as a "uniform language of value throughout the civilized world."[24] Indeed, his magazine, *The Economist*, had argued in 1866, "We see no reason why each State should have a separate money."[25] But when a Belgian delegate had raised the idea of reminting all national coins and creating an entirely new universal unit at the Paris conference, the U.S. and British delegates had rejected the idea because of the significance of these names to citizens of their countries.[26]

In addition to reducing international transaction costs, the idea of a world monetary union was also seen to have wider political significance. One of its early American supporters argued in 1857 that it would foster a more peaceful, cosmopolitan world society: "Next to a universal language, everywhere spoken and everywhere understood, it will as eminently conduce to general peace and general good understanding, among nations, as any other measure which can be devised."[27] In 1868, one of the most prominent American advocates of the Paris proposals, John Sherman, made a similar case in defending the need for a universal monetary standard: "Nothing is better for the peace of nations than unrestricted freedom of intercourse and commerce with each other."[28] The key French advocate of a world monetary union, Félix Esquiron de Parieu, also argued that it would produce "the gradual destruction in the economic order of one of these frequent barriers which used to divide nations, and whose reduction facilitates their *mutual moral conquest*, serving as a prelude to the pacific federations of the future."[29] Bagehot echoed these sentiments in 1866, arguing that the use of a common money (which he also hoped would have common imagery) would help to dissolve national identities: "All Englishmen would lose some of the exceptional national feeling which retards their progress, which makes them look at others as strange, which makes them think us singular too. If civilization could make all men of one money, it would do much to make them think they were of one blood."[30]

These arguments linking monetary reform to a change in political

---

[24] Quotes from Royal Commission (1868, 115, 108). See also Bagehot ([1868] 1978, 71–75).

[25] Quoted in Einaudi (2000, 296).

[26] Russell (1898, 60–62).

[27] Mr. Tyson in *Congressional Globe*, Feb. 24, 1857, 284.

[28] Quoted in Russell (1898, 97). See also Royal Commission (1868, 205).

[29] Quoted in Einaudi (2000, 286) (italics in original).

[30] Quoted in Perlman (1993, 318).

identity are reminiscent of those we examined in the previous chapter. Just as territorial currencies were seen to foster national identities, a world monetary union was viewed as a tool to cultivate cosmopolitan identities. Interestingly, some of the same people who had earlier made the nationalist case now made the cosmopolitan one. Only a few years before, Senator Sherman had argued in favor of a national bank note on the grounds it would foster American nationalism, as we saw in the last chapter.[31] There was no contradiction involved here. As Hobsbawm notes, most economic liberals in the nineteenth century embraced political nationalism, but ultimately viewed the nation as a stepping-stone on the way to the construction of a more cosmopolitan global community.[32] The Italian finance minister who proposed unifying Italy's coinage demonstrated this way of thinking well in 1862. After noting how a common coinage would foster an Italian national identity, he concluded: "This [unification of currency] . . . is a step towards the unity of the type . . . which . . . will open up communications with other nations in order to arrive at that result which is the desire and the want of all peoples!—the uniformity of the monetary system in Europe and among all civilized nations!"[33]

Despite widespread support for the Paris proposals in 1867, they were never implemented. The failure of the initiative has been attributed to France's indecisiveness, Britain's lack of enthusiasm, the wariness of the U.S. Congress, and the decision of Germany after unification to adopt a gold standard on a basis that was not easily reconcilable with that of other nations. Not until Luca Einaudi's recent study, however, has there been a detailed analysis of the politics surrounding the proposal. He argues persuasively that underlying these various circumstances was a similar political division in most countries. In support of the initiative were free traders and internationalists, while standing opposed were bankers (who feared losing exchange profits associated with multiple currencies), protectionists, and nationalists.[34]

Nationalist opposition was particularly significant. Einaudi and others note that many in Germany and Britain were suspicious that French interest in the Paris initiative reflected its desire to expand French political influence.[35] But fears also were expressed that the Paris proposals would un-

---

[31] Treasury Secretary Chase was also a supporter of universal coin proposals (Russell 1898, 19–20, 42–43, 93).

[32] Hobsbawm (1992). Even nationalist critics of free trade, such as Friedrich List, embraced the construction of a cosmopolitan world community as a worthy final goal of humanity.

[33] Pepoli (1862, 303).

[34] Einaudi (2000).

[35] Russell (1898, 117), Nugent (1968, 63), Einaudi (2000, 300).

dermine national identities. In the early 1870s, for example, there was strong opposition in U.S. Congress to what John Sherman called a "practical utilitarian" proposal to remove the eagle from some U.S. coins and replace it with words indicating the intrinsic fineness and weight of the coin, a move designed to support the universal coin initiative. One member of Congress expressed the nationalist opposition in the following way: "I would not leave it to anybody to remove from the eyes and the thoughts of the people those symbols of nationality which have stood this country in such good stead on many a hard-fought day by land and sea; and which may have to do the same service in the same way for many generations to come."[36]

The British delegates to the conference also noted their resistance to proposals that would change the British monetary system, which was, in their words, "approved by experience and rooted in the habits of the people."[37] In testimony to a royal commission that was then established to examine the issue, other critics picked up on this theme. One opponent, John Bowring, argued that the slight lowering of the pound's value would pose a threat to the national identity, because of the "spirit of nationality" that "surrounds the pound sterling" as a result of its status as "a long-existing standard of value, recognized by everybody." He also noted:

> If it be considered what the power of the pound and of the penny is on the public mind . . . its importance as a representative of value will be recognized. . . . Our language, our literature, our proverbs, are permeated with these associations. . . . All this shows the extent to which this idea of the pound and the penny has become an almost universal presence—a sort of national inheritance. . . . The pound and the penny are scriptural words, associated with our earliest and most irradicable thoughts.[38]

Nationalists were also often effective in warning against the domestic transaction costs involved in adjusting to the new monetary standard. In Britain, this point was made strongly by the influential 1868 royal commission that recommended against Britain's participation in the Paris initiative. In addition to the costs involved in recoining all existing gold sovereigns, the commission reminded the country of the inconvenience it would experience if the pound's value was lowered slightly to correspond to the French system. This move would force everyone across the country to have to readjust to their accounts; salaries, rents, debts, and prices would all need to be increased slightly to compensate, thereby creating

[36] *Congressional Globe,* January 17, 1873, 672, 679.
[37] U.S. Government (1868, 326).
[38] Quotes from Royal Commission (1868, 133, 134, 130).

"the possibility of serious discontent for a time."[39] An important report from the U.S. congressional Committee on Finance in the same year made a similar point in advising against the idea of adjusting the value of the U.S. dollar downward slightly to match the French standard.[40] These arguments reminded citizens that the lofty goal of reducing international transaction costs could be achieved only by increasing domestic transaction costs, albeit only temporarily. Faced with the choice between domestic and international stability, policymakers chose the former. The German decision after unification provided a further example of how the goal of domestic national monetary consolidation took precedence over that of global monetary integration.[41]

The Creation of the LMU and SMU
Despite the failure of the Paris proposal, the cause of creating monetary unions in this period was not entirely lost. Two more limited, regional monetary unions in Europe were formed, which lasted until the 1920s. The first was the Latin Monetary Union (LMU) created in 1865 by France, Belgium, Italy, and Switzerland. The catalyst for its creation was the introduction of fiduciary silver coinages in these countries in the early 1860s. Before this time, each country's silver coins had circulated in the other countries' territories because of their close economic links and because each had gradually adopted monetary systems based on the units of account set out by France in 1803. When Switzerland and Italy first created fiduciary silver coins in 1860 and 1862 respectively, their coins quickly flowed into France and Belgium where they were initially accepted by the people and by public offices because of this tradition. But because the coins no longer had full metallic value, they were soon "giving rise to disputes and doubt in transactions between private people" in France.[42] When France also created fiduciary silver coins in 1864, the problems multiplied. The new French coins had a similar fineness as Italy's fiduciary coins but a slightly higher fineness than Switzerland's. For this reason, the French government now decided to refuse to accept Swiss fiduciary coins at public offices, a move that quickly discredited them and had widespread economic consequences, especially in border regions: "Circulation was impeded, and the ancient and precious uniformity so long enjoyed by France, Belgium and Switzerland had vanished. Frontier trade was impeded, and travelers were subjected to inconvenience."[43]

---

[39] Royal Commission (1868, xiv).
[40] Ibid., 316–18.
[41] Russell (1898, 117).
[42] Ibid., 28.
[43] Willis (1901, 40).

In these ways, the introduction of fiduciary coinages was beginning to bring an end to circulation of foreign coins within each country's territories, just as it did in other countries across the world in the nineteenth century. The difference in these four countries, however, was that their governments actively resisted this trend. In 1865, Belgium, which had not yet created a fiduciary coinage, proposed that a monetary convention be signed that enabled the silver coins of each country to continue to circulate in an orderly fashion. The other three countries agreed and the Latin Monetary Union was quickly created. Under its provisions, the four countries agreed to create fiduciary coinages with the same fineness and weight as French coins (although each country continued to place distinct images on their own coins) and to allow all gold and silver coins of the member countries to be accepted at public offices in the other countries. They also agreed to limit the number of fiduciary coins that each country could issue. In 1866, France invited other countries to join the LMU, and many countries soon applied including Greece, Spain, Austria-Hungary, Romania, Serbia, Bulgaria, the Pontifical State, and San Marino. In the end, only Greece was accepted, although many of the other countries did eventually adopt a monetary system modeled on the French system.[44]

What explains the choice of these countries to take active steps to *encourage* the circulation of foreign coins?[45] The choice partly stemmed from the kind of liberal enthusiasm for monetary unions that we have already examined. Policymakers in Italy, Switzerland, and the other poorer states who applied to join the LMU also hoped that the creation of a stable monetary link with France might encourage lending from Paris capital markets. In addition, in France, the LMU was seen by some as a tool to expand French influence in Europe. The nationalist opposition that torpedoed the Paris proposals of 1867 was not as present in these various countries. Nationalists often saw the joining of the LMU as a way to cultivate French political support for various initiatives they were undertaking. The absence of nationalist opposition in the original member countries might also have reflected the fact that the monetary union did not require any major adjustment of their domestic monetary systems, unlike the situation in Britain and the United States. In many poorer countries that applied to join the LMU, a major adjustment of the monetary system *was* required, but it was one that reinforced nationalist goals. As Einaudi notes, most of these states had

[44] Ibid., 82–84, Einaudi (1997; 2000, 287–88).
[45] For the points in this paragraph, see Willis (1901, chs.5–6), Flandreau (1995), Einaudi (2000), Pepoli (1868 [1862], 301).

chaotic monetary systems that "were plagued by old and clipped to-kens, by a multiplicity of foreign and debased units." He continues: "By adopting the franc and renaming it according to local customs—as lira, peseta, drachma, lei, dinar, or leva—the weakest European states could create a modern and orderly national currency and dispel monetary chaos."[46]

The other monetary union, the Scandinavian Monetary Union (SMU), had similar origins. It was created first between Sweden and Denmark in 1873 and then expanded in 1875 to include Norway as well. Some of its provisions were the same as the LMU: all countries were required to pro-duce coins with identical fineness, while the imagery on each country's coins could remain distinctive. But other provisions were more ambitious. These coins were not just accepted by all three governments but made legal tender throughout the union. Members also adopted the gold stan-dard with a new common unit of account (the Krona) and new common subsidiary units (ore), which marked a break from past practice in all three countries. And the union eventually began to encourage bank notes to circulate between the three countries.[47] Once again, the creation of the SMU was driven partly by economic liberals. The idea first emerged from a conference of Scandinavian economists in 1872 after it had become clear that the Paris initiative had failed. There were also specific interests who stood to gain. The three countries had close economic ties, and the SMU was particularly helpful in border regions where the circulation of each other's coin and even notes had already been quite common.[48] Some au-thors state that union also drew support from the strength of pan-Scandi-navianism, an ideology that was powerful in the mid-nineteenth century, particularly in Sweden.[49]

If this explains the origins of the SMU and LMU, what explains their long endurance in the years before World War I? In the SMU case, the union worked very well and the countries saw little reason to abandon it. For the LMU, however, circumstances were rather different. Very soon after its creation, it was disrupted by Italy's decision to make its currency inconvertible between 1866 and 1882. Speculators quickly exported enor-

---

[46] Einaudi (2000, 288). See also Martín Aceña (2000, 126).

[47] DeMarais (1986). The three central banks created a formal clearing system for each other's notes in 1885 and then increasingly began to accept each other's notes at par (Heckscher 1930).

[48] See Nielsen (1933), De Cecco (1992), Henriksen and Kaergard (1995).

[49] See Nielsen (1933). This point should not be overstated since Norway initially re-fused to join the SMU in 1873 because of the opposition of nationalists in the Norwegian Parliament who worried about the very fact that the SMU was linked to the idea of pan-Scandinavianism (Larsen 1948, 427, 434, 460).

mous amounts of Italian silver coin into the other LMU countries where it would still be accepted at par, a situation that caused consternation in these countries. As the recipient of most silver coins from other countries (not just Italy), France made it clear that any country quitting the LMU would be expected to redeem all these coins in gold, a position formalized in a 1885 revision of the treaty. This made the option of quitting the LMU very difficult for other countries because of the expense that would be involved, particularly in an era when the price of silver was dropping. Although France periodically insisted on one-off redemptions of foreign fiduciary coins, it refused to consider ending the LMU. In Willis's words, it preferred not to give up its "monetary hegemony" over other member states and continued to absorb member country's fiduciary coins as a way of ensuring that "the countries of the Latin Union were bound firmly to France by the difficulty of redeeming their coin."[50]

The Absence of Monetary Union in North America
The way in which an inconvertible currency could disrupt monetary integration would soon be witnessed again during World War I. It was also apparent in North America in the 1860s. In the scholarly literature on mid-nineteenth-century monetary unions, the case of the United States and Canada has received little attention, but it makes for an interesting comparison. Between 1854 and 1866, the United States and the Canadian colonies shared a free trade agreement that produced demands for closer monetary links between the two countries, particularly in Canada. In the early 1850s, the Canadian colonies were formally on local "sterling" standards, but the refusal of the British to issue currency for them left the colonies relying on a diverse collection of coins and notes issued by foreign governments, private firms, and local municipalities. When the Province of Canada finally declared its intention to produce its own coin based on a new standard in 1853, the issue of Canada's monetary relationship with the United States was immediately raised.

In the early 1850s, trade with the United States was expanding rapidly and the free trade agreement was about to encourage it further. But transactions with the United States were complicated and costly for Canadian merchants because the relationship of monetary values under the existing "sterling" standards did not always correspond easily with those of the U.S. dollar standard. These complications were compounded by the fact that U.S. silver coins had become widely used within Canada, although they were not legal tender after 1853.[51] Indeed, many domestic bank notes

[50] Willis (1901, 142, 181). See also De Cecco (1992).
[51] Shortt (1986, 489–90, 496–97).

began to be produced with values listed in both sterling and U.S. dollars, and the U.S. dollar was used widely as a unit of account in the private sector and even sometimes in local government.[52] In this context, the government recognized the need to simplify the monetary relationship between Canada and the United States as part of its project of creating a new monetary order. The decision was taken to adopt a decimal-based "dollar" standard that was modeled on and directly equivalent to the U.S. system. The British government and some Canadian "loyalists" opposed this choice, preferring a British-style standard based on the "royal" with shillings and pounds. But the decision prevailed because of the desire to facilitate trade with the United States and because dollars were already so familiar.[53]

Although the Province of Canada aligned its monetary standard with the United States, why did it not go further and create a formal "monetary union" allowing the circulation of U.S. coins during the period of the free trade agreement? Canadian policymakers had already created a similar standard as that of the United States, and U.S. coins were already circulating widely in the country even if they were not legal tender. Why then not formalize this situation with a monetary union of the kind that European countries were creating? In fact, Canada chose the opposite course, becoming increasingly hostile to the circulation of U.S. coins in Canada. This was demonstrated first when the United States created a silver fiduciary coinage in 1853, a move that prompted the Province of Canada to revoke their legal tender status in the province.[54] Although they continued to circulate widely, this new silver fiduciary coin increasingly frustrated Canadian policymakers in the 1860s. Indeed, when the new Dominion of Canada was created in 1867, one of the top priorities of the new federal government was to rid the country of U.S. coins. As noted in chapter 1, the government launched a massive and expensive operation to remove all U.S. currency from domestic circulation in 1870–71. At a time when many European countries were moving to encourage the circulation of each other's coins, why did Canada adopt the opposite policy course?

Some of the reasons were nationalist ones. As one member of Parliament who supported the withdrawal argued: "We had heard a good deal lately about adopting a national policy, and was it not humiliating that we should be compelled to carry on the commercial transactions of the country in a depreciated foreign currency? If we were to be a nation, we should have a currency of our own."[55] But a key reason was also the fact that the

[52] See Province of Canada (1855, 9).
[53] Shortt (1964, 126; 1986, 429, 444, 472–78, 486, 491).
[54] Shortt (1986, 489–90).
[55] Thomas Oliver quoted in Government of Canada (1975, 464).

U.S. currency had lost its convertibility into gold at the beginning of the Civil War in 1860. As in Italy, this move prompted speculators to export large amounts of U.S. silver coinage to Canada where the coins had long been accepted at face value. The influx of these silver coins quickly came to be seen as a "silver nuisance" in Canada by merchants and the general public. Since these coins were no longer convertible into gold, Canadian merchants realized the risk of accepting them at face value and began to take the coins only at a discount. The uneven use of discounts created considerable confusion and inconvenience for the general public, and the poor suffered particularly because their wages were often paid in U.S. silver coin. In these circumstances, it is easy to see why the idea of a monetary union was not popular and why the Canadian government moved quickly to eliminate U.S. coins from domestic circulation.[56]

The move, of course, did not satisfy everyone. Brokers in Montreal who made large profits from handling depreciated U.S. silver coin opposed the decision to remove U.S. coin, demanding the right to operate in whatever currency they chose. Indeed, they plastered signs across Montreal attacking the finance minister who planned the withdrawal of the coin. The individual in charge of carrying out the operation even feared that he would be "kidnapped or worse."[57] When the government first began to discourage further importation and acceptance of U.S. coin in 1867, some federal politicians also worried that these moves might offend the United States. But this internationalist sentiment carried less weight in Canada than it did in Scandinavia or the LMU countries. The response from the supporters of the operation was clear: "The sooner we ceased to express fears of offending the United States in legislating for our advantage the better. (Hear, hear) We had heard so much of this sort of talk lately, that the Americans would begin to imagine that we could not get on without them."[58]

Conclusion

The two most prominent principled arguments against territorial currencies from the nineteenth and early twentieth centuries are important to recall. Not only did they exert political influence in this historical period, but they also foreshadowed some sources of contemporary disillusionment with territorial currencies. Today, two prominent critics of territorial

---

[56] Shortt (1986, 559), Weir (1903), Mercator (1867, 28), Government of Canada (1967, 178, 281; 1870, 869; 1975, 465).

[57] Quotes from Weir (1903, 157). See also Weir (1903, 148–57, 252–53), Shortt (1986, 558–59).

[58] Mr. Bodwell in Government of Canada (1967, 281).

currencies are once again free bankers and advocates of currency unions, and many of the arguments put forward by these critics are similar to those found before the First World War.

In the mid nineteenth century, advocates of currency unions spoke up for the need to reduce international transaction costs in an era when international economic integration was intensifying. The same is true today, although I will examine in chapter 10 how global financial integration is more of a driving force behind monetary unions today than it was in the mid-nineteenth-century period. In the nineteenth century, free bankers spoke out against territorial currencies because they were not compatible with a liberal commitment to free markets. Today, when economic liberalism has once again emerged as a dominant ideology around the world, it is not surprising that this argument in support of free banking has reappeared prominently. In the current period, however, the free banking movement has also gained new strength from a widespread liberal dissatisfaction with the way territorial currencies came to be managed during much of the twentieth century. This experience has only confirmed in free bankers' minds the truth of their nineteenth-century argument that territorial currencies were likely to be mismanaged by political authorities. Indeed, this sentiment has also encouraged many contemporary liberals to endorse other alternatives to territorial currencies such as currency unions or dollarization, as we shall see in chapter 10. Before we can leap ahead to the contemporary era, however, we must turn to examine the history of the interwar period in order to understand why most economic liberals turned their backs on the idea of free banking and currency unions in that era.

7

The Coming of Age of Territorial Currencies in the Interwar Years

If the need for a territorial currency remained contested before 1914, it became much less so during the interwar period. By 1939, most independent countries had established these monetary structures and political support for the two key challenges examined in chapter 6 had collapsed. In this chapter, I seek to explain the popularity of territorial currencies in this period. I begin with the views of liberal policymakers who were influential during the 1920s, especially those from the dominant financial powers of the time, the United Kingdom and United States. Although they sought to rebuild the prewar monetary order, these figures showed little enthusiasm for currency unions and free banking. Because these two powers encouraged the creation of central banks with monopoly note issues in every independent country in the world, their rejection of free banking was particularly important. This initiative reflected a belief similar to Peel's in 1844 that these institutions were needed to restore and maintain the international gold standard. Liberals recognized, furthermore, that support for currency unions would be hard to sustain after the messy unraveling of existing unions in the years after World War I and in the context of growing nationalist sentiments.

In the second section, I examine why policymakers who were less enthused with economic liberalism also embraced territorial currencies. While liberals sought to restrain governmental influence in the monetary sector, these policymakers were often driven by more nationalist and statist goals of the kind that we examined in some contexts during the pre-1914 period. In the macroeconomic realm, they embraced central banks with a monopoly note issue for "liberal nationalist" reasons and, by the 1930s, even "macroeconomic activist" ones. They also saw the consolidation of territorial currencies as useful for their goals of constructing national markets, maximizing seigniorage benefits, and strengthening national identities.

The hegemony of territorial currencies in the interwar period should not be overstated. In countries that had already consolidated territorial currencies, two new kinds of challenges emerged. The first came from the sudden growth of foreign currency use in countries experiencing high inflation. The second challenge involved the rapid emergence of subnational local currencies in many countries during the Great Depression of the early 1930s. In both cases, the challenges were short-lived, as political authorities responded to them in ways that were designed to restore a consolidated territorial currency. Nonetheless, these challenges demonstrate the continued contestation of territorial currencies and also foreshadowed challenges in the contemporary period.

The Liberal Rejection of Currency Unions and Free Banking

At the end of World War I, the prewar international monetary order lay in ruins. Warring countries almost everywhere had abandoned the gold standard, introducing inconvertible currencies and often exchange controls. Stable money and balanced budgets had been replaced by inflationary conditions and large fiscal deficits, often financed by central banks whose independence from the state no longer existed. More generally, the liberal monetary values that had been so dominant before the war were now challenged in all countries, especially by political parties on the left, which had gained influence with the extension of electoral franchise. In this context, economic liberals and their allies believed that economic and political stability could only be restored by returning rapidly to prewar liberal monetary policies. Led by powerful policymakers in Britain and the United States, they encouraged and cajoled governments around the world to return to the gold standard, abolish exchange controls, and restore balanced budgets and independent central banks. This dramatic initiative to restore the prewar world began at two prominent international monetary conferences held under League of Nations auspices in Brussels in 1920 and Genoa in 1922, and then continued throughout the 1920s, achieving considerable success by the end of the decade. Historians have analyzed this political initiative in detail, but they have devoted less attention to a question that is key for this book. If liberal policymakers were so keen to restore the prewar monetary world, why did they actively reject two ideas that had been prominent in liberal circles in that earlier period: currency unions and free banking?[1]

Rejecting Currency Unions

The rejection of currency unions has been particularly neglected in existing literature. The rejection was especially interesting because there were many proposals for currency unions put forward at this time. At the 1920 Brussels conference, delegates and other interested observers floated proposals to create an international bank note and fiduciary coin that would

[1] For literature on the liberal initiative in the 1920s, see for example Eichengreen (1992), Meyer (1970), Pauly (1997), Leffler (1979), Silverman (1982), Costigliola (1984), and Clarke (1967, 1973).

circulate in all countries and be issued by an international bank, perhaps controlled by the League of Nations.[2] Two years later at the Genoa conference, proposals of this kind resurfaced.[3] The Romanian delegation to the League even brought forward a formal proposal in September 1922 for the unification of the currencies of all League countries.[4] There were also similar kinds of proposals at regional levels. Citing the 1867 Paris conference, the prominent American economist, Edwin Kemmerer, suggested the creation of a pan-American coin in 1916 that would circulate across the Americas.[5] One British financier—J.H. Darling—was also active in promoting the idea of a common central bank and currency for the British Dominions and entire British Empire in the early 1920s.[6] Similarly, the powerful League of Nations financial committee discussed several times whether it should be promoting regional currency unions in Europe. In 1922, the influential French member of the committee, Mr. Avenol, wondered aloud whether European countries whose currencies were not convertible into gold should be encouraged to create a currency union around a "European dollar," a union that, he noted, would be larger than the LMU.[7] Similarly, when Albania requested assistance to establish a central bank in 1923, one member of the committee, Mr. Parmentier, suggested that it might be better to create an international bank of issue with a head office in Geneva, which would issue an international currency to Albania and other interested European countries through branches in these countries.[8]

Many of the arguments in favor of these proposals for currency unions

[2] See the proposal of the Guatemalan delegate, Jean Van De Putte (1920) as well as Silverman (1982, 282) and Paul Einzig, "International Monetary System," Sept. 16, 1920, Doc. no.275, Dossier no.275, LN; "Monsieur A. Gyr Wickart's Proposal for an International Bank Note, etc., Correspondence Concerning" Economic and Financial 1921, class no.10, document no.12286, LN. At an earlier League meeting in May 1920, a Spanish representative had suggested the creation of an international unit of account linked to gold to act as the basis of League budgets (The Conference Forum, no.3, Oct. 2, 1920, C40/1035, p.21, BOE).
[3] See Senex (1922); S.P. Ford, "The Genoa Economic Conference: A Scheme, Worth Considering, for Re-establishing International Finance, Peace and Prosperity," *Suggestions of Mr. S.P. Ford for the Establishment of an International State Bank, Economic and Financial,* Class no.10, Doc. no.14522, LN; F. Lodi "Bank of the Nations" Letter to Sir Eric Drummond, secretary general of League of Nations, August 28, 1922, in *Monetary Questions,* E.F.S./373 A-207, Financial Committee, Economic and Financial Committee, Sept. 17, 1922, LN.
[4] E.F.S. 374.A.208, Oct. 11, 1922, Financial Committee, Economic and Financial Committee, LN.
[5] Kemmerer (1916), Rosenberg (1999, 102).
[6] See R. Hawtrey "Empire Currency," July 1923, T208/70, PEO.
[7] Financial Committee, 7th Session, 3rd Meeting, June 7, p.8, E.F./Finance/7th Session/P.V.3, June 9, 1922, LN.
[8] Financial Committee, 11th Session, Geneva, Aug–Sept. 1923, 2nd Meeting, Friday August 31, LN.

were similar to those advanced by liberals during the nineteenth century. Supporters hoped that currency unions and international currencies would reduce international transaction costs, especially by eliminating the kind of exchange rate instability that was hampering international trade and investment at the time. Like liberals in the nineteenth century, they also hoped that an international currency would "create International goodwill" at the global level or, in the case of Kemmerer's regional proposal, "Pan-Americanism."[9] A new argument for currency unions—which has emerged more prominently in our own time, as we shall see in chapter 10—was put forward by Mr. Parmentier: these would prevent governments from pursuing inflationary policies. He argued that a key advantage of his proposal for a currency issued by an international bank would be "the diminution of the possibility of the national governments concerned using the bank in their own country for unsound financial purposes." He pointed out that it "would put the currency of the country concerned outside the power of events in that country."[10]

Despite the continued enthusiasm for monetary unions and international currencies in some quarters, key liberal policymakers in the League and elsewhere rejected these ideas. At the Brussels conference, a resolution passed unanimously stating: "We believe that neither an International Currency nor an International Unit of Account would serve any useful purpose or remove any of the difficulties from which International Exchange suffers to-day."[11] Members of the League's financial committee also rejected the proposals of Avenol and Parmentier. Kemmerer even backed away from his 1916 proposal during the 1920s entirely and indeed played the lead role in consolidating national currencies and national central banks throughout Latin America (as we shall see below).[12] And the proposal for a British Empire currency was strongly rejected by British officials. Finally, and just as important, the two existing monetary unions—the LMU and SMU—both unraveled during the early 1920s, leaving the only currency union in existence by the late 1920s a new one created in 1921 between Luxembourg and Belgium.[13]

To understand this turn of events, let us begin by examining the reasons for the collapse of the LMU and SMU. The unions ended primarily because of the difficulties of making them work in the context of incon-

---

[9] Quotes from Ford (1922) and Kemmerer (1916, 71).

[10] Financial Committee, 11th Session, Geneva, Aug–Sept. 1923, 2nd Meeting, Friday August 31, p. 4, LN.

[11] League of Nations (1920, 20).

[12] Rosenberg (1999, 103, 287 fn.26).

[13] For the latter, see Financial Committee, 11th Session, Geneva, Aug/Sept 1923, 6th Meeting, Sept. 3, F/11th session/P.V.6/1, Financial Committee, 3–4, LN.

vertible currencies during and after World War I. In the previous chapter, we saw the difficulties encountered by the LMU when Italy's currency had become inconvertible: its fiduciary coins were exported in massive numbers to the other member countries who then worried about Italy's willingness to redeem these coins. When all LMU and SMU currencies were inconvertible during and after World War I, a similar problem emerged. Fiduciary silver coins of all union members flowed in large numbers to the country with the least depreciated currency. In the early years after the war, this country was Switzerland in the case of the LMU, and its policymakers worried not just about the future redemption of LMU coins but also the domestic inflationary impact of importing them. When Switzerland banned the importation of LMU coins in 1920 and withdrew existing LMU coins from domestic circulation, the monetary union's fate was sealed. It was soon formally wound down when Switzerland and Belgium withdrew in 1926 and 1927 respectively.[14] In the SMU, Sweden was the recipient of the Norwegian and Danish fiduciary coins in this period and it initially insisted that their governments ban the export of fiduciary coins to Sweden. When this was not effective, Sweden began to return fiduciary coins to the two countries for redemption at their nominal value in gold Swedish kronor. Given the size of fiduciary coins involved, this was an expensive proposition for Norway and Denmark, and the resulting frustrations in all three countries prompted them to agree in 1924 to end the legal tender of each others' fiduciary coins, thereby effectively ending the SMU.[15]

These unpleasant experiences likely influenced the thinking of liberal policymakers who rejected currency unions at meetings such as the 1920 Brussels conference. In the records and minutes of the Brussels conference, including those of the currency committee that produced the resolution cited above, I have been unable to find an explanation or commentary on this resolution. But in a pencil draft at the subcommittee stage, an explanatory statement was initially included, following the resolution, that stated "experience has shown that . . ."[16] This statement may have been a reference to the fact that the experience of the SMU and LMU was already a very frustrating one for the member countries by late 1920. Two years later, one Swedish central banker reflected on what his country had learned from its experience with the SMU: "With this experience before

[14] See Conant (1969 [1927], 786), Bartel (1974).

[15] Although gold coins remained legal tender in each other's countries, such coins were no longer circulating in all three countries and thus the SMU had been de facto dissolved. For the SMU experience, see Bartel (1974), Nielsen (1933), Bergman, Gerlach and Jonung (1993), Heckscher (1930).

[16] T172/1108, 213, PRO.

our eyes, it can easily be understood, that we in Sweden entertain no hopes of solving present currency-problems by international conferences and conventions. We are afraid of conventions, the consequences of which we cannot foresee. They will restrain our free action and in all probability, like the Scandinavian currency-convention, break to pieces, when they are most needed."[17]

There was in fact one more frustrating experience with a monetary union during this period that deserves mention because of its dissolution around the time of the Brussels conference. When the Austro-Hungarian Empire broke up after the war, the common currency of the old empire had initially remained in place.[18] Quite soon after, however, the new Austrian government began pressuring the Austro-Hungarian Bank, which produced the empire bank notes, to finance its deficits. Many of the other newly independent countries immediately objected to this abuse of the bank's note issue, and they worried about its inflationary consequences. When they were unable to stop the bank's activities, some began in 1919 to dismantle the currency union by placing a national stamp on all existing notes within their respective territories and converting all deposits and government bills into a new national monetary unit. Their actions encouraged an influx of unstamped money into Austria, prompting even that government to stamp its notes. The process of liquidating the bank and introducing distinct new national bank notes in all the countries of the old empire continued throughout 1920, the year of the Brussels conference.

If these troubling experiences undermined support for monetary unions, so too did the strong influence of nationalist sentiments after the war. Although many liberals may have supported currency unions, they saw them as politically unrealistic in the postwar period. British officials, for example, dismissed Darling's proposal for a common currency and central bank within the British Empire on the grounds that it did not take account of growing nationalist sentiments in the empire. In an internal memo, the influential Bank of England official Otto Niemeyer, reminded others of the difficulties he had encountered simply getting Australia and India to cooperate with the Bank of England. More generally, he asked: "Does he [Darling] imagine Canada giving up the dollar, or India the rupee?"[19] Similarly, Kemmerer's decision to back away from his 1916 common currency proposal during the 1920s reflected his new recognition that the maintenance of nationally distinct monetary units was "a natural reasonable function of a sovereign state."[20]

---

[17] OV50/19, W. Moll memo, May 1922, p. 12, BOE.
[18] See Dornbusch (1992), Garber and Spencer (1994).
[19] Memo, April 4, 1925, T172/1499B, p. 372, PRO.
[20] Kemmerer quoted in Rosenberg (1999, 103).

Most members of the League's financial committee also rejected Parmentier's 1923 proposal for a common currency for League-supported countries such as Albania on practical political grounds. Janssen, the Belgian representative, noted: "M. Parmentier's idea was theoretically possible and even desirable, but was for the moment impossible politically. . : . the whole of M. Parmentier's suggestion was based upon an international conception of currency which was fundamentally opposed to the whole spirit of nationality in matters of currency use." The Swedish representative, Wallenburg, made the same point: "The Albanians looked upon a bank of issue of their own as one of the essential attributes of their national independence. Probably, even if the Committee advised them not to create one, they would go their own way." The South African financier Henry Strakosch, noted that even the closely linked Baltic states had rejected the idea of the common central bank (with Lithuania and Latvia establishing their own central banks in 1921 and 1922 respectively) because of "[n]ational considerations." He argued:

> If this was the case with three countries so naturally assimilated as Latvia, Estonia and Lithuania, how much more unlikely was it that countries as wildly different as Albania, Danzig, and Poland would see their way to such an arrangement? Every bank of issue had an intimate connection with the political conditions of the country at any given moment. For example, the raising of the bank rate was a measure which if imposed by nationals of the country was tolerable, but which, imposed from without by an international control, would meet with enormous opposition. There would also be opposition from the governments concerned, which would thus see diminished their opportunities for borrowing from the bank of issue. However attractive M. Parmentier's idea might seem in theory as a safeguard against this possibility, [Strakosch] thought the only practical safeguards were those laid down at the Conferences of Brussels and Genoa, namely, a bank of issue as independent as possible of the Governments, with statutes drawn up on what all banking experience had shown to be sound lines.[21]

The British and American Push for Central Banks with Monopoly Note Issues
In addition to rejecting monetary unions, prominent liberal policymakers also did not support the idea of free banking after the war. This preference was made very clear at the 1920 Brussels conference, at which the following resolution was passed unanimously: "In countries where there is no central bank of issue, one should be established."[22] A very similar resolu-

---

[21] Three quotes from Financial Committee, 11th Session, Geneva, Aug.–Sept. 1923, 2nd Meeting, Friday August 31, p. 5, p. 6, p. 7, LN.
[22] League of Nations (1920, 9).

tion was passed at the Genoa conference two years later as well as at other international conferences such as the 1932 Ottawa Commonwealth Conference and the 1933 World Economic Conference.[23]

Particularly supportive of these resolutions were British officials, led above all by Montagu Norman, the governor of the Bank of England between 1920 and 1944. Indeed, Norman was so keen to see central banks created abroad that he even refused to visit countries that did not yet have them.[24] During the 1920s, he and other British officials such as Niemeyer and Strakosch pushed for the creation of central banks with monopoly note issues in all countries that received assistance and advice from the League of Nations financial committee (a committee that was widely viewed as under the control of Britain).[25] These countries (and the dates of their central banks' establishment) included Austria (1923), Hungary (1924), Danzig (1924), Bulgaria (1926), Greece (1927), and Estonia (1926–27). During the 1930s even after the gold standard's collapse, Bank of England officials continued to play a key role in setting up central banks with a monopoly note issue in countries such as Canada (1934), New Zealand (1933), El Salvador (1934), and Argentina (1935).

Sharing Norman's enthusiasm for central banks during the 1920s were prominent liberals in the other leading financial power after the war, the United States. One of these was the head of the U.S. Federal Reserve, Benjamin Strong, who worked together with Norman in developing fourteen "general principles" of orthodox central banking that could be promoted abroad.[26] The American who played the leading role in pushing for the creation of central banks abroad, however, was Princeton economics professor Edwin Kemmerer, who had been involved in a Philippine monetary reform of 1903–6 (see chapter 8) and also in the establishment of the U.S. Federal Reserve.[27] His advisory missions abroad, often tacitly supported by the U.S. government, helped to establish central banks in various countries in Latin America, including Chile (1925), Colombia (1923), Ecuador (1927), Bolivia (1928–29), Peru (1922), and Guatemala (1926). He also provided monetary advice elsewhere on missions to Mexico in 1917, South Africa in 1924–25, China in 1929, Poland in 1926, and Turkey in 1934. His advice to introduce balanced budgets, central banks with monopoly notes, and "sound" monetary policies was the same from country

---

[23] See Stokes (1939, 71), Neufeld (1964, 233).
[24] Sayers (1976a, 156).
[25] See De Cecco (1995, 119), Einzig (1932, 67).
[26] See Sayers (1976b, 74–75; 1976a, 156).
[27] See Drake (1989), Eichengreen (1994), Rosenberg (1999).

to country; indeed, Drake notes that "hardly a word in his reports varied from Poland to Bolivia. In purely technical terms, he could have delivered most of his laws by mail."[28]

What explains the enthusiasm of these British and American liberal policymakers for the creation of central banks with monopoly note issues around the world? Like Peel in 1844, they sought to insulate national monetary management from the control of domestic political forces in order to preserve the automatic workings of the gold standard. Given the new political conditions after the war, they argued that domestic monetary stability could only be restored by delegating monetary policy to independent central banks with a monopoly note issue.[29] Discussing the impact of the trend of "increased popular representation," Strakosch put it this way: "The trend of political evolution the world over . . . is in a direction which makes it less safe to entrust governments with the management of currencies than it may have been in pre-war days."[30]

In countries where a monopoly note issue had not existed, the creation of central banks with note monopolies would also provide greater national macroeconomic control that could be used to support the goal of restoring and maintaining the gold standard. While Peel had wanted the central bank simply to adjust the national note issue according to the level of gold reserves, central banks were assigned a more sophisticated role by British and American policymakers in the 1920s. In the event of a trade deficit, central banks were meant to increase their interest rate to attract short-term capital flows to cover the imbalance and to encourage the appropriate national macroeconomic adjustment over the longer term. The advocacy of a financing role for short-term capital flows, in effect, endorsed one of the "liberal nationalist" goals outlined in chapter 3: that of insulating the national economy from volatile short-term fluctuations in the balance of payments. But the endorsement was a very limited one because central banks' policy in this area was still meant to be nondiscretionary and automatic.[31] The 1922 Genoa conference also endorsed the idea that central banks were needed to facilitate international cooperation that could promote international monetary stability, a goal strongly supported by U.S. and British officials.[32]

---

[28] Drake (1989, 25).

[29] De Cecco (1994, 3), Boyle (1967, 205–6), Einzig (1932, 96).

[30] Henry Strakosch to Basil Blackett, Oct. 17, 1925, T176/25B, p. 3, PRO.

[31] This new view of the appropriate role of central banks was first outlined by the influential first interim Cunliffe Committee report for the British government in August 1918. In Flanders' (1989, 69) words, "A reading of Cunliffe . . . leaves one with the impression that a not very sophisticated computer could easily have been a central bank in their sense."

[32] For Strong's support of central bank cooperation, see Chandler (1958, 247), Leffler (1979). For Norman, see his "Central Banks" Feb. 25, 1921, OV50/1, BOE.

Given these goals, it is still necessary to explain the insistence on monopoly note issues. As U.K. Treasury official Ralph Hawtrey pointed out, a note monopoly was not actually necessary for central banks to obtain domestic macroeconomic control in modern financial systems where the money supply was primarily influenced by deposit money created by private banks through their lending activities. Most established central banks during the interwar period simply allowed the note issue to increase or decrease automatically in response to the public's need for hand-to-hand currency.[33] They controlled their country's money supply instead through interest rate changes, reserve requirements, or open market operations designed to influence private bank behavior. How then was the insistence on monopoly note issues justified?

Some analysts noted that a note monopoly did in fact help central banks to control deposit creation of private banks. For example, De Kock argued that if a credit expansion encouraged banks to borrow notes from the central bank in order to meet the demand for currency, the central bank could influence their credit creation by regulating this borrowing.[34] Others pointed out that inflationary pressures in many countries during the war and the early postwar period had been caused by fiscal deficits financed through note issues.[35] Still others repeated the nineteenth-century "currency school" argument that profit-maximizing behavior among competitive note issuers would encourage an overissuing of notes.[36] Hawtrey himself argued that a monopoly issue would encourage a centralization of the country's gold and foreign exchange reserves, thereby easing the task of stabilizing the exchange rate and covering temporary payments deficits.[37] He also argued that a monopoly note issue would strengthen a central bank's ability to act as a lender of last resort and thereby minimize financial instability, although he acknowledged that this role did not actually require a note monopoly.[38]

If these various arguments supported the case for a note monopoly, were there no liberal defenders of free banking left during the interwar period? A few economists associated with the ultra-liberal "Austrian school" of economics, such as Ludwig von Mises and Vera Smith, did remain committed to free banking in this period. Smith's 1936 Ph.D. thesis in support of free banking, written under Friedrich Hayek's supervision at

---

[33] Hawtrey (1932, 116); see also Plumptre (1940, 33–34).

[34] De Kock (1939, 23–40); see also Smith (1990, 9, 189).

[35] De Cecco (1994, 11–21).

[36] See Kisch and Elkin (1928,74), a book that carried a foreword from Norman.

[37] R. Hawtrey, "Inter-Imperial Exchanges," July 1921, PRO T208/39. See also Rosenberg (1999, 152).

[38] Hawtrey (1932, 131). See also H. Strakosch, "The Principles of Central Banking," May 21, 1921, OV50/1, BOE.

the London School of Economics, made the case this way: "To those who would prefer to place their trust in semi-automatic forces rather than in the wits of central bank managers and their advisers, free banking would appear to be by far the lesser evil."[39] But for most liberals, the urgency of the objectives of restoring price stability and the international gold standard strengthened the case for central banks. Many liberals also recognized the political reality that strong sentiments of nationalism and state intervention into the economy in this period worked in favor of central banks, whether they liked it or not. Indeed, even Smith concluded: "It is unlikely that the choice [of free banking] can ever again become a practical one. To the vast majority of people government interference in matters of banking has become so much an integral part of the accepted institutions that to suggest its abandonment is to invite ridicule."[40]

Also important were the specific preferences of liberals in the leading financial powers, the United Kingdom and United States. Their desire to see central banks established abroad partly reflected the fact that a central bank had come to be accepted as normal and desirable within their own countries before World War I. But it also reflected some national interests. Policymakers from both countries hoped that new central banks abroad— particularly in countries that created gold-exchange standards—would hold their reserve balances in London and New York, thus increasing the importance of these financial centers. Norman and Strong also hoped independent central banks might be a "channel for communication and influence" for British and American policymakers.[41] Indeed, many central banks established with British and U.S. assistance had foreign "advisors" on their boards of directors or their staff, a practice that had been sanctioned at the 1920 Brussels international monetary conference.[42] As Plumptre's detailed analysis in 1940 of the creation of central banks in the British Dominions concluded: "The desire in England for a chain of Empire central banks was a latter-day expression of financial imperialism . . . the essential purpose was the same: the maintenance and extension of London's influence and control."[43]

Before ending this discussion of the link between note issue reforms and monetary stability, one final development should be noted. In the 1920s, countries in the League of Nations sought to bolster monetary sta-

[39] Smith (1990 [1936], 192).

[40] Ibid., 195. See also von Mises (1953 [1924], 396–97).

[41] Quotation from Costigliola (1984, 197).

[42] The resolution endorsing central banks stated that if "the assistance of foreign capital were required for the promotion of such a bank [of issue], some form of international control might be necessary" (League of Nations 1920, 9).

[43] Plumptre (1940, 193).

bility not only by endorsing monopoly note issues but also by devising ways that the counterfeiting of these notes might be prohibited through an international convention for the first time. With the growing use of paper money and increased trade between countries, cross-border counterfeiting had become increasingly common, and it threatened the goals outlined at the Brussels and Genoa conferences. Czechoslovakia, for example, had found that widespread counterfeiting of its currency in Hungary had undermined its efforts to stabilize its currency between 1922 and 1926. As a League document put it: "A very large number of business transactions depended upon the faith in the national currency and, if this confidence was destroyed, the whole organisation of the country could be completely upset."[44] As early as 1922, police in different countries across Europe began to cooperate with each other in order to curb cross-border counterfeiting, and by 1927 police agencies from fifteen different countries were involved.[45] At a League-sponsored conference in 1929, thirty-five countries agreed to an international convention that required each to establish a central police office for combating counterfeiting and encouraged international cooperation among these offices. The task of enforcing the convention was given to Interpol, an international police organization created in 1923 that had already been issuing regular periodicals with information about counterfeiting.[46]

The View from the Countries Creating Territorial Currencies

What was the precise impact of the British and American push for the creation of central banks with monopoly note issues in independent countries around the world? At first glance, their efforts appear to have been remarkably successful since most independent countries had created such institutions by 1939. In fact, their influence should not be overstated since local policymakers in these countries were usually keen to introduce central banks anyway. In some instances, the latter's motivations were similar to the liberal goals of U.S. and British policymakers, that is, they sought to promote domestic monetary stability and the smooth functioning of the international gold standard. But many policymakers in Europe, Latin America, the British Dominions, and parts of Asia were driven by quite different goals. Like many prewar policymakers, they often favored note monopolies—and other territorializing monetary reforms—because of na-

---

[44] League of Nations (1930, 53). For the Czechoslovakian experience, see 222–23.

[45] M. Pella, "La Cooperation Des États Dans La Lutte Contre Le Faux Monnayage," Comité Mixte Pour La Repression Du Faux Monnayage, Société Des Nations, F.M.4, Genéve, June 23, LN.

[46] League of Nations (1930).

tionalist and statist goals linked to macroeconomic control, transaction costs, fiscal motivations, and the strengthening of national identities.

Beginning with macroeconomic motivations, the creation of central banks was often designed to strengthen the country's ability to pursue state-led rapid economic development. In many Latin American countries receiving Kemmerer's advice, Drake points out that policymakers supported the establishment of a central bank primarily because it would help attract U.S. loans that could be used to strengthen state institutions and economic infrastructure necessary for national development.[47] De Cecco also notes how central banks set up in the early 1920s in Latvia and Lithuania were given not just traditional tasks outlined by Norman and Strong, but also a role as development banks that could allocate short-term credit to industry and agriculture.[48] The same was true of the new central bank created in Iran in 1927. Indeed, that bank was also established to encourage the spread of the national currency across the entire country in order that monetary policy could be used to foster economic development. The foreign-owned Imperial Bank of Persia, which held a note issue monopoly in the country before the new central bank took it over in 1930, had made its notes redeemable only at the branch where they were issued.[49]

Many countries that established central banks in the interwar period were in fact inspired by the goal of wresting monetary control away from foreign banks. Turkey's nationalist government was keen to establish a central bank in 1930 partly to end the influence of the foreign-controlled Ottoman Bank, which had held the note issue monopoly since 1863.[50] Mussolini's decision to grant a note monopoly to the Bank of Italy in 1926 was also part of a broader initiative to reassert the central state's power over two rival (non-note-issuing) foreign-controlled Milan banks that had challenged the bank's dominance of the monetary system since the 1890s.[51] In Latin America, Tamagma notes that central banks were created in this period partly as "a determined effort by the various countries to bring to an end the dependence of their monetary and credit systems on foreign banks."[52] Similarly, in New Zealand, where four of the country's six banks were Australian, the government hoped that the central bank created in 1933 could reduce the influence of Australian monetary conditions on the country's exchange rate by centralizing gold and foreign exchange reserves and forcing private banks to hold reserves with it.[53] In

---

[47] Drake (1989).
[48] De Cecco (1994, 10).
[49] Minai (1961, 17, 159, 172), Jones (1986, 44, 202, 219).
[50] Keyder (1981, 104–5).
[51] Forsyth (1993).
[52] Tamagna (1965, 36). See also Drake (1989, 39–41, 94).
[53] Plumptre (1940, 170).

Canada, too, the prime minister supported the creation of a central bank in 1934 partly because he hoped it would lessen the country's dependence on New York banks that he believed controlled the value of the Canadian dollar.[54]

During the 1920s, most nationalists remained broadly committed to the liberal goal of maintaining currencies convertible in the gold standard. In the wake of the Great Depression of the early 1930s, however, the kinds of activist macroeconomic policies advocated by Attwood and Fichte increasingly came into fashion. Keynes was, of course, the most prominent figure to defend intellectually the need for more activist monetary policies in the 1930s. During the early 1920s, he had already attacked the gold standard, arguing that floating exchange rates allowed countries to preserve domestic price stability unencumbered by an external constraint. He also called attention to the fact that floating rates provided countries with a quicker and less politically charged manner of adjusting to external macroeconomic shocks in context of more inflexible domestic wages and prices.[55] By the time of his 1936 *General Theory*, Keynes went much further to argue that monetary policy should accommodate the need for countercyclical fiscal spending as a tool of national macroeconomic planning.[56]

In this new intellectual climate, countries that had not yet created central banks and consolidated territorial currencies had a new rationale for doing so. Without these monetary reforms, it was not possible to pursue this kind of activist monetary planning. Even countries with more conservative governments were forced to respond to the new context. In New Zealand and Canada, for example, the conservative leaders who introduced central banks were motivated not just by the nationalist goals cited above, but also by pressure from more left-wing forces who gained strength during the Depression and demanded more activist monetary policy.[57] Indeed, in both countries, the central bank was quickly nationalized after only several years of operation by new governments that were more committed to activist monetary management.

In addition to these macroeconomic motivations, territoralizing monetary reforms were also linked to the strengthening of national identities in many countries. The establishment of a central bank, for example, was sometimes seen as a move that could strengthen the country's currency and thus contribute to its international prestige. This was apparent in Turkey's decision to create a central bank and Mussolini's 1926 move to

[54] Stokes (1939, 65), Plumptre (1940, 170).
[55] Keynes (1971 [1924]).
[56] Keynes (1936).
[57] Stokes (1939, chs.3–4), Plumptre (1940, 162).

grant a note monopoly to the Bank of Italy. Both actions were designed to help these countries join the gold standard, but key policymakers saw this goal in nationalist rather than liberal terms. To them, adopting the gold standard symbolized the creation of a strong currency that contributed to national prestige.[58] More generally, the existence of a central bank came to be seen in the interwar period as a symbol of a modern, independent nation-state. This notion was, of course, reinforced by the resolutions at Brussels and other international conferences calling for central banks in all countries. Across Latin America, the creation of the Federal Reserve System in the United States in 1913 also provided an important "demonstration effect" that encouraged central banks to be established in that region in the 1920s.[59]

As before World War I, the importance of territorial currencies as carriers of national symbols also provided a rationale for territorializing monetary reforms in this period. One Canadian member of Parliament supported the effort to abolish private bank notes in 1934 on the basis that "it will be a great advantage to do away with those bills that at present going right and left having on them pictures of many gentlemen, some of them good, honest people, some of them high-class crooks who should be in penitentiaries, but whose pictures occupy the place of that of the sovereign on these bills."[60] In Ireland, too, symbolic reasons were partly behind the decision to start replacing British currency with a distinctive coin and notes in 1926–27. As one member of the country's Banking Commission argued, the new legal tender notes were required "to show our nationality," which was done through representative symbols of Irish rivers on one side of the notes and the image of a female figure resting on a harp with hills and lake in the background on the other (see figure 14).[61] The coins too were seen as "silent ambassadors of national taste" by W. B. Yeats who chaired the committee deciding on their design, which featured a harp on one side and various images of Irish animals on the other.[62] Monetary reforms introducing the gold standard in peripheral countries during the period were also sometimes accompanied by a renaming of the currency to reflect nationalist values; in Guatemala, the currency was re-

[58] Keyder (1981, 99). De Cecco (1995), Stringher (1927). Von Mises (1953 [1924], 244) argues that Knapp's state theory of money had encouraged the idea in the 1920s that a strong currency was "an economic expression of the respect or prestige of the State."

[59] Quotation from Meisel (1992, 100) who analyzes the Colombian case. See also Yaeger (1990, xx).

[60] Mr. Bourassa in Dominion of Canada (1934, 4244).

[61] Quotes from Moynihan (1975, 81, 124–28). See Hewitt (1994) and McGuinty (1993) for a discussion of the nationalist use of images of women on paper money.

[62] Moynihan (1975, 24–32).

Figure 14. Irish bank note from 1928. Photograph courtesy of The British Museum. © The British Museum.

named after the national bird, quetzal, at the time of the introduction of the gold standard in 1926.[63]

Fiscal motivations were significant in encouraging territorializing monetary reforms in some instances. A desire to gain seigniorage revenue played a significant role in Ireland's decision to introduce its own coins and notes.[64] In New Zealand, Plumptre argues that the principal catalyst for creating a central bank in 1933 was the fact that private banks were charging well above market rates in their lending to the government and were not supporting the government's plans for debt conversion.[65] Similarly, the League's financial committee noted that part of the interest of the Albanian government in creating a central bank in the early 1920s was the fiscal one of using the bank to support government spending.[66]

Finally, the desire to reduce intracountry transaction costs also prompted reforms that helped create territorial currencies in this period. In Columbia, where the note issue had previously been quite heterogeneous, merchants who sought greater uniformity in the currency sup-

---

[63] Kemmerer and Dalgaard (1983, 33).

[64] Moynihan (1975, 24, 58, 64, 73, 144–45).

[65] Plumptre (1940, 169).

[66] Financial Committee, 11th Session, Aug-Sept 1923, 7th meeting, Sept. 4, F/11th session/P.V.7/1, LN.

ported the creation of a central bank with a monopoly note issue.[67] The Mexican government's decision to make the Bank of Mexico's notes sole legal tender in 1935 was also driven by its goal of reducing internal transaction costs; in this case, costs that might stem from a sudden shortage of currency. Established in 1925, the bank's notes had hardly been used until the government demonetized gold and stopped silver coinage during the 1931 currency crisis, a move that forced the population to turn to the bank's notes as the only form of money whose supply could increase.[68] But the full-weight silver peso still retained an important place in Mexico's monetary system until a dramatic increase in the world silver price in 1934–35 threatened to encourage a mass export of these coins. To avoid the drastic economic disruption that would be caused by a sudden shortage of currency in circulation, the government demonetized the coins, exchanged them for new one-peso notes, and declared Bank of Mexico notes to be sole legal tender.[69]

The sudden rise in the world silver price in 1934–35 also prompted an important consolidating monetary reform in China for a similar reason. Up until 1933, the country's currency had remained very heterogeneous, with multiple currency standards, note issuers, and various silver and copper coins with fluctuating values. In 1933, the central government had attempted to create a uniform national standard and silver coinage, but the impact of this reform throughout the country was often limited because of the central government's lack of political authority.[70] The more dramatic move came in 1935 when full-weight silver coins were demonetized, new standardized fiduciary coins were introduced (in 1936), and the government announced its intention to give the Central Bank of China (created in 1928) a note monopoly. One prompt for the reform was fiscal; by moving to a fiduciary form of money, the government could monetize some of its debts.[71] The more important motivation for the reform, however, was the fear of a mass export of the silver coins because of the changing silver price.[72] The move was initially quite successful. It had been assisted by support of powerful British banks and the British government, as well as by "a strong public patriotic spirit, engendered by Japanese aggression."[73] But the monetary unification of China remained incomplete

---

[67] Drake (1989, 35–36, 44).

[68] Maxfield (1990, 60).

[69] Bett (1957, 81–82).

[70] See "China Committee Report on Silver, 1935, "Memorandum by Mr. H. Kano, July 15, 1935," T188/107, 68–69, PRO.

[71] Selgin (1992).

[72] Young (1971).

[73] Chang (1970, 158).

because of the political disunity in the country and the coming of war
with Japan two years later.[74]

Two Brief Challenges to Territorial Currencies

Although territorial currencies were increasingly put in place in most independent countries during the interwar period, their hegemony as a model
for organizing money was not complete. One challenge came from the monetary practices of colonial powers that will be examined in the next chapter.
But even in countries that had already established territorial currencies, two
other challenges to territorial currencies emerged. To begin with, some countries that experienced high inflation during the interwar period found that
foreign currency use within their territory became very significant. One of
the most dramatic examples of this "currency substitution" came during the
German inflation of the early 1920s when foreign currencies—especially U.S.
dollars, sterling, and Swiss francs—were used very widely as units of account, stores of value (including as foreign currency bank deposits), and even
as media of exchange in their paper form. Near the height of the hyperinflation in August 1923, one analyst estimates that the value of foreign currency
circulating in Germany was almost ten times the value of German marks in
circulation.[75] During the Austrian inflation of the early 1920s, a similar phenomenon took place, with many citizens beginning to hold and use U.S. dollars, Swiss francs, or Czech crowns in bank note and bank deposit form.[76]

These experiences showed that use of fiduciary money would not always be restricted to the country in which it was issued. In the nineteenth
century, fiduciary coins, because they were less likely than "full-weight"
coins to be accepted abroad, often helped consolidate territorial currencies. Their value did not depend on their metallic content but rather on
some knowledge of the trustworthiness of the government that issued
them. The experiences in the 1920s, however, demonstrated that this point
should not be overstated. In contexts of domestic inflation or political instability, a domestic fiduciary currency appeared much less trustworthy
than a foreign fiduciary currency, especially if the latter was issued by a
dominant power and was widely recognized as a stable currency. This les-
son had already been learned in many poorer countries, especially those
that had not yet consolidated a territorial currency and where monetary
heterogeneity was already present.[77]

[74] Pomeranz (1993, 67); Rawski (1989, 169–71).
[75] Holtfrerich (1986, 304).
[76] Van Walre de Bordes (1953 [1924], 190–91).
[77] Inflationary conditions in early-twentieth-century Guatemala, for example, encouraged the widespread use of U.S. dollars, a practice that only ended with the 1926 monetary
reform that established a gold standard and monopoly note issue (Kemmerer and Dal-

For states that had previously consolidated a territorial currency, the growing use of foreign currencies during the interwar period was worrying and actively resisted. The German government, for example, initially banned the use of foreign currencies for domestic payments and retail pricing in October 1922. It quickly recognized, however, the ineffectiveness of the ban in a context where the population had lost trust in the national currency because of accelerating hyperinflation.[78] This trust was only restored with the introduction of a dramatic anti-inflationary stabilization program the following year. In his authoritative work on the inflation, Holtfrerich argues that the central goal of this stabilization program was in fact to end the use of foreign currencies, which had been seriously undermining the ability of the state to earn seigniorage revenue.[79]

The second kind of challenge to territorial currencies in the interwar period came from the growth of subnational "local currencies." As we saw in chapter 1, local merchants and towns often produced their own local monies before the creation of territorial currencies in contexts where there was a limited supply of reliable official currency. The same motivation prompted a reemergence of local currencies. During the German inflation, for example, many towns and merchants began to issue their own "emergency money" to satisfy the need for a more reliable low-denomination money.[80] The more dramatic growth of local currencies took place during the Great Depression of the early 1930s when deflationary conditions in many countries left the national currency in short supply. In this context, thousands of local currencies issued by towns and merchants began to appear across Europe, North America, and Latin America. The small town of Worgl in Austria issued one of the first and most famous in mid 1932.[81] Faced with enormous local unemployment, the town's mayor decided to pay for public works with a large sum of locally issued notes denominated in the national currency and backed fully by a bank deposit of the same sum of national currency. The innovative feature of the notes was a requirement that holders of the note buy a special stamp every month to put on the note in order for it to remain valid. This idea had been borrowed from the writings of Silvio Gesell, who had argued that this

gaard 1983, 23). Similarly in Poland before its monetary consolidation in 1926, Kemmerer (1926, 27) observed "large quantities of foreign paper money in circulation in the country" including U.S. notes.

[78] Feldman (1997, 397), Schacht (1978 [1927], 52, 66–68).
[79] Holtfrerich (1986, 313).
[80] Schacht (1955, 184), Feldman (1997, 410). During World War I, many German towns had also issued low-denomination paper notes and coins to cope with a shortage of reliable currency.
[81] See Lietaer (2001, 153–56).

kind of "stamped money" could prevent economic downturns by discouraging hoarding because it ensured that the money effectively depreciated over time.[82] The initiative worked; in order to avoid paying the stamp, holders of the notes in Worgl spent them quickly, even paying their taxes in them early. The rapid circulation of the notes succeeded in generating a small economic boom in the town and the revenue earned from the stamps was also used to support a local soup kitchen.

The Worgl "economic miracle" soon attracted worldwide attention with many towns emulating its experiment. It also was given academic respectability by the prominent American monetary economist Irving Fisher who noted that it could help increase the velocity of money. He argued that efforts by the Federal Reserve to boost the economy by easing U.S. monetary conditions were ineffective because businesses would not invest unless consumers began buying again. Stamped scrip addressed this problem, he noted, because it would "give buying power to the consumer, *and supply the compulsion to use it.*"[83] He began advising many U.S. towns to introduce stamp scrips and even tried to interest President Roosevelt in backing these experiments.[84] There were soon hundreds of locally issued scrip currencies in existence in every state of the union (see figure 15). Indeed, according to one estimate at the time, as many as 1 million people may have been involved in these schemes by March 1933.[85]

The attraction of these local currencies was obviously that they seemed to offer some way out of the desperate economic conditions of the time. But it is worth noting that some supporters had broader ideological goals. Gesell, for example, had seen "stamped money" as part of a larger initiative to create a "free-economy" that was an alternative to communism and unfettered capitalism. Some communities in the United States also saw local currencies as a tool to create an alternative society; the National Development Association of Salt Lake City, for example, hoped the issuing of scrip would help build a "cooperative commonwealth" that would replace the "profit system."[86] In contrast to local currency movements today, however, the attraction of local currencies in this period did not seem to be linked to their "localness." Gesell preferred to see stamped money issued by the national state rather than local towns.[87] Fisher agreed, arguing that

---

[82] Gesell (1934).

[83] Fisher (1933, 65). Italics in the original.

[84] Allen (1977, 574–75), Fisher (1933).

[85] Weishaar and Parrish (1933, ch.7). As noted in chapter 1 (footnote 61), isolated mining and lumbering towns had often used scrip widely in the United States before the Depression.

[86] Weishaar and Parrish (1933, 47).

[87] Gesell (1934, 56–59).

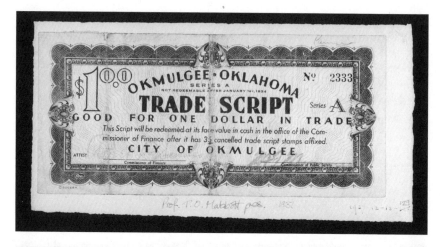

Figure 15. Example of U.S. scrip note from early 1930s. Photograph courtesy of The British Museum. © The British Museum.

a national issue of stamped scrip would "get the scrip *spread* over a maximum territory in a minimum time."[88] Two other American supporters of local currencies, Weishaar and Parrish, also argued that, because so many essential products in the United States had to be mass produced, the economic decentralization fostered by these forms of money could not last for long.[89] The movements were thus not rejecting territorial currencies per se; instead, they were simply advocates of alternative monetary man-

---

[88] Fisher (1933, 60). Italics in the original.
[89] Weisharr and Parrish (1933, 98).

agement who were concerned that the national state was not responding to the economic crisis adequately. It is perhaps not surprising, then, to find Keynes, one of the most famous advocates of a new more activist approach to national monetary management, praise their ideas. In his *General Theory*, he wrote that "the future will learn more from the spirit of Gesell than from that of Marx."[90]

These monetary experiments did not last long in most countries and almost none had survived by the time World War II broke out. In some cases, the currencies were overissued and lost the confidence of those who had used them.[91] More important, however, was the fact that national authorities quickly became concerned about their growth and shut them down. In Austria, the central bank banned local scrip money in 1933 on the grounds that this form of money threatened its monopoly in the monetary sphere. The move provoked a lawsuit from citizens, but the Supreme Court eventually upheld the central bank's position, declaring it a criminal offense to issue "emergency money." In November 1931, after losing a court battle, the German government cited the same rationale when it also used emergency law to outlaw a locally issued stamped currency titled Wara. This currency had also been inspired by Gesell's ideas, and Fisher estimates it had been handled by as many as 2.5 million people between 1930 and 1931.[92] In the United States, Roosevelt also soon prohibited local "emergency currencies" by executive decree, a move that Bernard Lietaer argues was prompted by advice he received about the potential decentralizing impacts of the further spread of locally issued emergency monies.[93] In each of these contexts, local currencies appear to have been seen as a threat to the power of the national central authorities. If the economic difficulties of the Depression were to be solved, policymakers appeared to prefer to solve them at the level of the nation-state.

Conclusion

The interwar years marked a period when territorial currencies were more popular than ever. Most independent countries that had not yet created them did so. As we have seen, their actions stemmed from a variety of motivations related to national macroeconomic control, national identities, fiscal objectives, and transaction costs. These motivations were often quite similar to those we encountered before World War I, although in the macroeconomic realm "liberal nationalist" and "macroeconomic activist"

---

[90] Keynes (1936, 355).
[91] Weishaar and Parrish (1933, 16).
[92] Fisher (1933, ch.4).
[93] Lietaer (2001, 151–57).

goals were now much more politically prominent. Moreover, the important challenges posed by advocates of currency unions and free banking before the First World War collapsed in this era. Prominent liberals lost their enthusiasm for the currency unions after the messy unraveling of the existing unions. Support for free banking was undermined not just by the new nationalist political context but also by the fact that powerful liberal policymakers from Britain and United States saw central banks with a monopoly note issue as necessary for their efforts to restore and maintain the international gold standard.

This is not to say that territorial currencies remained completely unchallenged in the interwar period. The rapid growth of the use of foreign currencies during periods of high inflation showed how trust in a territorial currency could be eroded rapidly if that currency was grossly mismanaged. The proliferation of local currencies in the early 1930s also showed how challenges to territorial currencies would continue to reemerge in the modern age when the supply of the territorial currency was scarce. Both phenomena are being experienced once again today, as we shall see in chapter 10. But as we shall also see, the rapid growth of foreign currency use and local currencies today is different in two ways. Each of these challenges to territorial currencies is being promoted for a broader set of reasons than was true in the interwar period, and public authorities today have also been much more tolerant of them.

8

The Monetary Dimensions
of Imperialism
Colonial Currency Reforms

The analysis in the previous chapter of the growing popularity of territorial currencies in the interwar period neglected regions of the world that
were under colonial rule. In this chapter, I examine their monetary experiences. In some respects, these experiences were similar to ones we have already examined. Before colonial rule, most of these regions had heterogeneous monetary systems that were characteristic of the preterritorial
monetary orders. A key goal of colonial economic policy in the late nineteenth and twentieth centuries was to transform these monetary systems
into ones that conformed more closely to the territorial currencies that had
been constructed in the "home" country. State-managed fiduciary
coinages were introduced and monopoly issuers of paper currency were
established. Colonial authorities also created new low-denomination
money that was integrated with the new official monetary system, and
they made concerted efforts to remove from circulation those forms of
money, such as foreign currencies or precolonial local currencies, that did
not conform to the new homogenous monetary order. Despite these similarities, the monetary structures created by colonial powers were not "territorial currencies." These regions did not, after all, have their own independent states; their monetary systems existed within the political
framework of an empire. Moreover, colonial powers sometimes encouraged the circulation of their own currencies in their colonies and often
joined distinct colonial jurisdictions within large single currency blocs.

Did imperial powers reform colonial monetary systems for reasons
similar to those that justified the creation of territorial currencies at home?
Historians of colonialism are very helpful in providing detailed studies of
various colonial monetary policies, but they have been less inclined to develop synthetic analyses of the common driving forces behind colonial
monetary policies. I provide such an analysis by exploring the role of the
four sets of motivations that were important elsewhere: those relating to
transaction costs, macroeconomic influence, seigniorage, and political
identities. These categories are indeed helpful in explaining the reasons

why colonial powers reformed colonial monetary systems along territorial lines. But because their goals were shaped in the context of the construction of an empire rather than a nation-state, the relative emphasis and specific content of the various motivations was often quite different than those we have seen in previous chapters.

Reducing Intra-empire Transaction Costs: Public and Private Concerns

In examining the motivations that drove colonial powers to transform colonial monetary systems, we must begin with the issue of transaction costs associated with economic interactions between colonial power and the colony. In chapter 3, we saw how, because of a desire to reduce international transaction costs, foreign economic interests from powerful countries often encouraged poorer countries to adopt a gold-based monetary standard in the late nineteenth and early twentieth centuries. When countries followed this advice, the effect was to encourage a territorialization of their monetary systems because the move was accompanied by the creation of a fiduciary coinage system, as well as often the removal of foreign coins and the creation of a monopoly note issue. A very similar dynamic took place in colonial regions.

One of the top economic priorities of colonial powers was to reduce currency-related transaction costs associated with economic transactions between the home country and the colony. By the end of the nineteenth century, all the major colonial powers had constructed domestic monetary systems based on the gold standard. Most of the regions they colonized, however, had quite different monetary systems. Some used currencies that were not easily convertible into the colonizer's home currency and whose value fluctuated considerably, even from one place to the next within a local region. This was true, for example, of the cowries used as a dominant currency across West Africa.[1] It was also true of the debased and quite chaotic copper and nickel coinages that Japan encountered in Korea during the years leading up to its conquest of the country in 1905.[2] Many other regions, including much of Asia, had currencies linked to a silver standard. When silver's price in gold began to drop in the late nineteenth century, this volatile exchange rate caused considerable confusion and uncertainty for those involved in economic transactions between the colonies and the imperial power.

In these contexts, imperial policymakers introduced new monetary systems in their colonies that were based on gold in order to reduce intra-em-

---

[1] See Austen (1987, 206), Ake (1981, 33).
[2] See Bank of Korea (1994, 446), Duus (1995, 139, 159–62).

pire transaction costs. Gold exchange standards—rather than pure gold standards—were introduced in most colonies in the late nineteenth and early twentieth centuries, beginning with the Dutch East Indies in 1877. In each instance, their introduction was associated with the creation of a modern state-managed fiduciary coinage. This move was also usually the catalyst for colonial authorities to demonetize various foreign coins.[3] In many instances, a monopoly note issuer was also created at this time. In British colonies, this issuer was usually a "currency board," whereas elsewhere the note issue was given to a private bank (e.g., Dutch East Indies and French colonies) or even a central bank (e.g., the Japanese colonies of Taiwan and Korea).

It is important to note that the desire to reduce intra-empire transaction costs related to both private and public sector economic activities. For some colonial powers, the primary goal was to encourage their private sector to become more engaged in trade and investment with their colonies. This motivation was key, for example, in the Dutch East Indies case as well as in the introduction by the Japanese of the gold exchange standards in its colonies of Taiwan and Korea in 1904–5.[4] In placing colonies such as India (in 1893) and Straits Settlements (in 1903) on gold exchange standards, the British shared this goal, but they also hoped to address public sector concerns. In the Indian case, the depreciation of silver relative to gold was playing havoc with the budget of the Indian colonial government. Its revenue was earned in silver, but it borrowed from Britain in gold and had to pay fixed payments—such as pensions and interest payments on debts—to Britain in gold. British officials in the colonial army and civil service also found silver's depreciation costly in terms of wages they received in India. Similar concerns played a role in the British decision in 1903 to introduce a gold exchange standard in the Straits Settlements.[5] They also were important in prompting the United States to place its new colony of the Philippines on a gold exchange standard in 1903. Because the colonial government received revenue in the local currency but paid salaries and suppliers from the United States in dollars, the uncertain gold-silver exchange rate of the time disrupted the colonial administration's finances. Not only was the depreciation of silver thus increasingly costly, but the uncertainty of the exchange rate also caused confusion and increased the temptation for fraud within the government, especially among remote officials who did not receive exchange rate information promptly.[6]

[3] See British policy in the Straits Settlements (Lee 1986), U.S. policy in the Philippines (Kemmerer 1916a), and French policy in Indochina (Conant 1969 [1927], 605–10).

[4] For the former, see van der Berg (1996 [1895]). For the latter, see Oh (1987) and Chang and Myers (1963, 441).

[5] Kemmerer (1916a), Bagchi (1997).

[6] Kemmerer (1916a, 281–98), Rosenberg (1985, 1999).

If intra-empire transaction costs were such a major concern to the private and public sector in imperial countries, why did these countries not simply introduce their own currencies in the colonies, as imperial powers had done in the past in many parts of the world? Some colonizers did adopt this strategy initially. Interestingly, however, almost all ended up abandoning it and creating distinct currencies in their colonies. Back in 1825, Britain, for example, had tried to encourage the sterling to circulate in its colonies as a way of eliminating complications associated with paying imperial troops in a variety of coins with fluctuating values vis-à-vis sterling. But in the face of considerable local resistance, it soon abandoned this strategy in most regions of the world in favor of creating locally distinct coins for many colonies.[7] Even in British colonies where sterling was widely accepted, such as those in West Africa in the late nineteenth century, the British eventually established an independent currency in 1912 and eliminated British coins from domestic circulation.[8] Similarly, after introducing the dollar into Puerto Rico, the United States moved very soon after to introduce a distinct currency for the Philippines in 1903.[9] This latter decision was also taken by Japan when it reformed Korea's and Taiwan's money. The French government also eventually abandoned its commitment to the use of French francs in its African colonies later in 1945 when it created distinct CFA currencies for various colonial regions (Equatorial Africa, West Africa, Somaliland, Madagascar, Reunion, St. Pierre and Miquelon), and these currencies were established with values of 1.7CFA:1FF (soon changed to 2:1 in 1948).

The decision of so many imperial powers to create distinct colonial currencies was especially curious because their business communities often opposed it on the grounds that it would increase intra-empire transaction costs. British merchants in West Africa in 1912, for example, almost universally opposed the decision to introduce a new colonial currency, because they worried about the new currency's long-term convertibility into sterling and they preferred the convenience of using British silver coins.[10] Indeed, the widespread use of British coin in the region was seen not just

[7] Chalmers (1893, 23–27).

[8] Greaves (1953, 51).

[9] In the U.S. protectorates of Cuba and Panama, however, U.S. officials did encourage the U.S. dollar to be used alongside these countries' national currencies. They did the same in the Dominican Republic after the United States intervened militarily there in 1904 to establish a "customs receivership." See Helleiner (2002). As is noted in chapter 9, U.S. officials turned their backs on this strategy in Cuba and the Dominican Republic in the 1940s, and advocated "de-dollarization."

[10] U.K. Government (1912a, 91). See also Newlyn and Rowan (1954, 30,38) Hopkins (1970, 122, 127, 131).

as a convenience but also something that gave British merchants a competitive advantage in local markets vis-à-vis other European merchants.[11] French businesses in the colonies also opposed the creation of the CFA currencies in 1945. Their opposition partly stemmed from the devalued exchange rate chosen for new CFA currency vis-à-vis the French franc (which raised the cost of imports), but it also reflected concerns about the future convertibility of the CFA into the French franc.[12] In the United States and Japan, too, there was often strong support in business circles, on the grounds of convenience, for the introduction of the home currency into new colonies such as the Philippines and Korea.[13]

Given these business preferences and the broader desire to minimize transaction costs within the empire, why were distinct colonial currencies created? Some reasons relating to the sharing of seigniorage and the broader symbolic role of money will be discussed below. In some cases, colonial rulers also anticipated resistance to their "home" currency from colonial populations because of the confusion the new currency would bring to pricing and accounting. As we have seen already, the British encountered this kind of resistance earlier in the nineteenth century and abandoned their initial efforts to promote sterling in the colonies for this reason. United States policymakers in the Philippines feared anger from the local population if the dollar were introduced instead of a distinct currency whose units were more similar to the familiar Mexican currency in use in the colony. American officials had just encountered this sentiment when introducing the dollar into Puerto Rico, and they feared a worse situation in the Philippines because of the tense political situation. As Kemmerer put it, the introduction of the dollar "would lead to frequent exploitation of the ignorant, too much bickering, and to criticism and suspicion of the American authorities."[14]

Also important, however, was the fact that the monetary systems of the colonizing countries were primarily made up of fiduciary coins and notes by the early twentieth century. British officials in West Africa anticipated two problems that could arise when these home-issued fiduciary forms of currency circulated widely in colonies. First, as the volume of British fiduciary coins in circulation across West Africa grew dramatically between 1901 and 1910, concerns arose about the stability of their value in the region. Because the face value of the coins was well above their metallic value and because they were not backed up by a local reserve of gold,

---

[11] Davies (1978, 57). For a similar view among Japanese merchants, see Duus (1995, 94).
[12] Onoh (1982, 39).
[13] Kemmerer (1916a, 258), Beasley (1987, 81).
[14] Quotes from Kemmerer (1916a, 303).

there was a risk that a crisis of confidence might produce a depreciation of their value. Second, the British Treasury back home began to worry at the same time about the potential consequences for the management of the British domestic coinage system as a result of the growing number of British coins in West Africa. If these coins were suddenly repatriated, this would complicate the domestic management of the fiduciary coinage and might even lead to a depreciation of the value of silver coins in Britain. As one report noted, the number of British coins being exported to West Africa from 1901 to 1910 was almost equal to that number of new coins being put into circulation in Britain.[15]

These two concerns encouraged the British government to create a new distinct currency for West Africa that would be managed closely by a currency board. The currency would be backed by a 100 percent reserve, thus guaranteeing that its value would be fixed permanently to that of the British pound. The West African currency board then acted as a model for other British colonial administrations. As noted already, British merchants opposed this solution in West Africa. They preferred to address the potential problems caused by unbacked British silver coins by simply creating a gold reserve in West African colonies to back up the fiduciary money in circulation.[16] This was the solution that French policymakers introduced in Africa in 1901 when they gave the Banque de l'Afrique Occidentale sole authority to issue French currency in its African colonies. To minimize the risk of France's domestic monetary system being disrupted by a sudden repatriation of fiduciary coins, the French government also controlled the transfer of francs from the colonies to France.[17] This, of course, increased international transaction costs for merchants in a different way, but it was a system that stayed in place until 1945 when the separate CFA currencies were created as a means of preventing wartime inflation in France from being exported to the colonies.[18]

If these various concerns encouraged imperial powers to create distinct colonial currencies, one more question arose: should each colony have its own currency or should there be common currency zones among the colonies? Many colonial powers opted for the first option, but the second option was also prominent. The British joined together their colonies in West Africa under one currency board; those in East Africa under another in 1919; and Malay, Brunei, and Singapore under a third in 1938 (then ex-

---

[15] U.K. Government (1912b, 7). See also Newlyn and Rowman (1954, 35–37), Hopkins (1970, 105–7).
[16] U.K. Government (1912b, 8).
[17] Baier (1980, 105), Hopkins (1970, 132).
[18] See Thompson and Adloff (1969, 278–79).

panded to include Sarawak and Borneo in 1950). Similarly, the French created common currency zones in West Africa and Equatorial Africa. Creating common currency zones cut down on administrative costs. It also helped to reduce transaction costs associated with economic transactions among colonies. In British West Africa, for example, European merchants favored a common note among the four colonies on the grounds that it would facilitate trade and remittances among them.[19] At various times, proposals had even been made to merge all British colonial currency boards into one as a means of fostering intercolonial trade and reducing remittance costs among the various colonies, although these proposals were never implemented.[20]

Domestic Transaction Costs and the Construction of Colonial Economies

Concerns about transaction costs were not restricted to those associated with economic interactions between colony and colonial power. The desire to reduce domestic currency-related transaction costs within each colony drove some territorializing monetary reforms. More than most previous colonizers, imperial powers in this period were committed to a massive transformation of their colonies' domestic economies. They set out to construct export-oriented economies that could supply commodities to support the industrialized home economies. The introduction of a new standardized colonial currency played an important role in encouraging this transformation to take place.

A particularly important colonial objective was to bring peasants into the new colonial economy as taxpayers, wage laborers in colonial enterprises, or producers of cash crops for export. To facilitate this objective of "extraverting" local economies, colonial authorities sought to replace precolonial currencies with a standardized money issued by the new colonial power.[21] The continued circulation of precolonial currencies allowed local inhabitants to maintain their localized and more self-sufficient precolonial economies. If a new colonial currency became the dominant currency, on the other hand, it would prompt inhabitants to enter the new externally oriented colonial economy. By requiring poll taxes to be paid in the colonial currency, for example, colonial authorities ensured that inhabitants were forced to earn that currency by working for colonial enterprises or

---

[19] U.K. Government (1912a, 16, 18–20, 24, 38, 96; 1912b, 12).

[20] See OV44/97, "Proposal for an Amalgamated Currency Board," Jan. 31, 1944 by Crossley, BOE; OV44/97 "Colonial Currencies," J. Fisher, Feb. 25, 1944, BOE. At this time, the Bank of England argued against the proposal, noting that the gains would be slight and it would generate considerable opposition from local colonial administrators.

[21] Quotation from Ofonagoro (1979, 640).

producing cash crops for export. For this reason, it is not surprising to find that this requirement was often vigorously resisted by the colonized.[22]

Precolonial currencies also included low-denomination forms of money that were viewed by colonial officials as problematic because their value was not homogeneous across the colony and not fixed to that of other forms of money in a stable manner. In many colonized regions, cowries were the dominant form of low-denomination money. From the standpoint of colonial authorities, they were not well suited for the kind of highly monetized and spatially extensive economy they hoped to construct. One problem was that their value often differed considerably from one locale to another according to local customs and market conditions. Equally important, their value fluctuated considerably vis-à-vis higher-denomination money because their supply was not centrally controlled. This was particularly a problem after the mid nineteenth century when new sources of cowry supplies (especially from Zanzibar) began to undermine their value dramatically.[23] In places such as West Africa where cowries served not just as low-denomination money but often as a standard of value, some scholars argue that the instability of cowry values had begun to prompt a considerable retreat into barter and subsistence. From the standpoint of colonial authorities, this trend worked against their goals of creating a more monetized economy.[24]

Colonial authorities encountered the same problems with other indigenous forms of low-denomination currency. In parts of Nigeria, British officials, frustrated by fluctuations in the value of local copper rods (manillas) that served as low-denomination money (sometimes as much as 50 percent between seasons), sought in the early twentieth century to substitute coin.[25] Another example comes from French Indochina where copper and zinc coins had been long used for low-denomination currency. As with cowries, there was no fixed exchange rate between these forms of money and the high-denomination silver money that was employed for long-distance trade. In the precolonial context, this dual monetary system posed few problems because the world of long-distance trade and that of local

[22] Arbin (1995), Jucker-Fleetwood (1964, 200), Suret-Canale (1971, 12, 59–60, 105, 131, 345, 348, ch.4), Weiskel (1980, 235–37).

[23] Hogendorn and Johnson (1986).

[24] See CO 520/8, Mr. Butler, "Currency in Southern Nigeria," Sept. 9, 1901, PRO; CO 879/66 letter of R. Moor to CO, July 7, 1901, p. 24, PRO. See also Suret-Canale (1971, 13–14), Ekejuiba (1995, 140–41), Austen (1987, 135), Fry (1976, 6), McPhee (1971 [1926], 233). Ofonagoro (1979) argues that the existence of "barter" in precolonial Africa has been exaggerated.

[25] Newlyn and Rowan (1954, 30–31); CO 879/66, letter of R. Moor to CO, July 7, 1901, p. 24, PRO.

peasant life did not overlap to a significant degree. But as the French began to construct a more integrated and monetized colonial economy, the variable rate of exchange between the two forms of money became increasingly problematic. For example, salary disputes began to erupt when wages were paid in copper and zinc coins but listed in silver coins. Attempts by the government to try to stabilize the rate of exchange also proved difficult.[26]

Another kind of low-denomination money that caused problems for colonial officials were privately issued tokens. Their issue proliferated in the late nineteenth century in colonies such as Puerto Rico where newly created plantations used them as a means of payment for their workers. Because plantation tokens were redeemable only at the plantation store, these tokens caused enormous resentment among the workers. Indeed, during the political upheavals of 1898 in Puerto Rico, Vaia reports that bands of rebels stole these tokens from hacienda owners and demanded their exchange into official coins. Some owners who refused to make the exchange saw their buildings burned.[27]

Faced with these various situations, colonial officials often made the reform of low-denomination money a high priority in the late nineteenth and early twentieth centuries, just as they had earlier within their own economies. In some cases such as Puerto Rico, the reform was dramatic; the United States immediately introduced its own low-denomination coinage to replace private tokens after taking control of the colony. In a region such as West Africa, colonial policy moved more slowly. French and British authorities initially attempted to manage the value of cowries by banning their importation and fixing an exchange rate between them and the official colonial coin. But when this proved difficult, they were demonetized altogether and new standardized, low-denomination coins that were linked to the official monetary system were brought in to replace them.[28]

In addition to addressing transaction costs associated with low-denomination money, colonial authorities hoped the introduction of new homogeneous colonial coins and notes would minimize transaction costs associated with commerce between interior regions where commodities were produced and the major cities or coastal regions from which they were exported. In West Africa, as the spatial scale of trade expanded, colonial authorities worried that cowries increasingly became an inconvenient form

---

[26] Lacaun (1944, 137–39).

[27] Vaia (1980).

[28] See Baier (1980, 106–7), Hogendorn and Johnson (1986, 137, 143–53), Suret Canale (1971, 115 fn28).

of money because of their weight and bulkiness. The British High Commissioner of Southern Nigeria argued in 1901 that traditional currencies "are so cumbersome as to be practically of no real assistance in the conduct of trade. . . . I am of the opinion that as long as the systems of barter and existing cumbersome native currencies continue in vogue, the expansion of trade is severely hampered. . . ."[29]

Colonial officials' concerns about domestic transaction costs also stemmed from their efforts to construct new territory-wide public fiscal systems. They worried about the accounting complications that would arise if tax collection and public spending were made according to different monetary standards in different parts of the colony. Initially, for example, British colonial officials in West Africa accepted taxes in cowries and other indigenous currencies; indeed, assistant residents in colonies such as Nigeria were required to pass an exam on how to enter cowries in official accounts as late as 1908.[30] But the fiscal complications arising from accepting taxes and making payments in multiple currencies soon acted as a motivation for the creation of a new standard colonial currency.[31]

The same was true in Korea where the pre-1905 monetary system was quite chaotic; different regions of the country used different standards, official coins varied widely in weight and value; and privately issued foreign and counterfeit currencies circulated extensively at varying values. Beginning in 1905, Japan launched a major monetary reform, ending the legal tender status of most precolonial coins and introducing a new standardized fiduciary coinage.[32] The Japanese official who administered this reform made clear that his central motivation was to reduce fiscal transaction costs. He argued that the creation of a standardized currency in the colony was a prerequisite for the establishment of a modern financial administration with a new uniform system of taxation and a new treasury. In Hosino's words, he "perceived that unless this was done any other reform in the fiscal systems was of little use or even hardly possible."[33]

Japanese colonial officials were frustrated not just by the heterogeneous nature of the Korean monetary system but also by inconveniences created by the bulkiness of the local currency. In one important region of the country, the dominant coins in circulation were very large copper coins that proved very difficult to transport over long distances. The problems this caused government officials, who needed to move money

---

[29] CO 879/66, letter of R. Moor to CO, July 7, 1901, 23–24, PRO. See also U.K. Government (1912a, 16), Vice (1983, 85), Fry (1976, 9).

[30] Hogendorn and Johnson (1986, 149).

[31] Austen (1987, 135).

[32] Hosino (1920, 57). See also Duus (1995), Bank of Korea (1994), and Ladd (1908).

[33] Hosino (1920, 51).

around the country, were considerable. One example is given by a Japanese writer: "To give an idea how cumbersome a money it was, the fact may be mentioned that, when the Japanese army bought timber up to yen 10,000 in the interior where yuchan [copper coin] was in use, the army had to charter a steamboat and fill her completely with copper cash to finance the transaction."[34] Indeed, already in the precolonial late 1890s and early 1900s, local Korean officials had begun converting Korean coins into the more convenient and portable Japanese currency—which had begun to circulate—when forwarding revenue to the central government.[35]

The desire of colonial authorities to create a spatially homogeneous currency should not be overstated. Their central goal, after all, was to create a colonial economy geared toward exports rather than an integrated national market. In British colonies, for example, colonial notes were usually convertible only at one office located in a major commercial center. As a result, colonial currency notes were frequently discounted heavily in more rural and remote areas.[36] In rural regions that were not well integrated into the emerging export-oriented economy, colonial authorities also often did little to address scarcities of colonial currency, and the use of indigenous currencies often persisted up until the 1940s and 1950s.[37]

It is also worth noting that not everyone associated with the colonial enterprise favored the reduction of domestic transaction costs within each colony. In West Africa, frequent references are made in British colonial archives to the opposition of European merchants to the introduction of new colonial currencies. In the absence of a standardized colonial coin, these merchants often traded with Africans on a barter basis, a situation that benefited them financially because it restricted the range of choice open to African customers and created opportunities for unusually large profits.[38] The Royal Niger Company also resisted the British colonial government's call for it to make more use of colonial coins in 1905 because it had mastered the use of cowries and now saw this as a competitive advantage vis-à-vis other European merchants.[39] In most colonies, this kind

[34] Hosino (1920, 54).

[35] Duus (1995, 273).

[36] Newlyn and Roman (1954, 45, 56–57), Baier (1980, 107–8), Howard (1978, 131).

[37] Onoh (1982, 26), Ofonagoro (1979), Suret-Canale (1971, 14, 155), Hogendorn and Johnson (1986, 150, 152–53), Baier (1980, 106), Ekejuiba (1995, 144).

[38] CO 879/66, letter of R. Moor to CO, July 7, 1901, p. 25, PRO; CO 520/8, Mr. Butler, "Currency in Southern Nigeria," Sept. 9, 1901, PRO; CO 879/66, Letter from Governor C. King-Harman to Mr. Chamberlain, "Further Correspondence Relating to the Currency of the West African Colonies," Oct. 1903, PRO; CO 520/14 R. Moor to CO, June 12, 1902, 2–3, PRO; CO 879/66, letter of W. Wallace to Mr. Chamberlain, PRO. See also Vice (1983, 13), Suret-Canale (1971, 13–14).

[39] Hogendorn and Johnson (1986, 149).

of merchant resistance received little official sympathy. But there were exceptions. The most dramatic case was the Belgian Congo.[40] In the Congo State, the government refused to introduce a colonial currency at all before 1908, even into Leopoldville. The use of all money was discouraged because it would have allowed Africans to break the link between selling produce to Belgian merchants and buying imports directly from them. The government was particularly concerned about preserving these barter arrangements in places where Belgian merchants had competition from other European merchants. In addition, the government was also concerned about the prospect of Africans paying taxes in money. While most colonial governments saw money-based taxes as efficient, the Belgian authorities worried that they would eliminate the possibility of forced labor on which the colony relied heavily.[41]

Macroeconomic Motivations

To what extent were colonial monetary reforms linked to the goal of acquiring a greater degree of control over the local monetary supply in order to influence macroeconomic conditions in the colonies? As in the home territories of colonial powers themselves, the decision to create note monopolies in colonies was often driven by this goal. This was most clearly evident in British colonies. Initially, note monopolies were established in British colonies such as Mauritius (1849), India (1861), Ceylon (1884), and the Straits Settlements (1899) for other motivations, especially that of restoring confidence in paper notes after private banks had experienced various kinds of crises.[42] But in the case of the establishment of the West African currency board in 1912 and those that followed, the central motivation for note monopolies in British colonies was usually a macroeconomic one. Note monopolies were given to currency boards whose operations were modeled on the 1844 Bank Act; the supply of notes was adjusted automatically in accordance with the levels of the colonies' reserves in order to ensure the external convertibility of the colonial currency and guarantee an automatic macroeconomic adjustment mechanism.

[40] Stengers and Vansina (1985, 344). Suret-Canale (1971, 100) also notes how French colonial authorities in West Africa often benefited from the shortage of official colonial currency because they would accept taxes in indigenous currencies at rates of exchange that were very favorable to them. Baier (1980, 108), too, notes that when they accepted taxes in French coin, colonial authorities could often then sell them in a black market for a profit because shortages gave these coins a premium.

[41] Interestingly, one of the arguments put forward by the British high commissioner for Southern Nigeria in favor of the provision of a colonial currency was that it would foster the emergence of a labor market and thus end slavery (CO 879/66, letter of R. Moor to CO, July 7, 1901, p. 24, PRO). The one place in the Belgium Congo that used money in 1908 was Katanga where local authorities had begged for it in order to pay Belgian workers.

[42] Chalmers (1893, 32), Lee (1986, 10–11), Gunasekera (1962, 71–72).

Most other colonial powers also established note issue monopolies in their colonies, and the issuers of these notes were increasingly called up to perform macroeconomic tasks. Interestingly, these tasks were sometimes more extensive than those of the British currency boards. Japanese colonial authorities had by far the most ambitious ideas about macroeconomic management in their colonies. In both Taiwan and Korea, Japan established central banks with considerable powers that would have shocked Montagu Norman. Like the British currency boards, the banks were committed to the external goal of maintaining the convertibility of the colonial currency into that of the colonizing power. But they also took on the internal objective of promoting state-led economic growth within the colony.[43] The Bank of Korea was created in 1909 with authority not just to regulate the domestic money market, but also act as a banker to the colonial government and finance public projects in the commercial, industrial, and agricultural sectors of the colony. As one Japanese official put it in 1920 in describing the Korean central bank (which had been renamed in 1911 the Bank of Chosen), "It has done a great deal more than a central bank, as such is understood in most countries, ought to do."[44] Even in India where the British established a central bank in 1935, there were few similarities to the Korean central bank. Bank of England officials had pushed for the establishment of a central bank in India not as a tool for economic development of the colony but in order to create a new conservatively managed monetary authority that would be independent of the rising power of Indian nationalists.[45] They had explicitly rejected the more interventionist, "developmental" role for a central bank that Japan was pioneering in its colonies and that Keynes had in fact endorsed two decades earlier in his official report recommending a central bank for India.

As part of its goal of promoting economic development, the Bank of Chosen also refused to follow the macroeconomic policies of British currency boards. When its gold reserves declined as a result of the colony's chronic balance of payments deficits, the bank was very reluctant to contract the money supply or even to increase its bank rate because "this could not be done without interfering with the industrial progress then going on, for which cheap money was most necessary."[46] Instead, it adopted an unorthodox strategy of bolstering its reserves by expanding its commercial bank business into Manchuria soon after World War I. In-

[43] For the developmental goals of the colonial state in Korea, see Kohli (1994).

[44] Hosino (1920, 198).

[45] This objective is highlighted well in some early internal British government correspondence on the issue; PRO T176/25B, Henry Strakosch to Basil Blackett, Oct. 17, 1925, p. 3, and the exchange of letters between Basil Blackett and Henry Strakosch, August 5 and Sept 28, 1925, PRO.

[46] Hosino (1920, 204).

deed, Woo notes that it was soon unclear whether its notes circulating in Manchuria were greater than those in Korea. The international activities of the Bank of Chosen were indeed remarkable; in addition to over twenty branches it set up in Manchuria, it even established an agency in New York.[47]

More generally, in comparison to other colonial powers, Japanese colonial authorities went to quite extraordinary lengths to finance industrialization in Korea. By the 1930s, Koreans were being forced to purchase government bonds whose proceeds were used to help finance large industrial projects of Japanese companies in the colony.[48] It had also encouraged the growth of modern financial institutions whose presence was felt throughout the colony. The Industrial Bank of Chosen was established in 1918 and by the 1930s it was providing low-interest loans to finance industrial and public projects.[49] Together with the Bank of Chosen, it dominated the financial sector with as many as seventy-four branches throughout the colony by 1938. As Woo puts it, Korea thus had "financial institutions remarkably developed for such an 'underdeveloped' colony."[50] Again, the contrast with British colonies was particularly dramatic. Most banks in British colonies served only the foreign trade sector and local savings were usually exported to London financial markets.

Enhancing Seigniorage?

I have already discussed some fiscal motivations that drove colonial monetary reforms. As we have seen, concerns about fiscal transaction costs played an important role in encouraging these reforms. These related not just to domestic fiscal operations of colonial authorities but also to their fiscal operations vis-à-vis the colonizing countries. I have not, however, yet discussed the seigniorage objectives of imperial powers. As we have seen, a key element in colonial reforms in the late nineteenth and early twentieth centuries involved the creation of monetary systems with monopoly issuers of fiduciary forms of money—both coins and paper currency. This monetary transition created much greater opportunities for seigniorage revenue. Indeed, in some regions such as much of West Africa where competitive suppliers of commodity-based money had previously existed, the colonial era introduced a monetary system in which seigniorage was earned by a public authority for the first time.[51]

---

[47] Woo (1991,26–28). See also Hosino (1920, 229).
[48] Kohli (1994, 1277).
[49] McNamara (1990, 42), Woo (1991, 29).
[50] Woo (1991, 30).
[51] Hogendorn (1996, 111).

To what extent did the goal of maximizing seigniorage act as a motivation for monetary reforms? There is no doubt that it played a role in some instances. The best-documented case involved the British decision to create a distinct currency for West Africa in 1912. We have already seen how this decision was driven partly by concerns about the impact of the growing British fiduciary silver coinage in West Africa on the colonial and British monetary systems. But we have also seen that it was not necessary to create a distinct currency to solve the problem: faced with a similar problem, the French had simply created a currency reserve to back francs circulating in the colonies and regulated the flow of francs to and from the colonies. As Newlyn and Rowan note, the most important reason for creating a distinct currency was that it provided a way for colonial authorities to share in seigniorage profits.[52]

Faced with large debts from railway construction, colonial governors of Lagos and the Gold Coast had first demanded a share of the seigniorage earned from British fiduciary silver coins circulating in their colonies as early as 1897.[53] Although an official committee agreed with this request in 1900, British Treasury officials strongly opposed it. They worried that it would be difficult to calculate the proper share of the profits to be allocated to the colonies (especially given the possibilities of repatriation) and that this arrangement would create a temptation simply to increase imports of coin.[54] To meet the colonies' seigniorage demands, the Treasury advocated the creation of a separate currency as the better solution. Indeed, as we saw in chapter 4, when the Treasury had refused a similar request from Australia in 1907, that country had proceeded to establish an independent currency two years later. Faced with the Treasury's position, colonial governors also became strong advocates of an independent currency. As the colonial secretary of Sierra Leone put it bluntly: "My sole idea of being an advocate of a special coinage would be for the Colonies to get the profit on it which the Mint at present gets."[55]

The creation of a new West African note issued by a currency board would also create some seigniorage revenue for the colonial government in the form of interest earned from the assets held as reserves when they were invested in Britain. Interestingly, however, the creation of the note issue was not supported primarily for this reason but rather because of

---

[52] Newlyn and Rowan (1954, 26–29, 33–35). See also U.K. Government (1912a, 1, 5, 12, 27, 37).
[53] Hopkins (1970, 121). Colonial authorities in the West Indies had made a similar request in 1891, but had been refused.
[54] U.K. Government (1912a, 11).
[55] G. Haddon Smith, ibid., 22. See also Loynes (1974, 11), Hopkins (1970, 122).

the benefits it would create for merchants.[56] In other British colonies, however, the desire to increase seigniorage profits did help support the creation of note monopolies. Colonial authorities in Ceylon were encouraged to create a government note monopoly in 1884 partly because it would ensure that seigniorage profits helped support the colony instead of going to British shareholders of the private bank issuers.[57] Later, in 1938, the Malay States sought to join the Straits currency board primarily to share the seigniorage profits from the circulation of the latter's note.[58]

What is interesting in each of these cases is that the goal was to maximize seigniorage revenue for the local colonial government rather than the home government in Britain. This is not to say that Britain was being overly generous to local colonial authorities. Before 1945, seigniorage gains for the colonies were restricted by a rule that currency boards had to cover the currency they issued with 100 percent reserve assets invested in London into British or other Commonwealth securities.[59] Indeed, by 1943, one Bank of England official acknowledged in an internal memo that this rule was "unduly onerous for the Colonies." He argued that its relaxation would help make new funds available to local governments because there would be a "once-for-all return" of the sterling securities that had been used to back the currency and because new unbacked fiduciary currency could be issued in the future.[60] As he hinted, a key purpose of the rule had been to reinforce London's status as an international financial center and sterling's position as an international currency. Other colonial powers had a similar motive. When establishing the new Philippines currency in the early 1900s, U.S. officials insisted that it be backed 100 percent and that the reserve assets be held in New York. Like the British, they hoped that New York's position as an international financial center would be bolstered by these reserve holdings. They also used the seigniorage profit created from introducing new fiduciary coins in the colony to back this strategy. All of the profit was used to establish the gold fund in New York that was used to defend the new currency's value.[61]

Before ending this discussion of seigniorage, one related issue deserves attention. For seigniorage earnings to be increased, political authorities should try to maximize the circulation of the money they issue and restrict that of any potential alternative currencies within the territories they control. For this reason, one might expect that colonial authorities sought to

[56] U.K. Government (1912a, 16).
[57] Gunasekara (1962, 73).
[58] Lee (1986, 16).
[59] Greaves (1953, 15).
[60] OV44/97, "A Fiduciary Issue for Colonial Currencies," by R. Kernshaw, Sept. 22, 1943, p. 1, BOE.
[61] Rosenberg (1985, 198).

demonetize precolonial currencies as a way of enhancing their seignior-age benefits. Indeed, Kirshner reports that Japan tried to eliminate all use of China's currency in regions it occupied after 1937 partly for this rea-son.[62] Interestingly, the demonetization process in some colonies may also have been pursued as a more direct means of undermining the economic position of the precolonial elite. One example comes from the Korean cur-rency reform of 1905 when the Japanese began to demonetize precolonial nickel coins that circulated very widely (they were fully demonetized by 1908). Noting that these coins were debased and widely counterfeited, the Japanese authorities offered to exchange them for new coins at only 50 percent of their nominal value, and some very debased coins received nothing at all. The move was controversial among Koreans, and some scholars have argued that it devastated the wealth of the Korean merchant class. In Eckert's words, it was "a coup de grace from which they never re-covered."[63] Writers disagree about the extent to which Japanese officials may have been driven by this goal of dispossessing local elites, given the other motives we have already examined.[64]

The demonetization of precolonial currencies in West Africa such as cowries and manillas also often provoked strong local protest. The de-monetization of cowries, in particular, produced significant losses for Africans, especially those who held much of their fortune in these forms of money. Without a formal monetary role, cowry shells could only now be sold for their lime content at very low values. In Ofonagoro's words, "pre-colonial monied families and many not-so-wealthy people were finan-cially ruined."[65] A more generous approach would have been to offer com-pensation by exchanging cowry shells for the new official coinage, an approach that was rejected at the turn of the century by British officials. They did finally adopt this approach much later in 1948–49 with respect to manillas when all previous efforts to end this currency's role in the local monetary system had failed. As part of major initiative to eliminate manil-las at that time, the British offered to purchase each rod at a rate above its metallic value. This "Operation Manilla" was costly for the British; the 32 million manillas purchased from the local population were sold for metal at loss of 284,135 pounds sterling. But Africans also incurred a loss because the price paid by the state was less than their local purchasing power.[66]

---

[62] Kirschner (1995, 60–62). He notes that the move was also designed to force trade with Japan and to delegitimize the Chinese government.

[63] Eckert (1991, 12). See also Oh (1987), Woo (1991, 26).

[64] For contrasting views, see Oh (1987) and Hosino (1920).

[65] Ofonagoro (1979, 652). See also Hogendorn and Gemery (1988, 139), Onoh (1972, 20), Guyer (1995, 15).

[66] Hogendorn and Johnson (1986, 154), Ekejuiba (1995), Vice (1983), Ofonagoro (1979, 643–46).

Influencing Identities

When examining the creation of territorial currencies in independent countries, we have seen how this monetary reform was often linked to the goal of strengthening national identities. Imperial powers were, of course, not driven by any desire to strengthen nationalist sentiments in their colonies. They did, however, see the acquisition of colonies as part of a broader mission of bringing what they considered to be "civilization" and the values of their "superior" culture to these regions of the world. To what extent were colonial monetary reforms also linked to these imperialist ideological goals?

They certainly played a role in encouraging colonial officials to withdraw some precolonial currencies in some regions. In Africa, the demonetization of currencies such as cowries and manillas was driven partly by the fact that they were seen by most colonial authorities as "primitive" forms of money that should have no place in the new social order they hoped to build.[67] More generally, Hopkins argues that in Africa "money was not only a means of assisting commercial transactions but also a medium of values: accepting colonial currencies was a symbol of submission; paying taxes in coin was seen by colonial rulers to be part of an educational process whereby their subjects would acquire new values of frugality, punctuality, and hence self-discipline."[68] His point is backed up by the British high commissioner of Southern Nigeria who argued in 1901 that "as far as Southern Nigeria is concerned, the establishment of a system of currency is of the utmost importance as a civilizing factor, apart altogether from other considerations, such as the so-called "profit" which render it the more desirable."[69] Similarly, in French West Africa, Baier describes how authorities believed that French money "was inherently superior to local currencies, and anything less than a full commitment to encouraging the use of metropolitan currency was thought to betray a lack of seriousness about the self-proclaimed civilizing mission of colonization."[70]

The symbolic value of the new currencies introduced into the colonies was also identified as important by some imperial powers. Wambui Mwangi shows how colonial bank notes issued by the Portuguese were particularly evocative of colonial domination and the "civilizing" mission. In Angola, notes issued in the early 1920s had a picture of "European explorers in the process of raising a monument surrounding by admiring Africans." By the mid-1940s, the images included a white man "tutoring

---

[67] Hogendorn and Johnson (1986, 150).
[68] Hopkins (1997, 584).
[69] CO 879/66, letter of R. Moor to CO, July 7, 1901, PRO.
[70] Baier (1980, 105).

the watching Africans in methods of agriculture," "an avuncular missionary sitting under a tree surrounded by attentive African children," as well as another in which an "African woman in a kneeling posture confronts a monument topped with the Christian cross" (see figure 16).[71] The British also paid considerable attention to the imagery on their colonial currencies. After the turn of the twentieth century, Hewitt notes how the most common images on currency board notes were those "in which portraits of British monarchs presided over exotic foreign landscapes."[72] Each landscape was distinct to the region in which it was issued and Mwangi shows in the case of the East African Currency Board how the landscape images reflected and reinforced colonial ideologies of conquest in that area. She also shows how, perhaps for this reason, Kenyan opponents of British colonial rule in the 1950s began to deface the currency notes, covering them with messages of support for the "Mau Mau" insurrection. This development quickly prompted the British to revise the note design to focus on images of economic development.[73] Elsewhere, the British also increasingly shifted to place detailed images of local inhabitants happily engaged in export-oriented economic activities. These kinds of images were also common on the notes issued in the Belgian Congo, the Dutch East Indies, as well as many of the CFA notes issued after 1945 by France.[74]

In the United States, the symbolic value of colonial currencies was also discussed. When the country acquired new colonies in 1898, one member of Congress argued that the U.S. dollar should be introduced there as a way of teaching the locals "the lessons of the flag and impress upon him the power and glory of the Republic."[75] As we have seen, this advice was followed in Puerto Rico, but not in the Philippines perhaps because U.S. policymakers there worried that the introduction of the dollar might in fact become a symbolic flash point for anticolonial sentiment in an already tense political situation. The Philippines may not have been the only place where symbolic considerations influenced the decision of colonial powers not to introduce their own currency into newly acquired colonies. Another may have been Korea, where the circulation of Japanese currency within the country had caused controversy in the precolonial period. In 1895, Duus describes how a Japanese initiative to encourage Bank of Japan notes to circulate in the country met with strong protest from Korean leaders on the grounds that it "would damage the national prestige."[76] This ex-

[71] Mwangi (2002, 38).
[72] Hewitt (1999, 97–98).
[73] Mwangi (2002).
[74] Mwangi (2002), Hewitt (1999, 110), Mevius (1981).
[75] Quoted in Kemmerer (1916a, 303).
[76] Duus (1995, 94).

Figure 16. Angolan banknote from 1947 with image of African woman kneeling before monument topped with a Christian cross. Photograph courtesy of The British Museum. © The British Museum.

perience led the Japanese government to be very wary of encouraging other Japanese banks to circulate their notes in Korea before 1905, fearing that any such move would be interpreted in Korea as an infringement of its sovereignty and thus undermine diplomatic relations.[77] After Japan seized control of Korea in 1905, this history may have played some role in discouraging Japanese officials from introducing the yen as the new currency of the territory. Indeed, when new notes were issued in 1905, the Japanese government encouraged the idea that they represented "the national currency,"[78] by insisting that their design be approved not just by the resident general but also by the local Korean finance minister, and that they include various Korean landmarks on them. Even after Korea was formally established as a colony in 1910, the notes continued this distinctive character with images of Korean figures on them.[79]

Conclusion

Like the territorializing monetary reforms we have seen in earlier chapters, monetary reforms in colonial regions were driven by a diversity of motives relating to transactions costs, macroeconomic influence, fiscal concerns, and political identities. Some of these motives resembled those

[77] Ibid., 164.
[78] Ladd (1908, 318).
[79] Bank of Korea (1994, 455).

we have already seen, such as the clear parallel between British macroeconomic motivations for creating monopoly note issues in their colonies and those that produced the 1844 Bank Act. Others, however, were different because colonial monetary reforms were driven by the outside interests of an imperial power rather than by those of local policymakers. The desire to minimize transaction costs, for example, was linked more closely to a desire to foster intra-empire economic transactions as well as the construction of an export-oriented economy designed to serve the colonizing country. Similarly, although monetary reforms were sometimes designed to help bolster seigniorage profits for local public authorities in the colonies, they undermined the local economic elite through the demonetization of indigenous currencies. Monetary reforms were also often intended to bolster certain political identities, but these were not nationalist ones but rather identities being promoted by the ideologies of imperialism.

We have also noted other ways in which monetary reforms were distinct in the colonies. Imperial powers sometimes joined distinct colonial jurisdictions within large single currency blocs, but this push for intercolony "currency unions" did not stem from the kind of liberal enthusiasm that had encouraged monetary unions in the nineteenth century. Instead it reflected imperialist goals of simplifying administrative rule and fostering intercolonial commerce. The circulation of indigenous currencies also often persisted long after efforts had been made to ban them. In some cases, this was because of the colonial power's lack of interest in eliminating them in remote rural regions. But it also often reflected a conscious effort by colonized peoples to retain precolonial monetary structures as a means of preserving local circuits of exchange, stores of wealth, and even identities.[80] They even served an important macroeconomic role in some contexts. In West Africa, for example, Vice notes that "the manilla offered a haven to local trade, sheltering it from the economic storms of the First World War and the subsequent depression," because palm oil prices were more stable when valued in manillas than in sterling in this period.[81]

One further note should be made about colonial monetary reforms. They transformed the domestic monetary systems of their colonies in a more far-reaching manner than colonial powers before the nineteenth cen-

---

[80] See Ekejiuba (1995, 142). See also many of the essays in Akin and Robbins (1999) for a excellent discussion of this issue in the Melanesian context where precolonial currencies often remained in use throughout the colonial and postcolonial period. See also Lambek's (2001, 750, 753–74) analysis of the use of precolonial coins in Madagascar.

[81] Vice (1983, 17).

tury had ever attempted. In part, for the various reasons outlined in this chapter, this reflected a new interest among colonial policymakers in reducing the heterogeneity of colonial monetary conditions. But the more ambitious colonial monetary initiatives were also made possible by the two developments outlined in chapter 2: the availability of new industrial processes for manufacturing coins and notes, and the emergence of nation-states. Regarding the latter, colonial administrations were not, of course, nation-states, but their economic, administrative, and coercive apparatus drew on the same techniques of statecraft as at home, techniques that enabled them to influence the kinds of money being used within a given territory much more effectively than previous colonial powers. In West Africa, for example, McPhee notes that the introduction of colonial currencies was quite effective because of the large economic presence of colonial governments in the daily lives of the colonized through public works projects and the imposition of poll taxes.[82] The coercive power of colonial states was also very important.[83] It was used not just to enforce legal tender laws and combat counterfeiting, but also to repress, often brutally, local resistance to policies such as the requirement of paying taxes in colonial currency.[84] Indeed, although the monetary reforms we have examined in previous chapters were often hotly contested, resistance to colonial monetary reforms was often more intense and long-lasting.

There were, however, limits to the power of colonial states. As noted already, their administrative power did not always reach deeply into more rural and remote areas.[85] They also lacked a feature we observed in nation-states. In chapter 2, we saw how "trust" in the state often helped political authorities introduce fiduciary forms of money that were important in constructing territorial currencies. Colonial states certainly often made use of "extensive propaganda" to convince locals of the trustworthiness of new forms of money.[86] But colonial inhabitants had many reasons to be very distrustful of colonial authorities, not least of which was that they had been offered no role in the colonial monetary decision-making.[87] This

[82] McPhee (1971 [1926], 237–39).

[83] See Woo (1991, 25).

[84] Suret-Canale (1971, 105, 131, ch.4).

[85] Kemmerer (1916a, 305) notes that one reason why the United States decided not to introduce the U.S. dollar directly into the Philippines was the danger of it being counterfeited in a context where "a strong secret service had not yet been extended throughout the country."

[86] Quotation from McPhee (1971 [1926], 237). See also Kemmerer (1916, 340) in the Philippine context and Craig (1955, 83) for Korea.

[87] Britain's Emmott Committee that recommended the creation of the West African Currency Board, for example, heard from twenty-two witnesses, none of whom were Africans (Newyn and Rowan 1954, 34).

distrust often played a significant role in undermining official efforts to impose colonial currencies. In eastern Nigeria, for example, Ekejuiba notes that there was a widespread distrust of the value and purchasing power of colonial currencies, particularly when many believed British rule would not last long.[88] This distrust, in turn, played a key role in enabling indigenous currencies to retain an important economic position for a long time in the region despite extensive British efforts to eliminate them.

[88] Ekejuiba (1995, 142–54).

9

The Final Wave
Post-1945 Macroeconomic Activism and Southern Reforms

Following World War II, almost all independent countries that had not yet created territorial currencies now did so. Most African and Asian countries emerging from colonial rule also finally created territorial currencies. In some cases, newly independent countries simply inherited a homogeneous and exclusive currency structure within their borders from the colonial period, a structure that now became a "territorial currency" because it corresponded with the political jurisdiction of an independent state. In other countries territorial currencies were not created until policymakers broke up large intercolony monetary unions.

Some of the rationales for creating territorial currencies in this period—such as maximizing seigniorage and strengthening national identities—were similar to those we have already seen. But some were new. One was the desire to *increase* international transaction costs, a goal that emerged when policymakers in newly independent countries decided to abandon colonial currency unions. The other was even more important: the goal of pursuing activist national macroeconomic management. In chapter 7, we saw briefly how the Great Depression and the Keynesian revolution in the 1930s began to give this idea more political respectability than it had previously had. After World War II, national macroeconomic management emerged as one of the central reasons for creating and having a territorial currency. In place of currency boards and the gold standard, policymakers in many Southern countries saw their nationalist economic and political goals served by activist macroeconomic planning, backed up by national capital controls, more flexible exchange rates, and politically controlled national central banks.

The politics surrounding these early postwar Southern monetary reforms have received little attention in the considerable scholarly literature about the politics of the postwar global monetary order. This chapter corrects this neglect. In the first section, I show that these reforms received important—and in some ways surprising—political support from the United States, the dominant financial power after World War II. Its support stemmed partly from the commitment of American financial advisors to an "embedded liberal" ideology and partly from a recognition of the geopolitical value of not challenging Southern nationalist monetary preferences. The significance of U.S. support is made clear through an examination of two contexts where it was not present: regions that remained under British and French influence. For their own ideological and geopolitical reasons, Britain and France strongly opposed many nationalist monetary reforms in their ex-colonies. Their attitudes, in combination with the ideological orientation and economic interests of some specific Southern governments, help to explain why reforms took a more limited and cautious form in some parts of the South in the postwar period. In the ex-French colonies in Central and West Africa, in particular, most countries chose to retain the CFA monetary unions that had existed in the colonial period.

America's New Money Doctors: The Southern Extension of "Embedded Liberalism"

In an important 1982 article, John Ruggie highlighted the central role of the ideology of "embedded liberalism" in influencing the construction of the global monetary order after the Second World War.[1] Led by British and American negotiators at the 1944 Bretton Woods conference, embedded liberals sought to build a different kind of global monetary order from the gold standard that "classical liberals" had endorsed. While remaining committed to an open, multilateral world economy, they no longer celebrated the discipline of the gold standard. Instead, they hoped to strengthen the capacity of national governments to pursue domestically oriented activist monetary policies of the kinds that Attwood had first endorsed in the nineteenth century. National policy autonomy was to be bolstered through adjustable exchange rates, the international provision of balance of payments financing, and the endorsement of capital controls. The international monetary system—centered around the newly created IMF and World Bank—would become more of a servant to the domestic Keynesian and welfarist goals that had emerged in many countries in the wake of the Great Depression of the 1930s.[2]

The role of Southern countries within the new "embedded liberal" international monetary order has received much less academic scrutiny than that of Northern countries. But the dramatic monetary reforms that produced territorial currencies in Southern countries in the early postwar years were linked by U.S. officials to the new "embedded liberal" commitment to domestic monetary autonomy. Explicitly rejecting Kemmerer's ideas from the 1920s, U.S. policymakers played a key role in backing these reforms through

[1] Ruggie (1982).
[2] Helleiner (1994).

various "money-doctoring" missions partly for this reason. Because of their country's dominant position in the postwar global monetary order, their support gave important strength to this trend of monetary reform.

Why did U.S. policymakers turn their backs on Kemmerer's ideas in the early postwar period? One might have expected the new thinking to come from the U.S. Treasury, which during the early 1940s, under the influence of Henry Morgenthau and Harry Dexter White, had become sympathetic to embedded liberal ideas in the international monetary context. In fact, however, the first criticisms of orthodox money doctoring in the South came in the early 1940s from the U.S. Federal Reserve. The Federal Reserve's interest in this issue was triggered by a 1941 request for advice on monetary reform from the Paraguayan government. In response to this request, the chief of the Latin American section of the staff of the Federal Reserve's Board of Governors—Robert Triffin—launched an extensive process of consultation over several years with financial officials from the United States, Paraguay, and other Latin American countries.[3] Out of this consultation process emerged the view among key Federal Reserve officials that a different approach to money doctoring would be necessary in the postwar period from that promoted by Kemmerer.

This new approach was first put into place in Paraguay in a set of monetary reforms in 1943–45, which the U.S. Federal Reserve described as "a fundamental departure from the central banking structures previously established in Latin America."[4] Triffin himself described the Paraguayan reforms, which included the creation of a new central bank and territorial currency in the country for the first time, as "revolutionary."[5] Triffin and other U.S. officials in a series of advising missions over the following decade actively promoted the Paraguayan model of reform in countries such as Ethiopia (1942–44), Cuba (1942), Guatemala (1945), the Dominican Republic (1947), Honduras (1950), the Philippines (1949), South Korea (1950), Ceylon (1950), and Saudi Arabia (1951–52).[6] In Kim's words, the new Bank of Paraguay's legislation "heralded much post-war central banking legislation that followed."[7]

---

[3] Triffin (1966a [1947], 16, 112–14).

[4] U.S. Federal Reserve (1945, 528).

[5] Triffin (1946, 25).

[6] Triffin (who was originally from Belgium), in his role as chief of the Latin American section of the Federal Reserve staff from 1943 to 1946, led many of these initial Federal Reserve "money doctoring" missions to Southern countries. Other U.S. officials involved in these missions included Bray Hammond, John Exter, Henry Wallich, David Grove, John DeBeers, Arthur Bloomfield, John Jensen, George Blowers, and Arthur Young. I should make clear that the new central banks set up under U.S. assistance did not always pursue the policies that U.S. money doctors advised.

[7] Kim (1965, 6).

Various publications by Federal Reserve officials in this period outline clearly their rationale for the new approach to money doctoring.[8] They argued that the interwar experience had highlighted the drawbacks of a passive monetary policy geared externally to respond automatically to changes in the balance of payments. In countries whose balance of payments were vulnerable to crop failures, dramatic changes in export markets, or volatile international capital movements, this "monetary automatism" was simply too costly in an economic and social sense. It magnified—rather than minimized—the impact of international instability on the domestic economy in this context, resulting in what Triffin called "unbearable and often unnecessary disruptions."[9] Triffin also noted that these adjustments might not even be equilibrating in the way that orthodox theory predicted for countries whose exports were concentrated in a few products with inelastic demand, or whose internal price levels were mostly determined by international prices of their exports and imports.[10]

In the new American view, what was needed, thus, was a form of monetary management that insulated the national economy from international disruptions rather than reinforced the latter's impact on the former. Whereas Kemmerer's banks (and colonial currency boards) had prioritized the external stability of the currency and international equilibrium, the new priority was domestic economic development. In the Guatemalan reform of 1945, for example, the Federal Reserve emphasized the goal of creating "guidance of monetary policy primarily by analysis of domestic developments, rather than in automatic response to changes in international reserves."[11] Similarly, one U.S. official involved in the 1950 Honduran reforms lamented how the monetary system had "not been used as an instrument to promote economic development" in the past, but that now it would be able to do so.[12]

To promote domestic economic development, U.S. money doctors made sure that new central banks were created in countries where they did not yet exist. In some instances (such as the Philippines or Ceylon), the new central bank replaced a colonial currency board as the monopoly

---

[8] U.S. Federal Reserve (1945), Triffin (1944, 1946, 1966a, 1966b [1947]).

[9] Triffin (1946, 74). The domestic money supply of Southern countries with currency boards or orthodox central banks might have been less dependent on changing balance of payments condition if trends in domestic private bank lending had counteracted the direction of monetary policy pursued by these monetary authorities. In reality, however, domestic private bank lending trends usually reinforced central bank or currency board policy because foreign banks that responded primarily to the needs of the foreign trade sector dominated the banking sector.

[10] Triffin (1946, 79–80). Triffin (1968) later developed a more elaborate critique of the working of the classical gold standard from the standpoint of poorer countries.

[11] Quoted in Laso (1957–58, 448).

[12] Vinelli (1950–51, 420).

issuer of currency. In other cases, the new central bank took over the note issue from several private banks, creating a monopoly note issuer for the first time (e.g., Honduras), or it displaced U.S. notes that had dominated domestic circulation (e.g., the Dominican Republic). The new domestic priority was then clearly written into the constitutions of the new central banks. The Paraguayan central bank, which became the prototype of the new approach, described one of its key purposes as "the development of productive activities."[13] A key goal of the central bank established in 1948 in the newly independent Philippines was also "to promote a rising level of productive employment and real income in the Philippines." Similarly, Ceylon's new central bank, set up in 1949, was designed to serve, among other things, "the promotion and maintenance of a high level of production, employment, and real income in Ceylon, and [t]he encouragement and promotion of the full development of the productive resources of Ceylon."[14]

To achieve these new domestic objectives, central banks had to have quite different charters than those written by Kemmerer. Their note issue and deposit liabilities were no longer regulated by rigid provisions linking them to gold or foreign exchange reserves. With this external constraint loosened, the national currency could be managed without such a strict connection to the condition of the balance of payments. To ensure that international economy did not disrupt domestic goals, central banks were also usually allowed to adjust the exchange rate within limits in certain circumstances and to control capital inflows and outflows. Triffin acknowledged that many economic liberals would regard the endorsement of the latter in particular as "highly unorthodox," but he reminded them that the new IMF Articles of Agreement now permitted and even encouraged capital controls.[15] Indeed, the principal negotiators of the Bretton Woods agreements, Keynes and White, had seen capital controls as a central element of the new "embedded liberal" monetary order.[16]

Federal Reserve officials also insisted that central banks be equipped with strong powers to promote the development of their national economies.[17] Central banks set up with Kemmerer's advice had usually been expected to influence the money supply through mechanisms such as discount rate changes and open market operations. In most Southern countries (as well as the British Dominions), U.S. officials noted that these

[13] Triffin (1946, 115).
[14] All quotations in Kim (1965, 15fn2).
[15] Quotation from Triffin (1966a [1947], 141).
[16] Helleiner (1994, ch.2).
[17] Indeed, in the case of Paraguay, Triffin (1946, 72) noted the powers of the central bank were "almost without precedent."

tools were ineffective because domestic financial markets were underdeveloped and foreign banks, which responded primarily to monetary developments only in their home country, dominated the banking system. To become more effective, central banks needed to be able to impose reserve requirements on private banks and control private lending, and perhaps even to lend directly to the public. Central bank involvement in lending to domestic firms was also advocated as a means to promote developmental goals more directly, especially in contexts where foreign banks dominated the domestic banking system and had engaged in little such lending. Interestingly, U.S. officials also did not oppose provisions that allowed central banks to lend to their own governments. The reasoning was that it was simply unrealistic to expect a central bank to behave otherwise in many developing countries.[18]

One final recommendation of U.S. money doctors was especially important in the context of the theme of this book. They encouraged Southern governments to eliminate the use of foreign currencies within their territory wherever that practice was still widespread. It was very difficult, U.S. officials argued, for a central bank to develop a strong and independent monetary policy devoted to national development unless the currency it issued held a monopoly position inside the country. In Paraguay, for example, an (outdated) Argentine currency standard and Argentine notes were widely used in private transactions and even in official accounts for paying taxes and duties. United States officials insisted that they be banned because the use of the foreign standard would "throw doubts upon the stability" of the national currency.[19] In the Dominican Republic, as mentioned above, the U.S. dollar had been the main monetary standard and official currency in use since 1905; even the creation of a national subsidiary coin in 1937 had not displaced the dollar from its dominant role. Along with his colleague Henry Wallich, Triffin now argued that the dollar should no longer be used on the following grounds: "the continued existence of dollar contracts and payments would deprive the monetary authorities of much of their power."[20] In Cuba where dollars had dominated the domestic monetary system since soon after the country became a U.S. protectorate in the early twentieth century, Wallich also noted that dollarization prevented the country's foreign exchange resources from being controlled in a centralized fashion to mobilize them efficiently for development goals. In addition, he highlighted how it made capital controls more difficult to enforce as well as created a situation

---

[18] Triffin (1946, 23).
[19] Ibid., 60.
[20] Wallich and Triffin (1953, 26).

where the country was "in effect making a loan to the United States."[21] In Honduras, too, where U.S. currency had been used widely for several decades (especially in the north where U.S. fruit companies played a prominent economic role), U.S. officials now recommended its removal. Indeed, they trumpeted the fact that "for the first time in its history, Honduras will then have nationalized its currency" and its government will be able to use monetary policy "to assist the growth of the national economy."[22]

The decision of U.S. Federal Reserve officials to turn their backs on Kemmerer and endorse quite unorthodox monetary policy and institutional reforms in Southern countries was controversial among some parts of the business community.[23] But it was in keeping with the new political support in the U.S. policymaking circles for "embedded liberal" ideas. Triffin and other economists in the U.S. Federal Reserve were clearly influenced by the Keynesian revolution that was underway. But even if U.S. officials were not themselves convinced by these ideas, they were forced to recognize their political power abroad. Across the world, monetary policy had moved during the 1930s and wartime decisively away from the classical liberal notion that monetary policy should be geared externally to respond automatically to changes in the balance of payments. In place of this "monetary automatism" was a new commitment to "autonomous monetary management" geared to domestic goals of monetary stability, full employment, and rapid growth. Triffin concluded from these changes that it was simply not politically feasible to try to return to orthodox policies: "Tomorrow's currencies will be managed currencies. . . . Any attempt to enforce rigid solutions patterned upon orthodox gold standard doctrines would be even more futile in the postwar than it already proved to be in the interwar period."[24]

This shift away from orthodox monetary policies had been particularly

---

[21] Wallich (1953, 45). See also ibid., 89–92, 154–56. A brief effort to introduce capital controls by a Cuban nationalist government in 1934 had been very ineffective because of the dollarized domestic monetary system (Díaz-Alejandro 1988a, 196). This nationalist government had also expanded the issue of Cuban currency as a way of capturing seigniorage profits that were lost to the United States through the dollar's circulation (Wallich 1950: 48, 84–87).

[22] Quotations from Vinelli (1950, 428, 420). For the history of use of the U.S. currency, see Young (1925, ch.9).

[23] In the Philippines, Cullather (1994, 81) notes the strong opposition of U.S. business to the introduction of capital controls in 1950 because it interfered with their ability to repatriate profits freely. The inflation that accompanied the monetary policy pursued by the new central bank of the Philippines was also strongly criticized by the U.S. business community (Hartendorp 1958, 255, 608).

[24] Quotations from Triffin (1946, 22; 1966a [1947], 144)

striking in Latin America, the region that strongly influenced the views of Triffin and other Federal Reserve officials. When declining export markets and the collapse of U.S. lending produced dramatic balance of payments crises in the early 1930s, most Latin American countries abandoned the gold standard and introduced trade and exchange controls rather than undergo dramatic deflations. Many of them also began during the 1930s to experiment with more activist monetary policies aimed at financing government spending and encouraging import-substitution industrialization. Exchange controls, which had initially been introduced as temporary measures, were often made permanent in order to allow this kind of monetary policy to be pursued independent of external constraints. Governments also became more directly involved—often via the central bank—in directing credit to the private sector as a means of promoting agricultural and industrial growth.

The new interest in these kinds of activist monetary policies in Latin America and other Southern countries stemmed not just from the kind of economic thinking Triffin put forward. It was also linked to broader nationalist goals. Liberal monetary policies pursued by currency boards, or the independent central banks established before the 1930s, were increasingly associated with the export-oriented economies favored by colonial or neocolonial interests. By contrast, new activist monetary policies were seen to support the project of import-substitution industrialization that had come to be seen in many Southern countries as a means to end their subordinate political position in the global economy. The liberal practice of maintaining 100 percent reserves to back the domestic currency was also now viewed as a measure that inhibited national development because it tied up precious funds and prevented monetary policy from being used to finance government spending. Indeed, inflationary deficit financing was sometimes seen positively as a way to mobilize domestic savings in contexts where taxation and borrowing did not provide adequate funds for ambitious nation and state-building plans.[25] More generally, the creation of new politically controlled central banks was often seen as a move bolstering the state's proper authority over the territory it governed and as a symbol of financial independence and national sovereignty.[26] In countries that had not yet consolidated territorial currencies, the expulsion of foreign currencies and the creation of monopoly note issues were seen in similar ways, as noted below.

In the early 1940s, U.S. Federal Reserve officials displayed a detailed understanding of the various policy innovations in Latin America during

---

[25] See for example Ahmad (1970, 23–25).
[26] Basu (1967, 52, 66), Asseily (1967, 4).

the 1930s. Triffin, in particular, was very knowledgeable about them and was explicit in acknowledging that they had strongly influenced his thinking.[27] He made a special point to frequently cite his debt to Raul Prebisch's "pioneering work" in this area.[28] Prebisch, who was head of the Argentine central bank between 1935 and 1943 and then became head of the UN Economic Commission for Latin America, was the leading theorist of the "structuralist" school of economic nationalism that advocated policies of import-substitution industrialization. Triffin recognized his importance by consulting him in detail on the initial Paraguayan reforms.[29] Other Latin American governments, such as that in the Dominican Republic, also invited Prebisch for consultations with the Americans as part of preparations for U.S.-led monetary reform programs.[30]

United States officials, thus, were very familiar with the policy changes that had taken place across Latin America during the 1930s and understood the extent to which the new approach to monetary policymaking had become politically entrenched in the region. To challenge this approach might not just be futile but also detrimental to broader U.S. geopolitical goals. In the important Paraguayan case, for example, U.S. monetary consultations took place at a time when U.S. policymakers were actively seeking through aid packages and diplomatic efforts to prevent the Paraguayan government from allying itself too closely with the Axis powers. Accommodating the nationalist leanings of the country's government, rather than challenging them, was a U.S. priority.[31] United States advisers played to nationalist sentiments when they advocated the elimination of the use of the old Argentine monetary standard on the grounds that it would help the country "reaffirm its monetary independence and sovereignty." They argued that the use of a foreign currency standard "has injured the prestige of the national currency both at home and abroad," and they encouraged the new currency to be called the "guarani," a name that "derives from the racial origins of the Paraguayan nation."[32]

By the late 1940s, geopolitical concerns in the new Cold War also en-

---

[27] Triffin (1944).

[28] Triffin (1966a [1947], 141fn.2).

[29] The head of the Bank of Colombia (Enrique Davila) was also very involved in Paraguayan consultations with Triffin, and both he and Prebisch even spent three months in Paraguay in 1943 and 1945.

[30] Triffin and Wallich (1953, 25).

[31] Gardner (1964: chs.6, 10) explains more generally how the threat of Axis influence prompted U.S. officials to take a more active and positive role in supporting Latin American nationalist goals of economic development and industrialization beginning in the late 1930s. The new U.S. monetary advice to Latin America fit this pattern perfectly.

[32] Quotations from U.S. Federal Reserve (1944, 46, 47).

couraged an accommodating approach toward economic nationalism in the South.[33] In the Philippines, for example, local politicians after the war sought to replace the colonial currency board with a powerful central bank that would introduce capital controls and pursue expansionary monetary policies.[34] These local demands stemmed not just from the goal of rapid industrialization and the pressing fiscal needs of the government, but also from broader nationalist sentiments that a currency board arrangement was "an unsuitable system for an independent Philippines."[35] Some U.S. officials were wary of the local demands for monetary reform and would have preferred to see more orthodox deflationary measures introduced. But Cullather shows how Cold War fears of the growing power of left-wing rebels in the Philippines prompted the United States to accept local objectives and not to press for deflationary measures that might have given political strength to the rebels.[36]

One further geopolitical benefit deserves mention. In countries emerging from European colonial rule, a more sympathetic approach to nationalist monetary reforms helped U.S. officials gain influence in the newly independent countries. Some ex-British colonies, for example, explicitly sought out U.S. "money doctors" instead of British ones because the latter favored the maintenance of colonial boards (for reasons explained in the next section). In Ceylon, for example, the currency board "was looked upon as a financial appendage of colonial government and was recognized as part and parcel of the system of colonial administration." The construction of a central bank was seen as necessary to achieve "economic freedom"; indeed, one supporter argued that it was more important than the Independence Bill. Even the ability to adjust the national exchange rate—not possible under the currency board arrangements—was seen in political terms by the minister of finance in 1949 as creating a "free currency, the content of which, the value of which, we and we alone can determine according to the best interests of the people of Ceylon."[37] Since U.S. officials were known to be more sympathetic to these nationalist goals, they were invited—instead of Bank of England officials—to help construct the country's first central bank. Indeed, local policymakers

---

[33] I have shown elsewhere the influence of the Cold War in encouraging U.S. officials to accept European and Japanese preferences for monetary and financial interventionism in the early postwar years (Helleiner 1994, ch.3).

[34] Cullather (1994, 63–66).

[35] Quotation from the U.S.-Philippine Finance Commission set up in 1946 to study the future of monetary arrangements (quoted in Golay 1961, 217).

[36] Cullather (1994, 64–71, 76, 81, 191).

[37] All quotations in Karunatilake (1973, 3, 8, 13).

made it clear that they wanted a central bank like that recently constructed under U.S. advice in Korea and the Philippines.[38]

In British-occupied Ethiopia during the early 1940s, a similar dynamic existed. At the time, the money in circulation within the country was a motley collection Maria Theresa thalers, traditional commodity-based small denomination money, Italian and British currencies, and currency issued by the Ethiopian state. Ethiopian policymakers sought to create an exclusive national currency for the first time in order to assert the state's authority over the whole country and create a monetary system that could be mobilized to promote rapid economic growth. The British were supportive of the objective of consolidating the national currency, but they pushed for it to be managed by a currency board with all its reserves in sterling assets. To the Ethiopians a currency board was unacceptable because it prevented them from pursuing their nationalist monetary goals and would also tie up foreign exchange that could otherwise be used to finance imports. They also saw the British proposal in highly political terms as an attempt to turn the country into a protectorate or colony of the United Kingdom. These fears were intensified by the fact that the British made clear that the new currency would be called the Ethiopian pound and the currency board's headquarters would be in London and be staffed with representatives not just of the Ethiopian government but also of the Bank of England and U.K. Treasury. To offset British influence, Ethiopian policymakers turned to U.S. officials for advice, recognizing correctly that the latter would support their goal of creating a powerful central bank that pursued more nationalist policies. Indeed, keen to see Ethiopia freed from British influence, U.S. officials provided advice that helped create Ethiopia's new central bank and currency, the Ethiopian dollar. They even secretly help print Ethiopia's first notes and provided the central bank with its first governors until 1959.[39]

A final example of the conflict between U.S. and British money doctors came in Saudi Arabia. The Saudi monetary system after World War II was heterogeneous, consisting primarily of various domestic and foreign full-weight silver and gold coins whose relative values fluctuated considerably. As far back as the 1920s, Saudi rulers had attempted to reduce the number of foreign currencies in use in order to simplify tax collection, but these efforts had often been resisted by local moneychangers and had been undermined by the state's weak control over its territory.[40] After oil was discovered in 1938, a more monetized economy emerged and the state established more sophisticated fiscal arrangements. In this context,

[38] Ibid., 5.
[39] Degefe (1995).
[40] Chaudhury (1997, 65–67).

the heterogeneity of the monetary system produced growing frustrations, especially for the government's own financial affairs and for those of foreign oil companies. When the British proposed during the war to establish a London-based currency board backed by the pound, however, the United States opposed the initiative, as did the Saudi government. Not until 1951–52 did a major monetary reform take place when the Saudi government requested and received U.S. assistance in creating a central bank, the Saudi Arabian Monetary Agency, that could stabilize the currency vis-à-vis the dollar and also act as a banker to the government.[41]

United States support for the new approach to monetary policy thus had both ideological and geopolitical roots. Regardless of its sources, U.S. support was important in encouraging nationalist monetary reforms across the South. Its importance stemmed not so much from the specific content of the advice provided by U.S. money doctors. Most of the countries that received U.S. advice were, after all, already committed to the course that U.S. money doctors recommended.[42] Instead, what was important was the simple fact that the political weight of the world's dominant financial power would not stand in the way of the reforms.

Discouraging "the Wrong Tendencies": Monetary Reforms in Ex-British Colonies

The importance of U.S. support is put into relief if we contrast it with some cases where it was not present. As mentioned already, British policymakers were quite opposed to activist monetary policies, and they went out of their way to advise newly independent, ex-British colonies not to implement them. Some countries—such as Ceylon, as we have seen—simply ignored this advice, but others had to listen because of continuing close economic and political ties to Britain. In these latter cases, the introduction of these monetary reforms took place more cautiously and slowly.

Why were British policymakers so opposed to the new approach to monetary policy in Southern countries? The opposition was partly ideological. At Bretton Woods, Britain had endorsed the new "embedded liberal" monetary ideas, but it had been the Treasury, led by Keynes, which had represented the country at the conference. The institution that took charge of British foreign monetary policy toward Southern countries in the early postwar period was the Bank of England. Despite the experience

---

[41] See al-Dukheil (1995), Young (1983), Knauerhase (1975). The government initially objected to the central bank issuing paper currency and silver fiduciary coinage, but paper currency was soon issued initially in the form of "pilgrim receipts" and then as a regular bank note by the 1960s.

[42] The same had been true of Kemmerer's missions (Drake 1989).

of the 1930s and the nationalization of the bank in 1944, its outlook remained largely orthodox throughout this period. The Bank of England's leading money doctors in the postwar period, such as J. B. Loynes, largely picked up where their predecessors in the interwar period had left off (with one exception noted below).

Equally, if not more, important in explaining British policy was its goal of preserving the sterling area and Britain's privileged position within it.[43] The sterling area consisted of a set of countries and colonies whose currencies were fixed to the British currency and which held most of their foreign exchange reserves as sterling balances in London. First emerging in the early 1930s after Britain left the gold standard, the area then became more closely knit during World War II with the introduction of common exchange controls and the pooling of foreign exchange reserves. After the war, the continued existence of the sterling area provided Britain with not just international prestige, but also important balance of payments support. This support came partly from the considerable foreign exchange reserves held in sterling in London by sterling area members; indeed, in the case of colonial currency boards, Balogh noted that this practice ensured that any increase in the colony's money supply resulted in a "de facto loan" to Britain (and often at below "market" rates since sterling balances earned very low rates of interest).[44] The absence of capital controls and exchange rate risk within the sterling area—when combined with limited local money markets—also encouraged private banks, companies, and individuals in many sterling area countries to export savings and liquid funds to London markets. When this export of local savings was offset by long-term loans back to the colony from London, there might be no net balance of payments benefit to Britain. But the arrangement still bolstered the City of London's role as an international financial center.

If countries turned to activist monetary policies, these benefits of the sterling area to Britain would diminish. Activist domestic monetary management might produce balance of payments deficits in those countries, which would force them to draw down their sterling reserves and sterling assets in London. Demand for sterling and sterling assets in London, and for sterling more generally, would also be reduced if national currencies were backed with less than 100 percent reserves or if reserves were held in local government securities. Similarly, capital controls and the creation of domestic money and capital markets might reduce capital outflows to

---

[43] Bangura (1983).
[44] Balogh (1966, 30).

London and reduce the dependence of Southern borrowers on London financiers.

British hostility toward the new approaches to monetary policy initially took an interesting form: opposition to the creation of central banks in newly independent countries altogether. Throughout the 1940s and 1950s, at the same time that the United States was advocating the creation of powerful central banks, British officials went to great lengths in their colonies to try to convince local policymakers not to create central banks and to maintain currency boards arrangements after they attained independence.[45] They even began to reform currency boards to try to accommodate criticisms of their operations.[46] Some currency boards, such as that in East Africa in 1955 and Malaya in 1960, were allowed to begin issuing some unbacked money. They were also permitted to invest their reserves in nonsterling assets such as local government securities and dollars around this time. The East African Currency Board began in 1960 to cultivate a local money market by discounting activities in the local Treasury bill market and by allowing banks to hold balances with it and offering clearance and settlement services. In addition, the headquarters of these operations were moved from London to the regions themselves and more local staff were recruited. Finally, colonial images on currency boards notes and coins were replaced with iconography more appropriate to newly independent countries in 1959 in the case of Malaya (the monarch was replaced by a fishing craft—see figure 17) and 1964 in East Africa (Lake Victoria appeared on the notes).[47]

The British opposition to central banks contrasted sharply not just with U.S. policy but also with the Bank of England's own policy during the interwar period. As we have seen in chapter 7, Montagu Norman had played a lead role in that earlier era in encouraging countries around the world to set up independent central banks where none yet existed (including in some colonized regions such as India). These banks, he had hoped, would help to insulate the management of money from political pressures and to preserve the international gold standard. Now that central banks had become associated with more activist monetary management, however, Bank of England officials wanted nothing to do with them. Central banks, they now argued, would only lead to inflationary pressures, bal-

[45] There were some exceptions. In the Gold Coast, Cecil Trevor (who had had experience with the Reserve Bank in India) unexpectedly recommended the creation of a central bank in a 1951 report, a conclusion that greatly annoyed the Bank of England and led them to insist that he not be allowed to provide advice to Nigeria (Uche 1997).

[46] See East African Currency Board (1967, 1972), Lee (1986, 20).

[47] For Malaya, see memos in T236/4420, PRO. See Mwangi's (2002) fascinating analysis in the East African context.

Figure 17. Malayan note from 1940, and Malayan and British Borneo note from 1959. Observe the replacement of the monarch with a fishing craft. Photograph courtesy of The British Museum. © The British Museum.

ance of payments crises, and capital flight as politicians controlled them to finance government deficits or pursue overly ambitious development plans. Bank officials also stressed that, in comparison to currency boards, central banks were more expensive to run and required a kind of expertise that was often not available in newly independent countries.[48]

---

[48] See East African Currency Board (1965, 7–11; 1966, 13), Uche (1997), Greaves (1953, 88–91).

It soon became clear to British officials, however, that most Southern governments disregarded these arguments and planned to establish central banks anyway. In part, Southern policymakers wanted a modern central bank for the symbolic reason that it was associated with political independence, as already noted.[49] Equally important, many policymakers in the South rejected currency boards because they precluded the kind of activist monetary policy that was seen as necessary to serve domestic goals of economic development. As Ghana's first finance minister put it, "A Currency Board is the financial hallmark of colonialism. And it is a dead thing as well, an automatic machine which has no volition of its own."[50] In Nigeria, which was one of the few British colonies to develop an indigenous banking system alongside the colonial one, it was also hoped that a central bank could support local banks in times of crises.[51]

In defying British preferences, these nationalists were sometimes supported by the United States, as we have seen in the cases of Ceylon, Ethiopia, and Saudi Arabia. Also important was the role played by the U.S.-controlled international financial institutions, the World Bank and IMF, which often made similar arguments as Triffin had.[52] Northern academic experts also often interfered with British efforts to preserve orthodox monetary arrangements. One of the more prominent was Thomas Balogh, a left-of-center Oxford economist who was very critical of currency boards on the grounds that they reinforced the export-oriented nature of Southern economies, encouraged capital outflows, and left Southern countries dependent on the judgments of London financiers to determine their creditworthiness.[53] His anti-imperialist analysis and his advocacy of powerful central banks in Southern countries appealed to many nationalist politicians in countries seeking to throw off British rule. In contexts such as Jamaica and Malaysia, British officials privately expressed their worries about the influence of his arguments on local debates concerning monetary reform.[54]

As it became clear that former British colonies could not resist the creation of central banks, British officials shifted their strategy. They accepted central banks, but insisted that they be managed in a conservative man-

---

[49] In Africa, see Bangura (1983, 49). In Malaysia, see Schenck (1993, 427).

[50] Gold Coast (1956–57, 852). See also Nkrumah (1965, 221).

[51] Uche (1997). Ghana's finance minister also criticized currency boards because they "could do nothing to assist in developing our own financial institutions" (Gold Coast 1956–57, 852).

[52] For the World Bank, see Schenk (1993, 412–13), World Bank (1962, 71–72). For the IMF, see Uche (1996, 157fn61).

[53] Balogh (1966).

[54] CO 1025/123, R.J. Vile to Mr. Marnham, Apr. 30, 1958, PRO; T236/5149, C. Lucas to J. Rampton, Jan 1. 1960, PRO.

ner. Currencies should be backed by 100 percent reserves and their convertibility into sterling should be guaranteed, they argued. They also opposed giving significant powers to the central bank, such as the power to control capital movements or to force commercial banks to hold funds at the central bank.[55] In the words of one British official in the Gold Coast (Ghana) in 1955, the objective was to ensure that the local government "does not set up a Frankenstein."[56] British officials also tried to appeal to nationalist sentiments in advancing these arguments in favor of an orthodox approach to monetary management. In the Gold Coast, Loynes argued that a stable and internationally convertible currency was crucial because "it is bound up with the international reputation of the Gold Coast as an independent country."[57] Other British officials were encouraged to stress how "the world is strewn with unsatisfactory Central Banks and shaky currencies and the combination of the two in any country is simply to replace political dependence by economic dependence, exemplified in foreign aid."[58]

When one looks at the kinds of central banks established in many ex-British colonies, it appears that the British were quite successful in advancing these arguments. Most of the central banks set up—with the exception of Ceylon—had initially quite conservative charters in contrast to those established under the U.S. Federal Reserve's guidance. They usually had only a limited fiduciary issue, no reserve requirements, strong sterling backing, and often no provisions for the use of capital controls or for direct lending by the central bank. This was even true of the central banks set up in countries such as Jamaica, where Balogh had initially had some influence, or Malaysia where the World Bank had called for more radical measures. Indeed, domestic critics argued that these were not real central banks but just another name for the old currency boards. As one Ghanaian critic put it, "If we are going to have a Central Bank we must have a Central Bank with 'teeth' and not a Central Bank which is only a channel for controlling the financial assets of their country by a foreign power."[59]

The conservative nature of these central banks partly reflected British pressure. But it also stemmed from the continued dependence of many of

[55] See Uche (1997).

[56] CO 1025/42 59/13/04, "Gold Coast Currency and Banking, Notes for Meeting on Sept. 14, 1955," p. 4, PRO.

[57] CO 1025/42 59/13/04, informal Report of J. B. Loynes to Minister of Finance, Feb. 21, 1956, p. 1, PRO.

[58] CO 1025/42 59/13/04, "Gold Coast Currency and Banking, Notes for Meeting on Sept. 14, 1955", p. 4, PRO.

[59] Gold Coast (1956–57, 711). See also 705–6.

these countries on London financial markets and links to the British economy. Policymakers were particularly concerned to cultivate confidence in their new national currencies in order to prevent capital flight and encourage international lending to their country.[60] A central bank with a conservative charter served this goal, as did public pronouncements of a commitment to conservative policies at the time of its establishment. In Kenya, for example, the central bank was set up with what one observer called "the expression of sentiments of impeccable respectability in monetary matters of which Mr. Montagu Norman would have been proud."[61]

If monetary reforms were usually quite limited at the time of independence in ex-British colonies, they often moved rapidly in a more nationalist direction in response to fiscal and economic pressures. In Ghana, for example, the government's desire in 1961 to accelerate economic growth and government spending led policymakers to allow the central bank to lend to the government more easily, to mobilize the foreign exchange reserves of Ghanaian residents, and to introduce capital controls.[62] Similar measures accompanied the introduction of Nigeria's 1962 development plan. Even the more conservative Kenyan government had begun deficit financing and tightened exchange controls by 1970. These episodes usually led to the results feared by British officials: the drawing down of sterling reserves, lessened dependence on London financial market, and often a break from the sterling area itself.

In discussing British monetary relations with its ex-colonies, I have not yet discussed the politics surrounding the break-up of the large colonial monetary unions that Britain had established earlier in the century. British officials generally preferred to see these unions continued at independence. An official report to the Colonial Economic Research Committee gave the following warning in 1953 to newly independent countries:

> the trend of modern conditions has been to make money essentially a national matter, so that its nature and its value are at once a reflection and an instrument of Government policy. In these circumstances the possession of an independent currency offers a country opportunities for financial virtuosity that appeal to tortuous planners of bureaucratic complex-

---

[60] Bangura (1983), Schenck (1993).

[61] Hazlewood (1979, 146). Similarly, Uganda's president opened its central bank with the following warning: "We must . . . work for every cent before the Bank can produce that one cent. The Bank is not, and will not be turned into a charity institution" (quoted in East African Currency Board 1966, 122).

[62] Interestingly, like Fichte, some Ghanaian politicians saw the introduction of capital controls in highly political terms as in keeping with Ghana's status as a "republic" (Bangura 1983, 99).

ity, and it has magnetic attraction for politicians tired of an impecunious
role, private and public. . . . But in all the long history of monetary movements there is no evidence that an independent currency provides a
country with an automatic remedy for its poverty, and no indication that
there is a magic formula, such as creating internal cover for its currency
issue, which alone will raise it to more prosperous heights. For a small
country, indeed, the successful management of its own currency may
prove to be one of the more difficult responsibilities of independence.[63]

These arguments were generally not well received in the ex-colonies.
The first monetary union to unravel was that in West Africa. Indeed, the
British were largely resigned to this breakup, accepting what Loynes
called "prestige and appearance" reasons why countries would want to
create national currencies at independence, as Ghana did in 1957, followed by Nigeria in 1958, Sierra Leone in 1963, and Gambia in 1964.[64]
Some Bank of England officials even acknowledged that, while British
banks and administrators had found the currency union useful, it had not
made much sense from an African standpoint since "it is not as though the
four territories have common frontiers and a large intra-area trade and
common Government financial policies."[65] British officials hoped, however, that the creation of these national currencies would not lead to, what
Loynes called privately, "the wrong tendencies." He wanted them to be
managed much as the common currency board had been, simply providing a "national façade for the currency."[66] As the acting British governor of
Sierra Leone put it in 1960, "Any reforms should be of a very conservative
nature."[67]

As these hopes were being dashed, British officials made more of an effort to preserve existing currency unions elsewhere. In East Africa, they encouraged newly independent countries to maintain the East African Currency Board.[68] This initiative soon failed, however, when Tanzania
announced its intention to withdraw and create a national currency in
1965, a move quickly followed by Kenya and Uganda in 1966–67. In Southeast Asia, the British also worked hard to preserve a currency union between Malaysia and Singapore after the former became independent and
created a central bank in 1959. Arguing that a common currency would

---

[63] Greaves (1953, 92).

[64] Loynes quotation from his 1961 report to Sierra Leone (CO 1025/127 E/57, Mar.
1961, p.8, PRO).

[65] CO 1025/39, J. Fisher "West African Currency Conference," to Galsworthy, Apr. 27,
1955, p.3, PRO.

[66] Quotations from Uche (1996, 151).

[67] CO 1025/127 S.F.P.9482, Acting Governor of Sierra Leone to Galsworthy, Oct. 7, 1960,
PRO.

[68] Onoh (1982, 42–43).

earn more confidence and preserve the close economic ties between the two former colonies, World Bank and IMF officials supported this goal. The British also supported this common currency in order to placate Singapore, a strategically important partner whose government feared currency instability in the region. The currency union eventually unraveled in 1967 when the two countries established separate national currencies.[69]

What reasons did ex-British colonies have for abandoning these currency unions? Loynes was certainly correct that most newly independent countries placed considerable symbolic value on the creation of a national currency. As Ghana's finance minister put it, "The issuing by any country of its own distinctive currency is recognized as one of the outward and visible signs of sovereignty—as visible, indeed, as the national flag. . . ."[70] Similarly, Sierra Leone's finance minister in his 1962 budget speech noted: "No independent country can regard itself as truly independent until it has its own national currency."[71] The symbolic value of the new national currencies was often reinforced by the names chosen for the currencies. In Sierra Leone, the government named its new currency the "Leone," despite the strong objections of Loynes who argued that it meant "discarding the pound which I should have thought had still great psychological value both inside and outside the country."[72] Other countries initially retained the names "pounds" and "shillings," but nationalists often protested this decision (as in Kenya),[73] or it was soon changed to reflect nationalist traditions (as in Ghana where a new currency was soon introduced called the cedi, a local word for cowry). The imagery on the new national currencies was also chosen to reinforce nationalist identities. In Ghana, the finance minister chose images of key economic activities such as cocoa growing and processing (see figure 18). Kenyan policymakers made a similar decision (see figure 19) which President Kenyatta explained in the following way: "When we look upon the bank notes which in a short time will officially go into circulation, we see several pictures showing Kenya's natural riches and the people working on them. This is indeed an indication where the country's economy, and the country's money as well, take its strength from. It is ultimately the productive work done by the people on which the growth and the balance of the national economy depends."[74]

[69] See Schenk (1993), Lee (1986, 62–68). The two countries retained an agreement until 1973 that their respective currencies could circulate in the other country as if they were legal tender.

[70] Gold Coast (1956–57b, 860). See also Gold Coast (1955, 1862–63).

[71] Quoted in Uche (1996, 157fn66).

[72] Quoted in ibid., 153.

[73] Republic of Kenya 1967, 1663–64.

[74] Quoted in East African Currency Board (1966, 118). A controversial issue in some countries was the question of whether to include a picture of the head of state on the money. Some countries made this choice (e.g., Kenya), while others did not.

Figure 18. 1957 Ghanaian note. Photograph courtesy of The British Museum. ©
The British Museum.

The desire for a more active monetary policy designed to serve national goals was also important in breaking up currency unions in some
former colonial regions. President Nyerere in Tanzania explained his
decision to initiate the breakup of the East African currency union and
create a national central bank on these grounds: "This change was not
decided upon for prestige reasons; the decision was made because it is
impossible to plan economic development properly if currency and
credit are not within the control of the planners—that is, of the government."[75] He had initially hoped for a federal East African central bank,
but when the prospects for this dimmed, he turned to a national solution as the most effective one to replace the East African Currency
Board.

Concerns about monetary management also played a role in the breakup
of the currency union joining Malaysia and Singapore. By 1967, Malaysia
policymakers began to want a more activist and expansionary monetary
policy than the joint currency board could provide. The Singaporean government did not share this concern and became one of the few countries in
the world in this period to keep a currency board backed by 100 percent reserves.[76] As an international trading entrepôt, it had good reasons to favor a

[75] Quoted in Rothchild (1968, 300).
[76] Others that maintained currency boards were Brunei and Hong Kong (until 1974 and
then resumed in 1983). In Singapore's case, a Monetary Authority was established in 1970
to do some central banking functions unrelated to currency issue.

Figure 19. 1966 Kenyan note. Photograph courtesy of The British Museum. ©
The British Museum.

stable currency. Singapore's finance minister from 1959 to 1971 also made
clear that his government's macroeconomic preferences had ideological
roots: "None of us [in the cabinet] believed that Keynesian economic policies could serve as Singapore's guide to economic well-being."[77] In addition

[77] Goh (1995, 181).

to these macroeconomic differences, the monetary union was also broken up for fiscal motivations. In particular, the Malaysian government expressed concern that the currency board's 100 percent backing of the currency locked up too many financial resources. It also had broader concerns about the distribution of the ownership and control of the reserves backing the currency between the two countries.[78]

Finally, concerns about transaction costs also encouraged these currency unions to unravel. We have seen in previous chapters how a desire to reduce international transaction costs often encouraged monetary unions. In this period, one motivation for leaving monetary unions was the opposite: to *increase* international transaction costs. In both Tanzania and Uganda, governments hoped the creation of a national currency would discourage financial flows within the region to Nairobi and thus reduce the concentration of East African financial services in that city. By creating an exchange rate risk, the introduction of national currencies might foster the growth of local capital markets in their territories, a goal that the introduction of capital controls would encourage further.[79] Some policymakers in Sierra Leone also hoped that the introduction of its national currency would allow the government to control cross-border movements of money more effectively. At the time, the government was trying to control remittances associated with the illegal diamond trade, which was costing it considerable revenue. While Sierra Leone remained in a common currency zone, capital controls could be easily evaded by smuggling notes across borders. But policymakers—including some British officials—argued that the creation of a national currency would make it easier to regulate these cross-border remittances.[80]

The similar motivation—with an interesting twist—also encouraged the creation of distinct national currencies in small countries in the Arabian Peninsula such as Kuwait, Bahrain, Qatar, and Oman. The main currency in use in these countries before their political independence was the Indian rupee. The desire to increase international transaction costs came not from these countries, but from the Indian government, which was frustrated in the late 1950s by the fact that this currency arrangement was undermining the effectiveness of its exchange controls. At the time, it was

[78] Schenk (1993); Lee (1986, 62), Goh (1972, 136–37).

[79] East African Currency Board (1966, 5–7, 25, 111, 114).

[80] Mr. Holland to Mr. Harding, May 27, 1960, CO 1025/127, p. 1, PRO; Acting Governor of SL to Galsworthy, Oct. 7, 1960, SFP 9482, CO 1025/127, PRO. Interestingly, in northern Ghana in the 1960s, the use of cowries reappeared as a means of smuggling money across borders in the context of national capital controls (Hogendorn and Johnson 1986, 153, 155).

trying to stop smugglers of gold into India from exporting their rupee earnings illegally to the Persian Gulf where the rupee was still freely convertible into sterling. In 1959, India decided that the best way to do that, while preserving the prestige of the rupee's wide circulation, was to introduce a new "external rupee" currency for circulation in the gulf region that was no longer legal tender in India. In the gulf region, however, the exchange of Indian rupees for the new external rupees was not well received. The latter were widely seen as a "second class" currency that might soon be devalued and a desire emerged for nationally issued currencies to be created.[81] Although the British hoped for a new common currency in the region, Kuwait, for seigniorage and nationalist symbolic reasons, chose to issue its own dinar managed by a currency board when it became independent in 1960.[82] The devaluation of the rupee in 1966 then acted as the prompt for other national currencies soon to be created in Bahrain, Oman, and Qatar.[83]

The Survival of the CFA Franc Zone

Not all colonial currency unions were dismantled in the early postindependence years. The most dramatic exception to this trend came from many ex-French colonies in West and Central Africa. At independence, most of these countries did not create national central banks and national currencies, but remained members of the two common currency zones that had existed under French colonial rule. The postindependence CFA franc monetary zones functioned in a similar way as had their colonial predecessors.[84] The CFA franc was convertible across the entire region with no capital controls existing among member countries. The notes and coins in use across each zone were also almost identical, with no national emblems on them[85] (with the exception in Cameroon which acquired its own note issue). All external payments of member countries were settled

---

[81] Quotation from A. Lamb to A. Walmesley, May 16, 1959, T236/5194, p. 2, PRO. See also Hallows "Persian Gulf Currency," Jan. 1959, 1, T236/5193, PRO; "Persian Gulf Currency," March 2, 1959, T236/5193, PRO; M. Johnston, "Persian Gulf Currencies," May 27, 1959, T236/5194, p. 4, PRO.

[82] S. Sawborn to Mr. Johnston, May 26, 1959; M. Johnston, "Persian Gulf Currency," June 1, 1959, T236/5194, p. 1, PRO.

[83] Edo (1975).

[84] See for example Chipman (1989, 208–16). The Central African CFA franc zone included Cameroon, Central African Republic, Chad, Congo, and Gabon, while the members of the West African CFA franc zone in the early years after independence were Ivory Coast, Dahomey, Mauritania, Niger, Senegal, and Upper Volta (as well as Togo after 1963).

[85] In 1962, each CFA franc note acquired a small country identification code (a letter following serial number), which enabled policymakers to analyze intercountry balance of payments situations. These payments situation were important in determining how much

through an "operations account" held at the French Treasury, which continued to cover all deficits emerging in these accounts. Even the name "CFA franc" was the same as the colonial currency, although the meaning of CFA had been changed from "Colonies Françaises d'Afrique" to "Communauté Financière Africaine."

How do we explain this anomalous experience? One part of the explanation is that the French government went to much greater lengths than had the British government to preserve the monetary structures in place in the colonial period. The French government's desire to maintain the CFA zone reflected the power of specific interest groups who benefited from the zone's existence as well as its broader concern with its status as a world power after the war.[86] The CFA zone also provided balance of payments support for France in much of the postwar period.[87] To increase the attractiveness of the CFA zone to African governments, the French government undertook a series of reforms of its operations in the postwar period. As the British had also done, the French initially relaxed the prewar requirement that CFA currencies be backed with 100 percent reserves in gold, FF, or convertible currencies and now allowed up to two-thirds of the reserve to be held in local assets.[88] They then went much further than the British to create regional central banks in Central Africa (1955) and West Africa (1959), which provided not only rediscount facilities for local banks but also short-term commercial credit (e.g., crop finance) and medium-term loans for development projects.[89] After independence, the French went one step further in 1962 to transform the regional central banks into intergovernmental institutions with a majority of Africans on the board (although the headquarters remained in Paris until 1972 and France retained an effective veto). At this time, each member government was also given more input into the central banks' decisions on the overall level of credit being allocated to their country as well as decisions on how this credit would be distributed to banks and companies within their country.

In these ways, the French attempted to accommodate Southern goals of using the monetary system more actively to promote economic development. But the price of these reforms was that the CFA zone remained a French-controlled monetary system. For this reason, many Africans con-

---

credit was allocated to each country by the regional central bank, as noted below (Robson 1968).

[86] Stasavage (2002), Chipman (1989).
[87] Joseph (1976), Balogh (1966, 46).
[88] Onoh (1982, 29).
[89] Robson (1968, 201–7).

tinued to see the CFA franc as "colonial money" and the CFA zone as a form of neocolonialism.[90] The extent of the 1962 economic reforms should also not be overstated. Credit from the central banks was refused to CFA countries that ran a consistent balance of payments deficit within the system, and CFA governments were still not allowed to run fiscal deficits (although French aid was available as a partial, albeit politically controlled alternative for financing government spending).[91] Given these constraints, it may seem surprising that more African governments did not break out on their own and create national currencies and national central banks as governments in ex-British colonies had done. To be sure, some countries such as Guinea and Mali did pursue this option, as is explained below. But the fact that more did not surprised many observers at the time, including this British Foreign Office official who was convinced in 1964 that the situation would not last: "In the longer term, the very conservatism of the Central Banks, and their inability under the present rules to play the part they ought to be playing in helping the countries they serve to establish their economic independence is, I should have thought, more likely to lead to moves of the kind Guinea and Mali have already taken."[92]

One reason so many African governments decided to remain in the CFA zone may have been that the French took a very tough stance toward countries that adopted a more independent course. Countries such as Guinea and Mali, which sought to break away from the CFA zone, found their broader security, trade, aid, and other economic links to France severed by the French government. African governments in the CFA zone thus appeared to face a starker choice than members of the sterling area has faced: either accept the CFA currency or face a sharp break in the relationship with France. For many elites, the prospects of losing security ties, aid support, and guaranteed access to the French market (as well as the stable and high prices paid by the French for these materials) were ones they were not willing to consider.[93]

This explanation is important, but it does not tell the whole story. An official French commission examining potential reforms to the CFA actually opened the door to the possibility of France allowing distinct national

[90] Quotation is from Joseph Tchunjang (quoted in Guyer 1995, 13). See also Nkrumah (1965, 20).

[91] As the French government's Jeanneney Report of 1963 noted, "France in effect renounces the possibility of refusing to finance initiatives taken unilaterally by African governments, in return the States accept a certain monetary tutelage, particularly in the matter of deficit financing" (quoted in Robson 1968, 207). Credit from the IMF and World Bank to national governments also complicated the fiscal arrangements in the CFA zone.

[92] OV100/3, R. J. O'Neil (FO) to W. Pattinson (Treasury), Jan. 16, 1964, p. 3, BOE.

[93] See Stasavage (2002), Chipman (1989), Joseph (1976), Kirshner (1995).

currencies to be created in its 1960 report. The commission even suggested that France would allow these currencies both to be devalued in situations of fundamental disequilibrium and to be defended by capital controls if such controls were necessary for economic development.[94] That African governments did not push more strongly for this kind of reform given French openness to it requires explanation. Indeed, when in 1961 the West African central bank floated the idea of creating distinct national bank notes for each newly independent CFA country in West Africa, the proposal was actually opposed by every African government involved.[95]

To account for the choice made by CFA countries, we must thus also look to the domestic ideological roots of the decision in these countries. Conservative governments whose commitment to nationalist ideology was much weaker than in other Southern countries at this time ruled most of the countries that stayed within the CFA zone. Many of their leaders had endorsed the goal of independence from France in only a lukewarm fashion, and they remained wedded to the assimilationist goals that the French had promoted in the colonial period.[96] A national currency and national central bank thus appeared to hold much less symbolic value for these leaders than it had for policymakers elsewhere.

The importance of the ideological orientation of African governments is also clear when one examines the countercases of Guinea and Mali. Soon after their independence, these two countries established a national central bank and national currency (in 1960 for Guinea and 1962 for Mali).[97] They also imposed capital controls, and the central banks were given considerable powers. In Guinea's case, for example, there was initially no provision for backing the currency whatsoever and no limitation on government borrowing from it. The five French banks in the country were also told to deposit 50 percent of their foreign currency holdings with the central bank, and when four of them refused, they were liquidated.[98]

This radically different approach to monetary reform from the other ex-

[94] OV100/19, "Summary of the Report of the Conseil Economique et Social on the Revision of the Structure of the Franc Zone Published in March 1960," summary by M. Hailstone, BOE. Other newly independent countries that had been members of the broader franc zone had established central banks and national currencies at independence, such as Tunisia and Morocco. By the early 1960s, they had also imposed exchange controls on transactions with France.

[95] OV100/20, C. M. Le Quesne to Foreign Office, Sept. 19, 1961, p. 3, BOE.

[96] Chipman (1989).

[97] Mali's departure from the CFA zone was not permanent. It reestablished an operations account with France in 1968 and rejoined the CFA zone fully in 1984 (Kirshner 1995, 152–53). Another country that pulled out of the CFA zone was Mauritania. It withdrew in 1973 and created a central bank in 1978 (Yansané 1984, 77).

[98] OV106/1, "Guinea," by J. Margetson, Mar. 25, 1960, BOE; OV106/1, 103–4, BOE.

French colonies was driven by the ideological goals of the two countries' leaders, Sékou Touré (Guinea) and Modibo Kéita (Mali). Unlike leaders in other ex-French African colonies, these two leaders were committed to a strong anticolonial nationalism. In the economic sphere, their ideas were in fact much more radical than the nationalist ideas that were prominent in the ex-British colonies and the countries that the United States was advising at this time. Influenced by the French Marxist economist Charles Bettleheim, they sought not just to build a national industrial economy but one that was organized on the basis of a revolutionary and ambitious form of national economic planning. Their commitment to planning and national economic self-reliance was, in fact, quite reminiscent of Fichte's thinking.

Like Fichte, both leaders saw monetary reform as crucial to their political and economic projects. In both countries, one key catalyst for creating an independent national currency was massive capital flight. Both leaders recognized that national capital controls could not be made effective while they remained part of a monetary union. The creation of a national currency would also allow the country to mobilize the monetary system behind its economic planning objectives, including those relating to government spending. In justifying the decision, Kéita complained of how French control of the CFA's central bank in West Africa was used to favor French monetary and commercial interests. With a national central bank and currency, the government could better direct foreign exchange and credit to serve national interests. In Touré's words, a national currency was "a means for us to control the economic activities of our society and to regulate the value of our social production."[99] Underlying these sentiments was a more general point that remaining in the CFA made these countries vulnerable to French influence.

The monetary change was also linked to national identities in both countries. When Kéita justified the creation of a national currency, he stated "monetary power is inseparable from national sovereignty . . . it is the indispensable complement of it, its essential attribute."[100] Referring to the creation of Guinea's national currency and central bank, Touré also argued:

> its importance is comparable, if not superior, to that of our choice of immediate independence in September 1958. This reform provides the basis upon which we can carry out our economic liberation, previously impeded by a financial system which remained that of the old régime,

---

[99] Touré (1979, 377). See also ibid., 371–79, Jones (1976, 162–63, 191–92), Yansané (1979).
[100] Quoted in Kirshner (1995, 152).

linked to the economic system of the colonizing country . . . Now that both the body—the national economy—and the blood which flows in the body—the currency—are under the sovereign control of our free Nation, it is up to us to see that the evil genius of colonial administration is superceded by the genius of human liberation.[101]

As noted already, the withdrawal from the CFA zone and the creation of a national currency in both countries met with a strong reaction from France as well as French banks in the countries. Domestic interests with ties to France also objected loudly. In Mali, some African merchants and others who favored De Gaulle demonstrated against the new currency, producing a violent clash with police and 250 arrests.[102] But the moves also found strong support among much of the population. One Bank of England official, highlighting the role that nationalism played in cultivating trust in the new currency, described the currency exchange in Guinea in the following way,: "Internal operation appears to be succeeding beyond all expectation . . . it is already evident that the country is behind the President and his colleagues in this operation. . . . The President's face on banknotes and his broadcast that these measures will give Guinea economic independence have obviously had considerable influence. This is a striking commentary on him and his party's authority in the country."[103] (see figure 20)

One final point needs to be made about the Malian and Guinean cases. Like many African nationalists, policymakers in both countries were committed to the goal of African unity. As part of this commitment, they had initially expressed interest in the idea of creating a common currency across the continent. In 1959, for example, Touré joined Nkrumah in proposing a common African bank of issue.[104] Keita's political party also called for an African monetary union and common market at its 1960 Congress.[105] When these ambitious goals could not be met, however, they became strong advocates of territorial currencies.

Conclusion

As we have seen, some of the motivations for creating territorial currencies in the years after World War II were similar to those in previous his-

[101] Touré (1979, 371, 373). Both countries initially preserved the name "franc" for their currencies, but when Guinea devalued and introduced a new currency in 1972, the name changed to the "syli," which means elephant in Soussou and which Yansané (1979, 142fn.35) notes "has been redefined by President Touré as the will of Guinea to destroy colonialism, neocolonialism, and imperialism."

[102] Jones (1976, 192).

[103] OV106/1, Mr. Hugh Jones to Foreign Office, Mar. 5, 1960, pp. 1–2, BOE.

[104] OV138/1, F.O. telegram no.174, May 8, 1960, from Conakry, BOE. For Nkrumah, Bangura (1983, 74).

[105] Jones (1976, 113).

Figure 20. 1960 Guinean note. Photograph courtesy of The British Museum. ©
The British Museum.

torical periods. Some, however, were new. Activist national macroeconomic management achieved a political prominence that it had never had
before. It now acted as a central motivation for creating territorial currencies in many Southern countries, and it was also endorsed by the leading
economic power in the world. The objective of increasing international
transaction costs had also rarely encouraged territorial currencies to be
created in the past, even though some thinkers such as Fichte and
Buchanan had supported this idea in the nineteenth century, as we saw in
chapter 3. Now, it emerged as an important reason for breaking up currency unions in Guinea, Mali, and some ex-British African colonies.

Before ending this chapter, it is worth noting that countries in the CFA
zones were not the only ones to be left without territorial currencies. In
the ex-British Caribbean, many small island states retained a limited currency union from the colonial period.[106] Belgium and Luxembourg also

---

[106] The British had created the British Caribbean Currency Board in 1950 involving
Trinidad and Tobago, British Guiana, Barbados, and the Windward and Leeward Islands.
In 1965, Guyana and Trinidad and Tobago withdrew to establish their own central banks,
and the remaining members replaced the currency board with the East Caribbean Cur-
rency Authority. In 1972, Barbados withdrew to create its own central bank. In 1983, the re-
maining members replaced the Currency Authority with the East Caribbean Central Bank
issuing the East Caribbean dollar. The members today are: Anguilla, Antigua and Barbuda,
Dominica, Grenada, Montserrat, St. Kitts and Nevis, St. Lucia, St. Vincent, and The
Grenadines. They are joined together also in the Organization of East Caribbean States
(Collyns 1983).

preserved their monetary union, and many other tiny European states such as Monaco, Andorra, San Marino, the Vatican, and Liechtenstein used currencies of nearby countries. After gaining their independence, various microstates in the Pacific used foreign currencies from Australia, New Zealand, and the United States, while Swaziland and Lesotho allowed the South African rand to circulate in their countries even after they created national currencies in 1975 and 1980 respectively.[107]

Two other interesting cases were Liberia and Panama, which used the U.S. dollar as their main currency. The role of the dollar in Liberia dated back to the Second World War when the arrival of large numbers of U.S. troops brought the dollar into widespread circulation, displacing British and West African Currency Board currency that had been dominant.[108] Even after the country established a central bank in 1974 to do bank supervision and provide banking services, it did not issue currency.[109] In Panama's case, the dollar had been widely used since 1904, soon after it became a U.S. protectorate independent from Colombia. At that time, Colombian coin had been withdrawn and a new national monetary unit (the balboa) with silver coins based on a gold-exchange standard had been established. But the United States had insisted that the unit correspond directly with the U.S. dollar and that U.S. gold coins be made legal tender because most American canal workers were being paid in these U.S. coins. Because Panamanian coins were usually in short supply, U.S. money soon emerged as the main currency in use.[110]

Although these various countries challenged the dominant practice of maintaining territorial currencies in this period, they were seen at the time as unusual cases. The point is worth highlighting because as territorial currencies are increasingly challenged today, some of these countries find themselves suddenly in quite a different position. Advocates of dollarization in Southern countries, for example, often now cite Panama as a coun-

[107] Collyns (1983), Collings et al. (1978). The rand is no longer legal tender in Swaziland, but it is in Namibia.

[108] Abdel-Salam (1970), U.S. Government (1963, 430–38).

[109] Not until the mid-1980s did the Liberian government begin to issue large amounts of coins (and then even notes in 1989) as a means of financing budget deficits. At that point, U.S. currency finally disappeared from circulation and the Liberian dollar began to trade at a discount vis-à-vis the U.S. dollar (Calvo and Vegh 1992).

[110] Grigore (1972), Stickney (1971), Rosenberg (1985, 185–86), Helleiner (2002). The dollar's dominant role in Panama was briefly challenged by the nationalist president Arnulfo Arias who came to power in 1940 as part of his broader challenge to the influence of the U.S. (and local oligarchs). He ordered paper balboa notes to be issued for the first time in the country's history and hoped to break the link between the balboa and the dollar. When his government was overthrown, however, this money was quickly withdrawn (LaFeber 1989: 73–77).

try to emulate. These advocates are usually skeptical of the benefits of activist monetary management, and they cite Panama's economic experience as evidence to support their view that it is not necessary. In the early postwar years, however, even Bank of England officials who shared this skepticism did not support the idea that Panama or Liberia were models to be followed. In advising Sierra Leone in 1961, J. B. Loynes explicitly rejected the option of adopting a foreign currency such as the pound or the dollar as nearby Liberia had done. In his view: "It would mean reverting to a more primitive form of money management such as existed in a degree, up to 1912; it would deprive both countries [Gambia and Sierra Leone] of useful income; and it would inevitably be an admission in Sierra Leone's case that the country did not trust itself to run its own affairs."[111]

[111] CO 1025/127 E/57, Mar. 1961, pp. 41–42, PRO.

10

The Current Challenge to Territorial Currencies

This book has explored the history of territorial currencies. As we have seen, these monetary structures do not represent in any way a "natural" way of organizing money. They became predominant only in the nineteenth and twentieth centuries; before that, money was organized quite differently. Moreover, throughout the nineteenth and twentieth centuries, territorial currencies have constantly been challenged. Indeed, some countries—such as the African members of the CFA franc zone—have never had a territorial currency.

If the historical perspective of this book reminds us of the relatively recent origins and contested nature of territorial currencies, what are the prospects for their future? As I noted in the introduction, these prospects look quite uncertain. In countries across the world, territorial currencies face many challenges in the contemporary period. Contemporary scholarship offers explanations for each of these distinct challenges, but what has been missing is a more general analysis of why territorial currencies are being contested in such a widespread fashion in the current era. In this concluding chapter, I develop this kind of analysis, drawing on the historical themes raised in the book.

The history is useful in two ways. First, it suggests this analysis should be built not on the basis of the popular theoretical framework used by many economists to analyze the geography of money: optimum currency area (OCA) theory. Instead, it points to the potential usefulness of a broader analytical framework that examines how the geography of money is influenced by technological and state structures as well as by political struggles in which currencies are seen to serve broader purposes than OCA allows for. Second, because none of the challenges being experienced today is entirely novel, the history that has been presented can help us address the following question: Are territorial currencies threatened today by the same developments that challenged them in the past, or are monetary transformations today caused by factors unique to the current era? As I suggest in this chapter, the answer lies somewhere in between.

The Widespread Nature of Challenges to Territorial Currencies

Before turning to this question, let us briefly review the various challenges to territorial currencies in the contemporary age. The first challenge comes from the new interest in monetary unions. Enthusiasm has been greatest in Europe, where most member countries of the European Union eliminated their national currencies altogether in favor of a supranational currency in 2002. But there is also growing talk of the possibility of monetary unions in other regions, a phenomenon that Paul Krugman has called a kind of "monomoney mania."[1] In North America, an active and high-level debate broke out for the first time in 1999–2000 on the subject of a common currency for the members of NAFTA.[2] In 2000, the leaders of six West African countries that are not part of the CFA zone outlined their commitment to create a monetary union within three years as a first step toward creating a larger monetary union among all fifteen member countries of ECOWAS (the Economic Community of West African States) by 2004.[3] Prominent calls for regional monetary unions were also heard in 1996 in East Africa as well as in 1997–98 among the South American member countries of the trade grouping Mercosur.[4] Although the prospects are much more remote, there have also been some calls for a common currency in the East Asian region, particularly in the wake of 1997–98 financial crisis.[5] Also noteworthy is the fact that prominent nationalist movements today who seek to create new independent states in these regions—such as that in Quebec or Scotland—are strong supporters of these supranational currency proposals. Their position signals an interesting departure from traditional nationalist movements that have understood the creation of a new territorial currency as an integral part of their project of building a nation-state.

Not since the mid-nineteenth century has there been this kind of interest in the idea of currency unions. In one sense, the kind of unions being proposed are more ambitious than those in the nineteenth century in that they involve replacing distinct territorial currencies entirely with new supranational currencies. At the same time, however, they are also less ambitious in that there has been little serious political attention given to the idea of a universal form of money. To be sure, some economic liberals

---

[1] Krugman (1999).

[2] Helleiner (forthcoming).

[3] Masson and Pattillo (2001, 1).

[4] For East Africa, see Michela Wrong, "East Africa Trio in Currency Link to Help Business," *Financial Times,* July 2, 1996. In the Mercosur region, Argentine President Carlos Menem promoted the common currency idea in late 1997.

[5] L. Lucas, "Asian Monetary Union is Mooted," *Financial Times* Dec. 31, 1998.

have raised this idea. *The Economist* magazine, for example, has proposed a global currency, echoing the enthusiasm of its earlier editor, Walter Bagehot, for the universal coin in the 1860s.[6] In the year 2000, the IMF also hosted a forum on the question "One World, One Currency: Destination or Delusion?" with prominent international economists as participants. But even the advocates of a global currency at the forum admitted that there was little chance of the idea being taken seriously in political circles.[7] There is, in other words, little prospect of an equivalent to the 1867 Paris conference taking place in the current era.

The second challenge to territorial currencies today comes from the growing use of foreign currencies within national territories. This trend first took off in the 1960s with a sudden and rapid growth of dollar deposits in London. As we have seen, foreign currency deposits had existed in places such as Germany and Austria in the 1920s, but the rapid growth of this "eurocurrency market" in London was quite unprecedented. The circumstances of its birth were also very different than those in the 1920s. Instead of reflecting efforts by domestic citizens to escape domestic inflationary conditions, the eurocurrency market was primarily an interbank market whose growth was carefully cultivated by the British state.[8] Although British residents could not hold eurodollar deposits and these deposits could not be lent to British residents, this activity still represented a challenge to the territorial principle in monetary affairs because foreigners were using British territory to conduct these foreign currency operations. Other governments housing leading financial centers soon followed the British lead, and eurocurrency bank deposits in Britain and elsewhere also soon involved other foreign currencies.

During the last two decades, foreign currency deposits have also become very widespread in many poorer countries across Latin America, Africa, the Middle East, and ex-Eastern bloc. In these countries, the phenomenon has not been restricted to an interbank market but has also involved many domestic citizens holding such accounts, again most often in U.S. dollars. In some cases, this "currency substitution" has even extended to widespread use of the dollar as a medium of exchange at the retail level, and foreign currencies have made up the bulk of the country's money supply.[9] This phenomenon has stronger parallels to the 1920s; individuals in these countries have turned to foreign currencies as a way to

---

[6] *The Economist* (1988).

[7] *IMF Survey*, Dec. 11, 2000, 391–93.

[8] Helleiner (1994, ch.4).

[9] Cohen (1998). A recent IMF study (Balino, Bennett, and Borenstein 1999) notes that dollars make up more than 50 percent of the domestic money supply in seven countries. They account for 30–50 percent in twelve others and 15–20 percent in many others.

insulate themselves from domestic economic and political uncertainty. But what has been novel today is the long endurance of currency substitution in many countries, even after dramatic anti-inflationary policies have been introduced. The phenomenon has also received official endorsement and even encouragement in many poorer countries. Dollarization in Latin America, for example, began to accelerate in the 1970s after some governments deliberately relaxed restrictions on foreign currency use as part of broader monetary and financial reforms. By the 1990s, some poorer governments had gone so far as to extend central bank guarantees to foreign currency bank deposits, create clearing and payments systems for domestic transactions in foreign currency, and grant foreign currencies full legal tender status.[10]

An even more dramatic step was recently taken by Ecuador and El Salvador when they each chose to abolish their national currencies and adopt the U.S. dollar in 2000 and 2001 respectively. Again, this choice was not unprecedented among independent countries: as we have seen, Panama has long used the U.S. dollar as its currency. But it did not abandon an existing national currency, and its policies were always seen as anomalous, linked to its close dependence on the United States. Now, as noted in the previous chapter, Panama is increasingly cited as an example to emulate. The choices of Ecuador and El Salvador also may not be isolated ones. Argentine president Carlos Menem suggested that his country move to "full dollarization" in early 1999 and similar proposals are being debated prominently in other countries such as Costa Rica, Guatemala, and Mexico. The U.S. Congress has also held prominent hearings on the question of whether the United States should be encouraging this practice.[11]

A third kind of challenge to territorial currencies has come from the growth of hundreds of subnational "local currencies" since the early 1980s in countries across the world.[12] These currencies serve as a means of exchange within a clearly defined local community network and are not convertible into the national currency or any other currency. As we have seen, local currencies of this kind were created in many countries during the early 1930s. In some instances today—as in the case of the well-known "Ithaca Hours" issued in Ithaca, New York—the local currencies are issued as a paper note, as they were during the 1930s. In more instances, however, the currency exists just as a bookkeeping entry to be used only by the local network of people (ranging from a few hundred to several thousand) who have become members of a Local Exchange Trading Sys-

---

[10] See Edwards (1993), Brand (1993), Savastano (1996), Sahay and Vegh (1995).
[11] U.S. Senate (1999), Schuler (2000).
[12] See Helleiner (2000).

tem (LETS) through the payment of a small membership fee. When transactions are conducted between LETS members, they are reported to a central accountant who credits or debits the respective accounts. Ceilings are often set for a maximum debit or credit in the system, but no interest is charged on debit accounts.

In some ways, these local currencies today pose less of a challenge to territorial currencies than they did in the 1930s because the overall number of people using them appears to be smaller. At the same time, however, the challenge is also greater because supporters do not see local currencies today as simply a temporary response to situations of economic distress as they generally were during the early 1930s. Instead, as I note below, local currency advocates are part of a sustained transnational movement that explicitly aims to challenge territorial currencies and use more "localist" monetary structures as a tool for permanent social change.

The final challenge to territorial currencies today is at the moment more of a possibility than a concrete reality. A number of analysts today are calling attention to the way in which new "electronic" forms of money may encourage private corporate currencies to be issued in the near future.[13] In the last few years, information technologies have begun to be used to create monetary devices carrying electronic representations of prepaid value, such as stored value cards (or "electronic purses") and software products that can make payments across computer networks (sometimes referred to as "digital cash"). In contrast to credit or debit cards, these devices do not access a bank account or credit line but rather represent general liabilities of the issuer. For this reason, some analysts are excited by the possibility that these new forms of money could be used to break the state's monopoly over currency. They argue that any corporation could potentially issue these new forms of money and that private issuers might provide customers with a choice of different national currencies— or even an entirely new private currency—in which to conduct banking or even retail transactions.

Particularly enthusiastic about this possibility are those seeking to revive interest in the merits of "free banking." Although support for free banking diminished after 1914, it has experienced a notable revival since the mid 1970s. Friedrich Hayek's 1978 work, *The Denationalisation of Money,* played a central role in this process. While nineteenth-century free bankers had assumed privately issued corporate currencies would be convertible into a common gold standard, Hayek went further in this work to argue that market forces should also determine the standard of value itself. His ideas have attracted a growing number of supporters, many of

---

[13] See Kobrin (1997), Cohen (2001), Weatherford (1998), Lietaer (2001).

whom have reinterpreted the history of nineteenth-century free banking experiences in a more positive light than conventional histories had portrayed them.[14] Many of these modern free bankers see the emergence of "electronic money" as the tool with which they can finally challenge directly the state's control over currency.[15]

It is clear, then, that we live at a time when serious questions are being raised about the future of territorial currencies. Each of these challenges has its opponents, and support for territorial currencies remains tenacious in many parts of the world. The creation of territorial currencies has also recently been a key goal of the new nation-states emerging from the break-up of the USSR, Czechoslovakia, and Yugoslavia (although foreign currencies are often used widely in these countries and some Eastern European policymakers have also made it clear that they hope to adopt the euro in the future). Although the trend should not be overstated, it is still an interesting one in the context of the history of the last two centuries. What are the sources of these challenges to territorial currencies today?

This question is difficult to answer at a general level because the nature of these challenges differs considerably in various parts of the world. The causes and implications of the introduction of a supranational currency in Europe may be quite different from those associated with currency substitution in Latin America or the growing use of local currencies in other regions. Also complicating the analysis is the varying intensity of the challenges to territorial currencies in different parts of the world. Despite these complexities, the fact that territorial currencies are being called into question in such a widespread manner in this era does call out for a more general analysis of the causes of this phenomenon. But on what theoretical basis should such an analysis be developed? Much of the literature produced by economists studying the changing geography of money today uses the optimum currency area theory as its starting point. My analysis of the origins of territorial currencies in this book, however, points out the limitations of this approach. As I have shown, territorial currencies emerged historically for a complex set of reasons that are not well addressed by the OCA theory. These monetary structures were a product of transformations in technological and state structures as well as political struggles over the proper scale of markets, competing macroeconomic ideologies, the fiscal capacity of states, and political identities. Using this historical analysis as a base, we can develop a general explanation of contemporary challenges to territorial currencies. The key question is: To what extent can the increasingly uncertain future of territorial cur-

---

[14] Hayek (1990), White (1984), Rockoff (1991).
[15] See many of the articles in Dorn (1997).

rencies be explained by challenges to the central structures and motivations that created national currencies historically?

Structural Changes: State Transformations and New Technologies of Money

Let us begin with the importance of technological and state structures. I have argued that two developments acted as key preconditions for the rise of territorial currencies: the application of industrial technology to the production of money, and the emergence of nation-states. Is it possible that challenges to territorial currencies are caused partly by transformations in both the technology of money and state structures?

I have already noted how many analysts see the emergence of new "electronic" forms of money as a development that could assist efforts to break the state's monopoly over currency. Predictions that new forms of electronic money will, on their own, allow the private corporate issuing of money should be viewed cautiously because these speculations assume states will be incapable of responding to this challenge. State policymakers have already indicated various ways that they could regulate electronic money issuers, including the option of prohibiting private issuers and issuing stored-value devices themselves.[16] More sophisticated analyses acknowledge this possibility but argue that states will find it hard to regulate e-money issuance because it could be issued from offshore locations in ways that are difficult for states to control.[17] Again, however, this threat should not overestimated. Money relies on trust, and it will be difficult to cultivate widespread trust in currency issued by unregulated offshore banks. Equally important, we should not forget the capacity of states to respond to this kind of challenge through international cooperation. We saw in chapter 7 how the threat of cross-border counterfeiting during the 1920s produced new innovative forms of international cooperation to combat the phenomenon. In the last decade, states have also developed sophisticated forms of cooperation to curb cross-border money laundering, including that from offshore locations, which could be mobilized to regulate international electronic money issuing.[18]

The significance of new electronic forms of money is not that they will spontaneously produce a world of free banking. As we saw in the nineteenth century, new industrial money did not create territorial currencies on its own. It did so only when it existed in a good "fit" with new state structures and political forces that were demanding this monetary struc-

---

[16] Helleiner (1998).
[17] Cohen (2001), Kobrin (1997).
[18] Helleiner (1999c).

ture. It is clear that various features of electronic money can support efforts to introduce free banking; indeed, even before the appearance of these products, Hayek himself argued that electronic technologies might help his cause by enabling shopkeepers to operate more efficiently in several different currencies simultaneously at the retail level.[19] But privately issued currencies will likely flourish only if their advocates are able to link this technological innovation to a successful broader political project.

In discussing how new technologies of money can encourage challenges to territorial currencies, we should not restrict our focus to the free banking movement. Well before the creation of electronic purses and digital cash, the application of information technologies to the monetary sector had already encouraged the growth of the "eurocurrency" market. Susan Strange notes how telex machines and the application of computerized accounting to the monetary sector facilitated the growth of eurocurrency activity.[20] These technological advances made it easier for U.S. banks to conduct offshore business in London in dollar-denominated bank deposits simply as bookkeeping operations. Many supporters of the local currency movement also point out that information technology has given their cause an enormous boost. Most LETS networks rely on advanced software programs to facilitate the bookkeeping operations associated with their members' transactions. Without these programs, the transaction costs associated with the recording of various credits and debits of hundreds of members would be enormous.[21]

If the changing technology of money may be supporting challenges to territorial currencies today in various ways, what about transformations in state structures? Answering this question is less straightforward. The success of the supranational currency project in Europe has obviously benefited from the new regional cooperative arrangements within which EU states now operate. The confidence of private actors in the trustworthiness of new offshore eurocurrency deposits has also been bolstered by the fact that leading states are cooperating to create sophisticated international regulatory frameworks and lender-of-last-resort facilities designed to promote stability in these and other international financial markets.[22] Although these specific patterns of close interstate cooperation are new, the fact that interstate cooperation can facilitate the creation of alternatives to territorial currencies is not historically novel. The creation and longevity of the LMU and SMU in the nineteenth century were also sup-

---

[19] Hayek (1990, 67–68).
[20] Strange (1976, 178).
[21] See Dobson (1993, 153), Lietaer (2001).
[22] See Kapstein (1994), Helleiner (1994).

ported by distinct patterns of regional interstate cooperation. The same has been true of more recent common currencies such as the CFA franc or the East Caribbean common currency.[23]

The link between changing state structures and the rapid growth of currency substitution in many poorer countries, however, is a more interesting one. Currency substitution has been most prevalent in those countries where the state's capacity to regulate and influence the activities of its citizens has been weakened by economic and political instability. In these contexts, as in Germany and Austria in the 1920s, citizens have often lost trust in the national currency. But the crises of state power have often been more severe and long lasting than those seen during the early 1920s. To be sure, some governments—Israel in 1985, some ex-eastern bloc countries in the early 1990s—have successfully reversed dollarization with regulatory changes and dramatic anti-inflationary programs, just as Germany and Austria were able to do in the 1920s.[24] But others have found this task much more difficult, and the state has often appeared quite powerless to stop the growing use of foreign currency.

In Russia, for example, David Woodruff has examined how political upheavals left the central state unable to assert its authority to enforce the use of the ruble across the country throughout much of the 1990s. This led not just to dollarization but also a proliferation of complex barter networks and quasi-currencies in various regions.[25] In many other countries with weak states, "de-dollarization" initiatives have either failed or been quickly reversed when they induced massive illicit capital flight.[26] Indeed, the fear of capital flight has often driven decisions by poorer states to legalize foreign currency use. As financial markets have become more globalized, wealthy asset holders in poorer countries have been increasingly tempted by opportunities to take their assets abroad in response to unfavorable domestic economic and political circumstances. In contexts where capital controls are not effective or the credibility of the state's economic policy is low, allowing foreign currency deposits has been seen as the only way to slow this exodus of capital and lure flight capital home.[27]

The widespread nature of currency substitution across many poorer countries of the world is, thus, often symptomatic of a pervasive weak-

---

[23] For a useful comparative analysis of these cases, see Cohen (1993).

[24] For Israel, see Bruno (1993). For the ex-Eastern bloc, see Brand (1993), Sahay and Vegh (1995).

[25] Woodruff (1999).

[26] See the cases of Mexico (1982), Peru (1985), and Bolivia (1982) analyzed in Calvo and Vegh (1992) and Maxfield (1992). Also significant has been a kind of hysterisis where currency substitution becomes difficult to reverse even after a successful stabilization.

[27] See Brand (1993), Ekejuiba (1995), Savastano (1996), El-Erian (1988, 93).

ness of the nation-state in these countries. In the years after World War II, there was considerable confidence that newly independent poorer countries would have few difficulties maintaining the territorial currencies they created in the postcolonial context. But this confidence is much less evident today. Not only has the globalization of finance made state control more difficult, but in the postcolonial era, many states have seen their "sovereignty" challenged in various ways.

Altering Transaction Costs in an Era of Intensifying International Economic Integration

To what extent are contemporary challenges to territorial currencies also being prompted by disillusionment with the motivations that drove policymakers to create territorial currencies in the first place? Let us begin with motivations relating to transaction costs. The issue of altering transaction costs certainly figures prominently among the motivations for many current challenges to territorial currencies. Recall that a key motivation for creating territorial currencies was to facilitate the emergence of national markets by reducing intranational transaction costs. Today, intensifying international economic integration has led to growing disenchantment with the constraints and limitations of national markets, a sentiment that has, in turn, extended to the territorial currencies that complement these markets.

The motivations for supporting the initial growth of the eurocurrency market in London during the late 1950s and 1960s provided an early example of this. As I have explained elsewhere, this monetary innovation initially derived much of its political support from internationally oriented economic interests in Britain and elsewhere who sought to create an "offshore" or "transnational" economic space in which to operate free from the kinds of national capital controls that had become popular during the post-1945 years.[28] More recently, as capital controls have been eliminated in many countries around the world, some supporters of international economic integration have promoted supranational currencies or "full dollarization" as another tool to eliminate international transaction costs. Some of their goals are quite reminiscent of mid-nineteenth-century enthusiasts for monetary unions; both then and now, policymakers have seen the unions as reducing international transaction costs associated with the exchange of national currencies and the comparison of prices across countries.[29] But much more prominent today than in the mid-nine-

---

[28] Helleiner (1994, ch.4).

[29] The European Commission (1990) has argued that the elimination of costs associated with actual currency conversions will bolster Europe's GDP by as much as 0.5 percent.

teenth century is the desire to eliminate exchange rate instability in today's atmosphere of very high capital mobility.

Indeed, it is no coincidence that discussions of monetary unions and full dollarization have accelerated in the wake of dramatic currency crises during the 1990s. As financial capital has become increasingly mobile, governments have found it increasingly difficult to maintain a credible fixed exchange rate or even a well-managed floating rate. Supporters of a common currency in Europe and North America have argued that this kind of exchange rate instability is undermining the project of accelerating regional economic integration. Many Latin American supporters of full dollarization also argue that exchange rate risks vis-à-vis the dollar must be eliminated in an effort to encourage foreign investment, stop flight capital, and eliminate uncertainty in debt repayments that are denominated in U.S. dollars.[30]

But if the key goal is to eliminate exchange rate risk, why is it necessary to abandon a territorial currency? In the nineteenth and early twentieth centuries, policymakers achieved this goal simply by ensuring that all currencies were tied to a common standard, gold. To the extent that the credibility of the peg to gold might be questioned, countries ensured that their national currencies were managed by independent central banks devoted to this goal or even currency boards. There has in fact been a dramatic increase over the past decade in the use of independent central banks and currency boards across the world partly for this same reason. But many countries have found that these reforms still did not do enough to establish credibility with volatile global financial markets. In Argentina, for example, Menem's interest in full dollarization stemmed partly from the fact that international financiers still charged an exchange rate risk premium on loans to Argentina during times of large external shocks despite the existence of a currency board since 1991.

The growing support for privately issued corporate electronic currencies is also driven by a motivation that differs somewhat from past concerns about international transaction costs. In this case, the goal is partly to reduce transaction costs in one of the most rapidly growing sectors of the global economy: e-commerce. A key feature of e-commerce transactions is that they take place in a kind of "cyberspace" that does not respect traditional sovereign borders of nation-states. It is not surprising, then, that participants in this commerce are searching for a kind of currency, such as privately issued electronic money, that is less tied to the sovereign nation-state.[31] But what about the concern expressed in the nineteenth

[30] See for example Hausmann (1999).
[31] Kobrin (1997). See also Lietaer (2001).

century that the coexistence of a number of different privately issued currencies will actually raise transaction costs? While acknowledging that modern free banking "might at times be slightly inconvenient," Hayek questions whether policymakers today should be as concerned about this as they were "when the money economy was only slowly spreading into remoter regions, and one of the main problems was to teach large numbers the art of calculating in money." In addition, he argues that only one or two privately issued currencies would likely become dominant in each large region of the world if free banking were introduced globally.[32]

Finally, support for local currencies has also been linked to a desire to change transaction costs in ways that facilitate the creation of new conceptions of economic space.[33] Unlike supporters of eurocurrencies, supranational currencies, dollarization, or e-currencies, however, supporters of local currencies are often reacting against the trend of international economic integration. Many of these advocates are inspired by "green" thinking that emphasizes various benefits of small-scale economic life, such as closer sensitivity to environmental issues and greater possibilities for meaningful democratic participation and community involvement. These benefits are thought to have been lost in larger international economic spaces and even national ones. The creation of local currencies is explicitly designed to foster this more decentralized sense of economic space by altering transaction costs in ways that encourage participants to foster intralocal trade and local self-sufficiency. Since local currencies are inconvertible outside the local network of participants, a holder of this form of money must search out local goods or services in order to spend it.

The way in which local currency advocates are promoting economic localism is somewhat reminiscent of localist resistance to the creation of territorial currencies in the nineteenth century. But it is quite different from the early 1930s experiences when local currencies were seen only as a temporary measure to alleviate economic distress. It is important to recognize that local currency advocates are not seeking to create an exclusively localized economic space with this form of money. It is very unusual for members of local currency networks to transact even a majority of their economic life within the network. Even individual payments by members are frequently made partly in local currencies and partly in national currencies (and local currencies are usually denominated in units that correspond one-to-one to the national currencies to facilitate this process). These practices reflect an endorsement by local currency advocates of a conception of economic space that is quite difficult from the exclusive

---

[32] Quotations from Hayek (1990, 111, 27).
[33] The following discussion draws from Helleiner (2000).

and homogeneous sense of national space that came to dominate economies in the age of national markets. Some local currency advocates, for example, have invoked Karl Polanyi's description of the parallel existence of local and transnational economies in the preindustrial age as a model for the kind of economic world they seek to cultivate.[34] In Bernard Lietaer's words, local currencies are designed to be "complementary" currencies that could coexist with national as well as even regional and global currencies.[35]

Changing Macroeconomic Priorities

Challenges to territorial currencies today also stem from some macroeconomic motivations. Particularly important has been a growing disillusionment with the kinds of activist national monetary policies that became popular during and after the 1930s. This sentiment has emerged partly out of the experiences of inflation that often accompanied those policies. Equally significant has been the recent influence of the rational expectations revolution in the discipline of economics. It undermined a key idea that had sustained support for activist monetary policies: the Keynesian notion that there was a long-term trade-off between inflation and unemployment. By emphasizing how experiences of inflation over time may encourage people to adjust their expectations, this new economic analysis suggested that activist monetary management would simply result in stagflation. To break inflationary expectations, it argued that authorities would have to reestablish their credibility and reputation for producing stable money by making a strong commitment to price stability. The need for this kind of credibility and reputation has also been reinforced by the enormous growth of international capital markets. The fear of the discipline these markets can apply against inflationary countries has helped to encourage a dramatic change of macroeconomic views.[36]

Out of these circumstances, many policymakers have embraced a "neoliberal" view that monetary policy has no long-term impact on real output and employment, and that the maintenance of price stability should be the primary objective of monetary policy. This disillusionment with activist monetary policies has also often extended to the use of the exchange rate to foster macroeconomic adjustments. Like Keynes in the 1920s, many policymakers still defend the use of floating exchanges as a tool to foster macroeconomic adjustments in a context where wages and prices are slow to adjust, or as a mechanism providing some autonomy to national poli-

[34] Rotstein and Duncan (1991).
[35] Lietaer (2001).
[36] Andrews and Willett (1997), Maxfield (1997).

cymakers seeking to pursue the goal of price stability. But others have questioned whether exchange rate adjustments have any lasting effect on the real economy. A devaluation, they argue, may simply produce inflation, if domestic citizens anticipate and react to its consequences.

The growing disillusionment with activist monetary management has played an important role in encouraging alternatives to territorial currencies to be considered. By eliminating a key macroeconomic rationale for wanting a territorial currency in the first place, this shift has made policymakers less resistant to the idea of giving these monetary structures up. In Europe, the shift from Keynesian to neoliberal monetary ideas was a key precondition for the move to monetary union; indeed, many policymakers saw currency union as a better way to achieve price stability than maintaining a territorial currency, because the union appeared to allow them to "import" the Bundesbank's anti-inflationary monetary policy.[37] Many advocates of monetary unions in other regions, such as North America, also subscribe to the new monetary orthodoxy and argue that there is little to be lost in this macroeconomic sense from the abandonment of a national currency.[38]

This shift in ideology has also been enormously important in putting the idea of dollarization and common currencies on the agenda in poorer countries. Today many policymakers in these countries have become more skeptical of the view popular during the early postwar years that discretionary monetary policy has a central role to play in promoting domestic economic development. They endorse arguments similar to those forward by Bank of England officials in that era: that growth is best fostered by maintaining price stability as the primary objective of monetary policy because this will encourage foreign investment, reduce the likelihood of balance of payments crises, and create a more stable macroeconomic environment for capital accumulation. Given the frequent volatility of exchange rates in some poorer countries, advocates of full dollarization also argue that exchange rates are not able to perform a useful adjustment function or provide autonomy for a country to pursue an independent monetary policy.[39] Not surprisingly, these new views have made policymakers much less resistant to the idea of adopting a common currency or the U.S. dollar than they had been in the early postwar years.

The changed thinking about monetary policy has not just made policymakers less resistant to alternatives to territorial currencies. It also encouraged them to see the abandonment of territorial currencies in a positive

---

[37] McNamara (1998).
[38] Courchene and Harris (1999).
[39] Hausmann et al. (1999).

light as a way to insulate money from arbitrary interference by politicians. Hayek's advocacy of the "denationalization of money" represents the most radical view of this kind. For most of his academic career, Hayek was an advocate of the international gold standard. The suspension of gold convertibility of the dollar in 1971, however, demonstrated how difficult it had become to preserve it when national governments in an age of mass democracy had become committed to activist monetary management aimed at domestic monetary objectives. If the gold standard could not be reintroduced, he concluded that monetary discipline might better be achieved by eliminating territorial currencies altogether. If people were given "choice in currency," Hayek argued, they would choose the most stable currency. Currency competition would thus discipline governments, forcing them to maintain the value of money they issued and restrain spending. In an age of mass democratic politics in which politicians were beholden to what he called "special interests," Hayek had essentially come to believe that the nation was no longer a community that could be trusted to manage national money according to his ideals.[40] Whereas many nineteenth-century liberals had worked closely with nationalists in building territorial currencies based on the gold standard, Hayek saw the need to make more of a choice; embracing territorial currencies might preclude the realization of liberal goals.

Written in the 1970s, Hayek's concerns about the way in which modern governments inevitably produce inflation now seem somewhat dated. Many countries have, after all, embraced neoliberal monetary goals over the past two decades without abandoning territorial currencies. They have simply come to manage their territorial currencies in a more neoliberal fashion or introduced currency boards in which discretionary monetary management is impossible.[41] But in countries where fears exist that neoliberal monetary policies may more difficult to introduce or sustain, support for alternatives to territorial currencies has often emerged for the reason Hayek stated. In poorer countries that have experienced very high rates of inflation, neoliberals have sometimes endorsed the circulation of foreign currencies because it helps "discipline" national macroeconomic policymakers and societal groups.[42] The decision by Argentina in 1991 to allow dollars to be used as legal tender, for example, was designed to send a signal to the population about the seriousness of the government's in-

[40] Quotation from Hayek (1990, 117).

[41] Interestingly, as in the pre-1931 era, the introduction of these policies has often been supported not just by economic liberals but also by nationalists who have wanted to recultivate "pride" in the national currency, expel foreign currency use, or to attract international investment (Helleiner 1999b).

[42] See Hanke and Schuler (1991, 35).

tent to reestablish the trustworthiness of the national currency by subjecting state monetary managers to the "competition" provided by a more "credible" foreign currency.[43]

This kind of motivation was also evident in the 1970s among Latin American policymakers who first encouraged dollarization by relaxing rules concerning foreign currency deposits. Although this move was often designed simply to curb flight capital, it also was frequently introduced as part of dramatic "neoliberal" economic reforms of the time. In the face of populist pressures from the left and dramatic political upheavals of the period, these neoliberal reforms were designed to radically shift the institutional context by encouraging market forms of discipline that would restore business confidence and promote neoliberal outcomes.[44] In the monetary sector, neoliberal reformers sought to replace activist monetary policies with a passive monetary policy that was determined by changes in the balance of payments. For this reason, some saw little reason to maintain the integrity of the territorial currencies. Indeed, in Chile in the late 1970s, Díaz-Alejandro notes that some reformers "dreamed of doing away with the national currency altogether, but feared the military might not wish to go that far."[45]

In Europe, some support for the euro has also had a similar motivation, particularly in neoliberal circles: abandoning the national currency in favor of the euro will prevent national policymakers from pursuing "outdated" Keynesian macroeconomic policies.[46] Some supporters of North American monetary union have explicitly stated their goal of "locking in" neoliberal reforms. In Canada, one of the more prominent advocates of a common currency, Herb Grubel, told a Canadian Senate committee: "I would like to have an institution that protects me against the future, when another generation of economists is rediscovering Keynesianism, or whatever threats there might be in the future."[47] Some neoliberals in both regions have also seen the abandonment of national currencies as a way to force domestic deregulatory policies that might have been difficult otherwise to promote politically. The elimination of exchange rate adjustments is seen by key European policymakers as a tool to foster more flexible domestic wages; in the European Commission's words, the euro will bring "increased labour market discipline" as devaluations can no longer be used to offset higher wage demands from workers.[48] In Canada, the elim-

---

[43] de la Balze (1995).
[44] Foxley (1983), Canitrot (1980).
[45] Díaz-Alejandro (1988b, 371).
[46] McNamara (1998).
[47] Government of Canada (1999, 35)
[48] European Commission (1990, 47).

ination of the devaluation option is seen as a move that will force manufacturers to bolster productivity and unions to moderate wage demands.[49]

The opposition to territorial currencies from these neoliberals on
macroeconomic grounds is a relatively new phenomenon. To be sure, free
bankers before World War I warned that political authorities would likely
mismanage monopoly note issues. But the dominant liberal view then
was that the danger of activist money management was best avoided simply by creating independent central banks or currency boards. Even Peel,
when faced with the threat of Attwood and his supporters, saw no reason
to abandon his goal of creating a monopoly note issue. Supporters of
monetary unions in the years before the First World War also never made
the argument that these unions were needed in order to insulate the management of money from political forces. Not until the 1920s did this argument first begin to appear among some thinkers in the League of Nations,
as noted in chapter 7. As Hayek's thinking suggests, the change of views
in some liberal circles was prompted by the fact that the arrival of mass
democracy brought with it strong demands for activist monetary management. In this new political context, liberals no longer felt so confident
that the management of money could be easily protected within the national context. With the emergence of neoliberal monetary views since the
1970s, this perspective gained many more adherents.[50]

But it is not just those opposed to activist national monetary policies
who back these alternatives to territorial currencies. Support has also
come from traditional advocates of activist monetary management who
have concluded that the nation-state's capacity to pursue this kind of
management in an age of global financial integration has been curtailed.
Some of them support the delegation of power to a supranational authority such as the European Central Bank, which might be able to challenge
the markets more effectively and insulate countries from their effects.
Supporters of local currencies also regard these currencies as able to promote macroeconomic priorities such as full employment that the nation-
state is no longer capable of serving. The reasoning is similar to that made
in the early 1930s: in both eras, local currencies facilitated economic transactions that were previously inhibited by monetary scarcity. LETS supporters today also argue that a stimulus may be created by the fact that
LETS networks provide the poor or unemployed with access to interest-
free credit (since no interest is charged on debits in the system). Similarly,
wealthier members of the network who are accumulating money will be

---

[49] Courchene and Harris (1999).
[50] I should make clear, however, that many neoliberals remain strongly committed to
territorial currencies.

encouraged to spend rather than hoard it because it does not earn any interest in the system. This latter feature of LETS is similar to the antihoarding device of stamped scrip, although not quite as dramatic in its impact.[51] Because of these various benefits, local currencies have often emerged most quickly in areas experiencing economic distress, such as high unemployment, as was also the case in the early 1930s.[52]

Interestingly, many national governments today have taken a different view of these local macroeconomic benefits of local currencies than did their predecessors in the early 1930s. As we have seen, national governments usually banned local currencies in that earlier era, preferring to see national-level solutions to the Great Depression. Today, however, many governments have not only tolerated them but often actively encouraged their growth because of their local macroeconomic benefits in an age when the national state is constrained by global financial markets from monetary activism. In Australia and New Zealand, for example, national governments have actively supported LETS, seeing them as a way of supplementing the state's social service role vis-à-vis the unemployed in a period of budget constraints and government cutbacks.[53] Indeed, Lietaer reports that the New Zealand central bank is the first national central bank to endorse LETS, seeing it as a way of reducing local unemployment in a manner that does not interfere with its national anti-inflationary objectives.[54]

New Fiscal Goals?

If the fiscal priorities of the nation-state played a role in encouraging territorial currencies to be created, are challenges to these currencies prompted partly by a departure from these priorities? David Glasner suggests that governments may be less committed to the fiscal benefits of a territorial currency today because of a changing security context. He notes that currency monopolies were particularly useful in the past for financing unexpected, short-term, and small-scale wars when other sources of quick finance were difficult to find. Their importance has diminished today, he argues, because changes in military technology (e.g., nuclear weapons)

---

[51] Local currencies today do not use Gesell's stamped scrip idea, but some advocates have suggested that they should, especially because it would be easy to implement in LETS systems via computers (e.g., Lietaer 2001).

[52] This kind of context in a region of British Columbia prompted the initial invention of the LETS idea in the early 1980s. As I note elsewhere (Helleiner 2000), some local currency advocates are also critics of the inflexibility of centralized national macroeconomic planning, arguing that only by decentralizing policymaking from the level of the nation-state to the local level can more democratic and accountable macroeconomic choices can be made.

[53] Williams (1996), Lietaer (2001, 164–66).

[54] Lietaer (2001, 215, 219–20).

and the advent of large standing armies now require constant, much heavier expenditures in peacetime.[55] In the European context, Goodhart speculates in a similar vein that the EU countries may have been more willing to give up national seigniorage privileges because of the lack of prospect of war between them.[56]

While these factors may be significant in some contexts, there is a more important fiscal consideration that explains some of the support for challenges to territorial currencies today. Many economic liberals hope that the abandonment of territorial currencies will constrain the state's ability to finance large budget deficits through money creation. This motivation is apparent among some supporters of monetary unions in Europe and North America and is also evident among many of those pushing for full dollarization in poorer countries of the world. Many supporters of privately issued corporate electronic currencies also see this as one of the central reasons to pursue this monetary reform.[57]

The role of this fiscal goal in undermining support for territorial currencies should not be overstated, however, since the enhanced tax collection and borrowing powers of modern states have greatly reduced the fiscal significance of currency monopoly. For most countries today, seigniorage revenue is only a small share of the country's GDP, usually below 1 percent.[58] The diminishing fiscal significance of territorial currencies may in fact help to explain why challenges to territorial currencies are less likely to be resisted on fiscal grounds than in the past. For countries experiencing dollarization, or considering abandoning their national currency, the costs of forgoing seigniorage revenue have often been raised as a possible objection, but the issue rarely seems to be decisive in influencing policy decisions one way or the other. Indeed, supporters of these initiatives are often able to argue easily that this loss will be clearly offset by other economic gains to be realized by their proposals.[59] The European Commission, for example, argued that the loss of seigniorage revenue generated by inflation in poorer EU countries will be more than offset by lower inflation premiums on these countries' borrowing in the new euro zone.[60]

Supporters of alternatives to territorial currencies have also noted that

[55] Glasner (1989, 45–50, 205; 1998).

[56] Goodhart (1995, 455).

[57] See Dorn (1997), Hayek (1990).

[58] Hausmann (1999). Fischer (1993, 8) notes that in late 1988, it was higher in some unusual cases such as Peru (6%), Jordan (8%), China (6%), Turkey (4%), Greece (3.8%). See also Fischer (1982).

[59] Schuler (2000, 14).

[60] European Commission (1990).

seigniorage revenue could still be found in alternative ways in the absence of a territorial currency, a point that policymakers in the nineteenth century had discovered too. The new European Central Bank, for example, will divide its profits among its shareholders, which are the national central banks of the participating countries. In advocating the adoption of the dollar in Latin American countries, Hausmann and Powell also mention that countries could still generate some seigniorage revenue in a fully dollarized economy through the use of nonremunerated reserve requirements on certain deposits (the "seigniorage" would be the interest earned on the reserves).[61] More prominent has been the suggestion that the United States might agree to share seigniorage as a way of reducing opposition to the adoption of the dollar.

What about the issue of fiscal transaction costs? As Goodhart notes, this issue has emerged in the European context.[62] Whereas European policymakers in the nineteenth century sought to lower transaction costs associated with administering emerging national-scale bureaucracies, their counterparts today worry about the impact of intra-European exchange rate instability on the operations of the Common Agricultural Policy (CAP), which still makes up such a large portion of the European Union's budget. When the values of European currencies have fluctuated dramatically against each other, the functioning of the CAP has been rendered very complicated. A desire to avoid these complications has played a significant role in prompting European governments to consider ways to eliminate intraregional exchange rate instability since the 1970s.

In countries experiencing currency substitution or the growth of local currencies, one might expect government opposition to these monetary developments on the grounds that they raise fiscal transaction costs. In fact, however, governments in these countries have generally not found their fiscal operation complicated by these monetary developments. The reason is simple: they have usually insisted that public fiscal operations—such as tax collection—continue to be done in the national currency. In many countries, transactions done in LETS networks, for example, are taxable at a fair market value, but the taxes must be paid in the national currency.[63] Similarly, even in countries where the state has endorsed the use of the dollar alongside a national currency, tax collection has been exempt. Argentina's dramatic monetary reform of 1991, for example, allowed all domestic transactions to be in dollars except for wages and taxes.[64]

---

[61] Hausmann and Powell (1999, 8).
[62] Goodhart (1995, 472).
[63] See Solomon (1996, 117–20).
[64] de la Balze (1995, 77).

New Kinds of Identities?

Finally, we are left with the question of the link between monetary reforms and political identities. Since territorial currencies were created partly to strengthen national identities, are their detractors today also motivated by the goal of promoting alternative forms of political identity? This motivation is clearly present in the case of the local currency movement. Their "green" advocates are often explicitly antagonistic to nationalism, and they see local currencies as way to promote more localist identities.[65] Creators of local currencies that use physical notes, such as Ithaca Hours, have done this partly by emblazoning the notes with images of the local environment and economy. The LETS networks, which do not employ physical forms of money, also often attempt to exploit the symbolic potential of money through the names assigned to them; in Britain, for example, Greenwich uses "anchors," Canterbury employs "tales," Totnes's currency is the acorn. At a more concrete level, local currencies are seen as fostering local identities by bringing local community members together through trade, just as nationalists argued of territorial currencies in the nineteenth century. Also paralleling nationalist thought is the view that local currencies may encourage a sense of collective identity among users because their value depends on a sense of trust that other members will accept the money. Across the front of Ithaca Hours bills, for example, is written "In Ithaca We Trust." In LETS networks, there is an added dimension of trust required for the proper functioning: members are trusted not to abuse the possibility of running large debit accounts which are then never repaid (and on which no interest is charged). Although some LETS networks try to reduce this possibility by setting maximum limits on debit balances, the problem of debts within LETS is also said to demonstrate the positive role that debts can play in encouraging a sense of commitment to the community. As the originator of the LETS idea, Michael Linton, puts it, LETS represent "a promise by people in the community to people in the community."[66]

Support for monetary unions in some regions also sometimes derives from a commitment to identities beyond the nation, just as it did in the nineteenth century. This is most evident in Europe where the creation of the euro was driven partly by political forces committed to a more "Europeanized" form of identity.[67] As one group of scholars put it, the euro has "acquired symbolic meaning as a cornerstone of European political unification."[68] More concretely, enthusiasts for European integration also hope

[65] Helleiner (2000).
[66] Quoted in Scanlan (1994, 40).
[67] Engelmann et al. (1997, 105).
[68] Ibid., 105.

that its introduction will encourage spillover effects—particularly the need for stronger federal fiscal arrangements—that foster further European political integration. In addition, many Europeans have seen the euro's introduction as an initiative that could bolster Europe's collective identity on the global stage.

Although those with a more "Europeanized" identity may be key supporters of this initiative, they have been quite hesitant to use the new currency in a symbolic sense to promote a collective identity. It would be difficult to argue, for example, that the imagery on the euro has been designed in a way that is meant to foster a strong sense of common European identity. Although the face of the coins has a common image of a map of the EU and the stars of the EU flag, each national government has been allowed to continue to decorate the obverse side with its own motifs and some have chosen traditional nationalist images for those motifs. The bank notes are also quite timid in their invocation of a new European identity. On their front side are images of windows and gateways, while the back of each denomination has a map of Europe and an image of a different bridge (see figure 21). The official EU website suggests that the former is meant to be "a metaphor for communication among the people of Europe and between Europe and the world" and the latter are "symbols of the spirit of openness and cooperation in the EU."[69] But nowhere do we find the kinds of images of a common history, landscapes, or culture of the kind that is found on most national bank notes.[70] In the words of one journalist, "The currency looks as if it has been designed for a 'Star Trek' episode about some culturally denuded land on Mars—not for the home of Socrates, Charlemagne, Martin Luther, Notre Dame, the Uffizi, Bach, Beethoven and Mozart."[71]

The limited use of imagery on the new euros to cultivate a common European identity undoubtedly reflects the limited extent to which political support exists for such a conception of identity within the EU. There is much stronger support among Europeans for the EU as a community that offers certain political rights and economic benefits than there is for the EU conceived as a unified people with a common identity that replaces the nation. For this reason, supporters of the euro appear much more comfortable discussing how it will promote "one market" than its role in cultivating a sense of "one people." In a 1995 publication discussing the intro-

---

[69] At http://europa.eu.int/euro/html/rubrique-defaut5.html?lang=5&rubrique=100.

[70] The EU website attempts to suggest that "the designs are symbolic for Europe's architectural heritage" but it quickly goes on to say that "they do not represent any existing monuments." It also notes that graphic symbol for the euro "was inspired by the Greek letter epsilon, in reference to the cradle of European civilisation and to the first letter of the word 'Europe.'"

[71] Zakaria (1999).

Figure 21. The new five euro note of the European Union.

duction of the euro, for example, the European Commission acknowledged briefly "for some people, the change will feel almost like a change
of identity," but felt compelled to add quickly that "national identity is not
in peril, however."[72]

This kind of defensiveness is also apparent among supporters of monetary unions and dollarization in other regions. In North America, supporters of monetary union are quick to acknowledge the nationalist opposition they anticipate to their proposals, leading some to emphasize that
each country could retain nationalist images on one side of the new common coins and notes.[73] Similarly, advocates of the adoption of the dollar in
Latin America have wondered aloud whether the United States might
help reduce nationalist objections to their proposals by replacing images
of past U.S. presidents on U.S. dollars with that of Columbus.[74] In countries that have experienced high levels of inflation or currency instability,
the argument is also sometimes made—and often successfully—that the
national currency is a liability rather than a source of national pride and
unity. In these contexts, it is suggested that abandoning the territorial currency in favor of a more stable, stronger currency will not undermine national identities. Many citizens in the poorer EU countries seem quite
happy to abandon their national currencies in favor of the euro for this
reason.

[72] European Commission (1995,48–49).
[73] Courchene and Harris (1999, 22).
[74] Hausmann et al. (1999, 19).

Another common argument is that a territorial currency should no longer be seen as a symbol of national sovereignty in an age when activist monetary management is passé on both theoretical and practical grounds. This has long been a common argument of Quebec nationalists who argue that they will not need a territorial currency on achieving independence.[75] The European Commission has made the same point: "For some, the transition to the single currency means a loss of national monetary sovereignty. But how much autonomy do monetary policies really have today in Europe? With capital moving freely between interdependent economies, an autonomous monetary policy is no longer a credible policy option. Member states will only lose a prerogative, which in practice they cannot use."[76] As in the nineteenth century, economic liberals who reject macroeconomic activism on theoretical grounds have also been less inclined to associate the value of popular sovereignty with the need for territorial currency. Indeed, one prominent American supporter of dollarization has gone further to question why the principle of national sovereignty should be more important than "the principle of 'consumers' sovereignty'—the freedom of choice that undergirds a market economy."[77]

The creation of the euro is also often invoked to argue that the existence of a territorial currency need not any longer be considered as a key part of the sovereignty of a nation-state. Indeed, the power of the European example in encouraging various alternatives to territorial currencies to be taken more seriously has been significant. In the nineteenth and most of the twentieth centuries, the creation of territorial currencies in leading states became a model—a kind of world culture—to be emulated elsewhere. Now, the creation of the euro has disrupted this culture. In regions outside Europe, supporters of monetary union frequently cite the European example to make this point. As one Canadian supporter of North American monetary union put it, "The euro is also signaling that in a progressively integrated global economy, currency arrangements are emerging as one of those supranational or international public goods, an international public good that will be fully consistent with the twenty-first-century notion of what national sovereignty will be all about."[78] Proposals in the early 1970s for a common European currency also played a role in encouraging Hayek to consider alternatives to territorial currencies.[79] The euro experience—as well as Hayek's writings—has also been used by local currency advocates to support their case that their alterna-

---

[75] See Lévesque (1979, 86).
[76] European Commission (1995, 4).
[77] Schuler (2000, 16).
[78] Courchene in Government of Canada (1999, 6).
[79] Hayek (1990, 23–24).

tive to territorial currencies deserves to be taken seriously. Indeed, in the EU, the Green party has actively campaigned against the euro on the grounds that a multitude of local currencies would be the better option.[80]

In short, some challenges to territorial currencies—particularly the creation of the euro—are being encouraged by groups seeking to cultivate collective identities above the national level, as was true in the nineteenth century (although the universal cosmopolitanism of nineteenth-century liberals is much less apparent in the current age). At the same time, the local currency movement represents a new political force seeking to undermine national identities from below. Challenges to territorial currencies have also gained strength because territorial currencies are no longer identified as clearly with national identities. This phenomenon is linked to some developments we have seen before. As noted in chapter 5, when the value of national currencies is unstable, they often cease to be linked to national identities. Similarly, classical liberals in the nineteenth century were often less inclined to recognize the link between territorial currencies and national sovereignty because they rejected the idea of activist monetary management. But the weakening of the link between national identities and territorial currencies is also a product of the new power of global financial markets and a rupture in the global culture, initiated by the move toward European monetary union and now accelerated by all of the various challenges to territorial currencies.

Conclusion

The widespread nature of the challenges to territorial currencies is one of the more interesting phenomena in the contemporary world. Perhaps because these challenges are so geographically uneven and heterogeneous in form, scholars have not devoted much attention to a general analysis of their causes. Drawing on the historical analysis, I have suggested that one way to examine these causes in a more general way is to explore the extent to which the broader historical structures and motivations that helped create territorial currencies in the first place are being transcended and transformed. This method helps us to begin to think through in a more systematic way what some of the common causes are of this phenomenon.

My analysis in this chapter is not designed to provide a comprehensive explanation of the growing challenges to territorial currencies. A more complete explanation of each challenge to territorial currencies would need to examine various circumstances unique to that particular situation; for example, we cannot understand the creation of the euro without examining the French-German political relationship. Moreover, to explain

---

[80] The Green Party (1994, 2), Helleiner (2000, 50fn.61).

the different ways that territorial currencies are being challenged and the different intensities of these challenges in each country, we must move away from this general level of explanation to examine regional- and country-specific variations in the factors cited above. Still, these explanations do provide a useful way of beginning to account for the widespread challenges to territorial currencies.

Since none of the challenges being experienced today is entirely novel, I asked the question at the start of this chapter: to what extent are the causes of these challenges unique to our era? As I have suggested, many of the causes are not new. The interest in currency unions is driven partly by intensifying international economic integration, close interstate cooperation, and the triumph of liberal economic ideas, each of which has also been significant to varying degrees in encouraging currency unions to be created in the past. Support for free banking today also comes from the same liberal quarters as it did before World War I. Currency substitution has grown in many poorer countries for similar reasons as it did during the interwar period: individuals have seen it as a way to cope with domestic economic and political instability. The growth of local currencies has also been prompted partly by spontaneous responses of local communities to a shortage of money, as it was in the early 1930s.

At the same time, a number of the causes of challenges to territorial currencies are unique to our era. One such cause is the growing use of "electronic money," which is playing a role in encouraging various challenges to territorial currencies. The widespread use of foreign currencies in many poorer parts of the world also reflects a more pervasive and long-lasting weakening of the authority of nation-states in these regions. The growing power of global financial markets has also been much more important in prompting interest in various alternatives to territorial currencies, as policymakers worry about exchange rate instability and their ability to pursue activist national monetary management. So too has been liberal disillusionment with the experience of activist national monetary management during the middle decades of the twentieth century. Challenges to territorial currencies have also been encouraged by new questioning of the link between territorial currencies and national identities, as well as perhaps by the changing security context. Finally, in two more specific contexts, the emergence of the green movement and the creation of the Internet have also encouraged new interest in local currencies and free banking, respectively.

These various causes of challenges to territorial currencies suggest that this monetary structure faces quite an uncertain future. This is less a dramatic development than some people might assume. As I have tried to show, territorial currencies have had a relatively short life, and they have experienced constant challenges in various regions of the world throughout their brief existence. To be sure, if we were soon to witness the passing away of territorial currencies, an important epoch in world history would have ended. But any predictions of the imminent death of territorial currencies should be viewed very cautiously. As noted already, support for territorial currencies remains strong in many parts of the world. Moreover, wherever contemporary challenges to this monetary structure have gained momentum, they have generated considerable opposition from many groups still attached to the idea that each state should have its own territorially homogeneous and exclusive currency. We can expect, then, that the future of territorial currencies, like their past, will continue to be influenced by political struggles in many diverse contexts around the world.

References

Archival Abbreviations

BOE   Bank of England archives, London, United Kingdom.
CNA   National Archives of Canada, Ottawa, Canada.
LN   League of Nations archives, Geneva, Switzerland.
PRO   Public Record Office, London, United Kingdom. CO (Colonial Files),
       T (Treasury Files), Mint (Mint Records).
USNA   United States National Archives, Washington, D.C.

Books and Articles

Abdel-Salam, Osman Hashim. 1970. "The Evolution of African Monetary Institutions." *Journal of Modern African Studies* 8(3): 339–62.

Abrams, Richard. 1995. *The Design and Printing of Bank Notes: Considerations When Introducing a New Currency.* IMF Working Paper no.26. Washington, D.C.: IMF.

Acres, W. Marston. 1931. *The Bank of England from Within, 1694–1900.* London: Oxford University Press.

Adelson, Howard. 1958. *The American Numismatic Society, 1858–1958.* New York: American Numismatic Society.

Ahmad, Naseem. 1970. *Deficit Financing, Inflation, and Capital Formation: The Ghanaian Experience, 1960–65.* Munich: Weltforum Verlag.

Ake, Claude. 1981. *A Political Economy of Africa.* Harlow: Longman.

Akin, D., and J. Robbins, eds. 1999. *Money and Modernity: State and Local Currencies in Melanesia.* Pittsburgh: University of Pittsburgh Press.

Allen, William R. 1977. "Irving Fisher, F.D.R., and the Great Depression." *History of Political Economy* 9(4): 560–87.

Anderson, Benedict. 1983. *Imagined Communities.* London: Verso.

Anderson, Patricia. 1991. *The Printed Image and the Transformation of Popular Culture 1790–1860.* Oxford: Clarendon Press.

Andrew, A. Piatt. 1904. "The End of the Mexican Dollar." *Quarterly Journal of Economics* 18: 321–56.

Andrews, David, and Thomas Willett. 1997. "Financial Interdependence and the State." *International Organization* 51(3): 479–511.

Angus, Ian. 1974. *Paper Money.* London: Ward Lock.

Arbin, Kwame. 1995. "Monetization and the Asante State." In *Money Matters,* edited by J. Guyer. London: James Currey.

Ardant, Gabriel. 1975. "Financial Policy and Economic Infrastructure of Modern States and Nations." In *The Formation of National States in Western Europe,* edited by Charles Tilly. Princeton: Princeton University Press.

Attwood, Thomas. 1964 [1816]. "The Remedy." In *Selected Economic Writings of Thomas Attwood.* edited by F. Fetter. London: London School of Economics.

———. 1964 [1826]. "On the Comparative Eligibility of a Reduction of the Metallic Standard or Bank Restriction Act." In *Selected Economic Writings of Thomas Attwood.* edited by F. Fetter. London: London School of Economics.

Austen, Ralph. 1987. *African Economic History.* London: James Currey.

Bagchi, Amiya Kumar. 1997. "Contested Hegemonies and Laissez Faire: Controversies over the Monetary Standard in India at the High Noon of he British Empire." *Review* 20: 19–76.

Bagehot, Walter. 1962 [1873]. *Lombard Street.* Homewood, Ill.: Richard Irwin.

———. 1978 [1868]. "A Universal Money." In *The Collected Works of Walter Bagehot,* edited by Norman St. John Stevas. London: *The Economist.*

Baier, Stephan. 1980. *An Economic History of Central Niger.* Oxford: Clarendon.

Balino, Tomas, Adam Bennett, and Eduardo Borenstein. 1999. *Monetary Policy in Dollarized Economies.* IMF Occasional Paper no.171. Washington, D.C.: IMF.

Balogh, Thomas. 1966. "The Mechanism of Neo-Imperialism." In *The Economics of Poverty,* edited by T. Balogh. London: Weidenfeld and Nicolson.

Bangura, Yusuf. 1983. *Britain and Commonwealth Africa: The Politics of Economic Relations, 1951–1975.* Manchester: Manchester University Press.

Bank of Korea. 1994. *Korean Currency.* Seoul: Bank of Korea.

Bank of New South Wales. 1954. *The Story of Currency in Australia.* Sydney: Bank of New South Wales.

Banyai, Richard. 1974. *Money and Banking in China and Southeast Asia During the Japanese Military Occupation, 1937–1945.* Taipei: Tai Wan.

Bartel, Robert. 1974. "International Monetary Unions: The Nineteenth-Century Experience." *Journal of European Economic History* 3(3): 689–704.

Beasley, W. G. 1987. *Japanese Imperialism,1894–1945.* Oxford: Clarendon Press.

Bell, John. 1953. *A History of Economic Thought.* New York: Ronald Press.

Bell, R. C. 1964. *Copper Commercial Coins, 1811–1819.* Newcastle Upon Tyne: Corbitt and Hunter.

Bendixen, Kirsten. 1967. *Denmark's Money.* Copenhagen: National Museum of Denmark.

Bergman, Michael, Stefan Gerlach, and Lars Jonung. 1993. "The Rise and Fall of the Scandinavian Currency Union, 1873–1920." *European Economic Review* 37: 507–17.

Bernard, B. W. 1917. "The Use of Private Tokens for Money in the United States." *Quarterly Journal of Economics* 31: 600–634.

Bett, Virgil. 1957. *Central Banking in Mexico.* Ann Arbor: University of Michigan, Bureau of Business Research, School of Business Administration.

Biersteker, Thomas, and Cynthia Weber, eds. 1996. *State Sovereignty as Social Construct.* Cambridge: Cambridge University Press.

Billig, Michael. 1995. *Banal Nationalism.* London: Sage.

Bodin, Jean. 1992. *On Sovereignty.* Edited and translated by Julian Franklin. Cambridge: Cambridge University Press.

Boeke, Julius. 1953. *Economics and Economic Policy of Dual Societies.* New York: Institute of Pacific Relations.

Boling, Joseph. 1988. "Building a National Currency—Japan, 1868–1899." *International Bank Note Society Journal* 27(1): 5–13.

Bonney, Richard. 1995. "Revenue." In *Economic Systems and State Finance,* edited by R. Bonney. Oxford: Clarendon Press.

Bordo, Michael, and Hugh Rockoff. 1996. "The Gold Standard as a 'Good Housekeeping Seal of Approval.'" *Journal of Economic History* 56(2): 389–428.

Bower, Peter. 1995. "Economic Warfare: Banknote Forgery as a Deliberate Weapon." In *The Banker's Art,* edited by V. Hewitt. London: British Museum Press.

Boyle, Andrew. 1967. *Montagu Norman.* London: Cassel.

Brand, Diana. 1993. *Currency Substitution in Developing Countries.* Munich: Weltforum Verlag.

Braudel, Fernand. 1985a. *The Structures of Everyday Life.* Translated by Sian Reynolds. London: Fontana.

———. 1985b. *The Wheels of Commerce.* Translated by Sian Reynolds. London: Fontana.

———. 1990. *The Identity of France.* Vol.2. *People and Production.* Translated by Sian Reynolds. London: Collins.

Briggs, Asa. 1948. "Thomas Attwood and the Economic Background of the Birmingham Political Union." *Cambridge Historical Review* 9(2): 190–216.

Broz, J. Lawrence. 1993. *The International Origins of the Federal Reserve System.* Ithaca: Cornell University Press.

Bruno, Michael. 1993. *Crisis, Stabilisation, and Economic Reform.* Oxford: Clarendon.

Bulmer-Thomas, Victor. 1987. *The Political Economy of Central America since 1920.* Cambridge: Cambridge University Press.

Calvo, G., and C. Vegh. 1992. *Currency Substitution in Developing Countries.* IMF Working Paper no.40. Washington, D.C.: IMF.

Canitrot, Adolfo. 1980. "Discipline as the Central Objective of Economic Policy: An Essay on the Economic Programme of the Argentine Government since 1976." *World Development* 8:913–28.

Capie, F., and G. Woods. eds. 1991. *Unregulated Banking.* London: Macmillan.

Carothers, Neil. 1930. *Fractional Money.* New York: Wiley.

Carson, Robert. 1986. *A History of the Royal Numismatic Society, 1836–1986.* London: Royal Numismatic Society.

Casasus, Joaquin. 1905. *Currency Reform in Mexico.* Translated by Louis Simonds. Mexico: Hull's Printing House.

Chalmers, Robert. 1893. *A History of Currency in the British Colonies.* London: Eyre and Spottiswoode.

Chandler, Lester. 1958. *Benjamin Strong.* Washington, D.C.: Brookings.

Chang, Han-yu, and Ramon Myers. 1963. "Japanese Colonial Development in Taiwan, 1895–1906." *Journal of Asian Studies* 22(4): 433–50.

Chang, Kia-Ngau. 1970. "Toward Modernization of China's Currency and Banking, 1927–1937." In *The Strenuous Decade,* edited by Paul Sih. New York: St. John's University Press.

Chaudhry, Kiren. 1997. *The Price of Wealth: Economies and Institutions in the Middle East.* Ithaca: Cornell University Press.

Checkland, S. G. 1948. "The Birmingham Economists, 1815–1850." *Economic History Review* 2d ser. 1(1): 1–19.

Chipman, John. 1989. *French Power in Africa*. Oxford: Basil Blackwell.

Cipolla, Carlo. 1956. *Money, Prices, and Civilization in the Mediterranean World: Fifth to Seventeenth Century*. Princeton: Princeton University Press.

Clain-Stefanelli, Elvira. 1985. "Copper Coinages and the Monetary Economy of the Early United States." In *Coinage of the Americas Conference*. New York: American Numismatic Society.

Clapham, John. 1966. *The Bank of England: A History*. Vol. 2. *1797–1914*. Cambridge: Cambridge University Press.

Clarke, Stephen. 1967. *Central Bank Cooperation 1924–31*. New York: Federal Reserve Bank of New York.

———. 1973. *The Reconstruction of the International Monetary System: The Attempts of 1922 and 1933*. Studies in International Finance no.33. Princeton: Princeton University, Department of Economics, International Finance Section.

Clough, Shepard. 1964. *The Economic History of Modern Italy*. New York: Columbia University Press.

Clout, Hugh. 1977. "Industrial Development in the Eighteenth and Nineteenth Centuries." In *Themes in the Historical Geography of France*, edited by H. Clout. New York: Academic Press.

Cohen, B. J. 1993. "Beyond EMU: The Problem of Sustainability." *Economics and Politics* 5(2): 187–202.

———. 1998. *The Geography of Money*. Ithaca: Cornell University Press.

———. 2001. "Electronic Money: New Day or False Dawn?" *Review of International Political Economy* 8: 197–225.

Colley, Linda. 1996. *Britons: Forging the Nation 1707–1837*. London: Vintage.

Collings, Francis d'A., et al. 1978. "The Rand and the Monetary Systems of Botswana, Lesotho and Swaziland." *Journal of Modern African Studies* 16(1): 97–121.

Collyns, Charles. 1983. *Alternatives to the Central Bank in the Developing World*. IMF Occasional Paper no.20. Washington, D.C.: IMF.

Committee on Next-Generation Currency Design. 1993. *Counterfeit Deterrent Features for the Next-Generation Currency Design*. Washington, D.C.: National Academy Press.

Conant, Charles. 1969 [1927]. *A History of Modern Banks of Issue*. New York: Augustus Kelley.

Cook, Peter. 1993. "Flash Money and Old-England's Agent in the Early Nineteenth Century." *The Cambrian Law Review* 24: 12–44.

Coppieters, Emmanuel. 1955. *English Bank Note Circulation, 1694–1954*. The Hague: Martinus Nijhoff.

Costigliola, Frank. 1984. *Awkward Dominion: American Political, Economic, and Cultural Relations With Europe, 1919–1933*. Ithaca: Cornell University Press.

Courchene, Thomas, and Richard Harris. 1999. *From Fixing to Monetary Union: Options for North American Currency Integration*. Toronto: C. D. Howe Institute.

Cox-George, N. A. 1961. *Finance and Development in West Africa: The Sierra Leone Experience*. London: Dennis Dobson.

Craig, Alan. 1955. *The Coins of Korea*. Berkeley: Professional Press.

Craig, John. 1953. *The Mint: A History of the London Mint from A.D. 287 to 1948*. Cambridge: Cambridge University Press 1953.

Cullather, Nick. 1994. *Illusions of Influence: The Political Economy of United States-Philippines Relations, 1942–1960*. Stanford: Stanford University Press.

Davies, Glyn. 1994. *A History of Money*. Cardiff: University of Wales Press.

Davies, P. N. 1978. *Sir Alfred Jones*. London: Europa.

Davis, Andrew McFarland. 1910. *The Origin of the National Banking System*. Washington, D.C.: Government Printing Office.

Davis, W. J. 1895. *The Token Coinage of Warwickshire*. Birmingham: Hudson and Son.

————. 1969. *The Nineteenth-Century Token Coinage of Great Britain, Ireland, the Channel Islands and the Isle of Man*. London: Seaby.

De Cecco, Marcello. 1992. "European Monetary and Financial Cooperation before the First World War." *Rivista di Storia Economica* 9: 55–76.

————. 1994. *Central Banking in Central and Eastern Europe: Lessons from the Interwar Years' Experience*. IMF Working Paper, October, WP/94/127. IMF: Washington, D.C.

————. 1995. "Central Bank Cooperation in the Inter-War Period: A View from the Periphery." In *International Monetary Systems in Historical Perspective*, edited by J. Reis. London: Macmillan.

De Cecco, Marcello, and Alberto Giovannini. eds. 1989. *A European Central Bank?* Cambridge: Cambridge University Press.

Degefe, Befekadu. 1995. "The Development of Money, Monetary Institutions, and Monetary Policy, 1941–75." In *An Economic History of Modern Ethiopia*. Vol.1. *The Imperial Era 1941–74*, edited by Shiferaw Bekele. Senegal: Codesria.

De Kock, Michiel. 1939. *Central Banking*. London: R. S. King.

De la Balze, Felipe. 1995. *Remaking the Argentine Economy*. New York: Council of Foreign Relations.

DeMarais, John. 1986. "The Scandinavian Monetary Convention of 1872." *NI Bulletin* 20(4): 84–86.

Deutsch, Karl. 1966. *Nationalism and Social Communication*. 2d ed. Boston: MIT Press.

Deyell, John. 1987. "The Development of Akbar's Currency System and Monetary Integration of the Conquered Kingdoms." In *The Imperial Monetary System of Mughal India*, edited by J. Richards. Delhi: Oxford University Press.

Díaz-Alejandro, Carlos. 1988a. "Latin America in the 1930s." In *Trade, Development, and the World Economy: Selected Essays of Carlos Díaz-Alejandro*, edited by Andrés Velasco. Oxford: Basil Blackwell.

————. 1988b. "Good-bye Financial Repression, Hello Financial Crash." In *Trade, Development and the World Economy: Selected Essays of Carlos Díaz-Alejandro*, edited by Andrés Velasco. Oxford: Basil Blackwell.

Dickinson, H. W. 1937. *Matthew Boulton*. Cambridge: Cambridge University Press.

Dixon-Fyle, S. R. 1978. "Monetary Dependence in Africa: The Case of Sierra Leone." *Journal of Modern African Studies* 6(2): 273–94.

Dobson, Ross. 1993. *Bringing the Economy Home from the Market*. Montreal: Black Rose.

Dodd, Nigel. 1994. *The Sociology of Money*. Cambridge: Polity.

Dominion of Canada. 1934. *Debates, House of Commons, 5th Session, 17th Parliament, 1934*. Ottawa: J. O. Patenaude.

Dominion of Canada Parliament. 1871. *Parliamentary Debates, 1st Parliament, 4th Session*. Ottawa: Ottawa Times.

Dorn, James, ed. 1997. *The Future of Money in the Information Age*. Washington, D.C.: Cato Institute.

Dornbusch, Rudiger. 1992. "Monetary Problems of Post-Communism: Lessons from the End of the Austro-Hungarian Empire." *Weltwirtschaftliches Archiv* 128: 391–424.

Doty, Richard. 1986a. "Matthew Boulton and the Coinage Revolution, 1787–1797." *Rare Coin Review* 61(Summer): 34–36.

———. 1986b. "'A Mint for Mexico': Boulton, Watt, and the Guanajuato Mint." *The British Numismatic Journal* 56: 124–47.

———. 1987a. "British Tokens and the Industrial Revolution." *World Coins* (April): S.3–37.

———. 1989. "Nationhood through Numismatics: Latin American Proclamation Pieces." *Coinage of the Americas Conference*. New York: American Numismatic Society.

———. 1994a. "Matthew Boulton and the Petersburg Mint." *Journal of the Russian Numismatic Society* 53 (winter): 18–44.

———. 1994b. "Boulton, Watt, and the Canadian Adventure." *Coinage of the Americas Conference, November 7, 1992*. New York: American Numismatic Society.

———. 1995. "Surviving Images, Forgotten Peoples: Native Americans, Women, and African Americans on United States Obsolete Banknotes." In *The Banker's Art*, edited by V. Hewitt. London: British Museum Press.

Dowd, Kevin. 1992. "Introduction: The Experience of Free Banking." In *The Experience of Free Banking*, edited by K. Dowd. New York: Routledge.

Drake, Paul. 1989. *The Money Doctor in the Andes: The Kemmerer Missions, 1923–1933*. Durham, N.C.: Duke University Press.

Dukheil, Abdulaziz M. al-. 1995. *The Banking System and Its Performance in Saudi Arabia*. London: Saqi.

Duus, Peter 1995. *The Abacus and the Sword: The Japanese Penetration of Korea, 1895–1910*. Berkeley: University of California.

Dyer, G. P. 1999. "The Modern Sovereign." In *Royal Sovereign, 1489–1989*, edited by G. P. Dyer. London: Royal Mint.

Dyer, G. P., and P. P. Gaspar. 1992. "Reform, the New Technology, and Tower Hill, 1700–1966." In *A New History of the Royal Mint*, edited by C. E. Challis. Cambridge: Cambridge University Press.

East African Currency Board. 1965. 1966. 1967. *Report*. Nairobi: EACB.

———. 1972. *Final Report of the East African Currency Board*. Nairobi: EACB.

Eckert, Carter. 1991. *Offspring of Empire: The Koch'ang Kims and the Colonial Origins of Korean Capitalism, 1876–1945*. Seattle: University of Washington Press.

Economist, The. 1988. "Get Ready for the Phoenix." *The Economist* 309 (January 9): 9.)

Edo, Michael. 1975. "Currency Arrangements and Banking Legislation in the Arabian Peninsula." *IMF Staff Papers* 22(2): 510–38.

Eggertsson, Thráinn. 1990. *Economic Behavior and Institutions.* Cambridge: Cambridge University Press.

Eichengreen, Barry. ed. 1985. *The Gold Standard in Theory and History.* New York: Methuen.

———. 1992. *Golden Fetters.* Oxford: Oxford University Press.

———. 1994. "House Calls of the Money Doctor: The Kemmerer Missions to Latin America, 1917–31." In *Money Doctors, Foreign Debts, and Economic Reforms in Latin America,* edited by Paul Drake. Willington, Del.: Scholarly Resource.

Einaudi, Luca. 1997. "Monetary Unions and Free Riders: The Case of the Latin Monetary Union (1865–78)." *Rivista Di Storia Economica* 13(3) (December): 327–62.

———. 2000. "From the Franc to the 'Europe': The Attempted Transformation of the Latin Monetary Union into a European Monetary Union, 1865–73." *Economic History Review* 53(2): 284–308.

Einaudi, Luigi. 1953. "The Theory of Imaginary Money from Charlemagne to the French Revolution." In *Enterprise and Secular Change: Readings in Economic History,* edited by F. Lane and J. Riemersma. London: George Allen and Unwin.

Einzig, Paul. 1932. *Montagu Norman.* London: Kegan Paul, Trench, Trubner.

Ekejiuba, Felicia. 1995. "Currency Instability and Social Payments among the Igbo of Eastern Nigeria, 1890–1990." In *Money Matters,* edited by J. Guyer. London: James Currey.

El-Erian, Mohamed. 1988. "Currency Substitution in Egypt and the Yemen Arab Republic." *IMF Staff Papers* 35(1): 85–103.

Elvin, Mark. 1973. *The Pattern of the Chinese Past.* Stanford: Stanford University Press.

Engelmann, Daniela, Hans-Jachim Knopf, Klaus Roscher, and Thomas Rissen. 1997. "Identity Politics in the EU: The Case of Economic and Monetary Union." In *The Politics of Economic and Monetary Union,* edited by Petri Minkinen and Heikki Patomaki. Boston: Kluwer.

European Commission. 1990. "One Market, One Money." *European Economy* 44.

———. 1995. *Green Paper: On the Practical Arrangements for the Introduction of the Single Currency.* Brussels: European Commission.

Feldman, Gerald. 1997. *The Great Disorder: Politics, Economics, and Society in the German Inflation, 1914–1924.* Oxford: Oxford University Press.

Fetter, Frank. 1931. *Monetary Inflation in Chile.* Princeton: Princeton University Press.

———. 1964. "Introduction" in *Selected Economic Writings of Thomas Attwood,* edited by Frank Fetter. London: London School of Economics.

———. 1965. *Development of British Monetary Orthodoxy, 1797–1875.* Cambridge: Harvard University Press.

Fischer, Stanley. 1982. "Seigniorage and the Case for National Money." *Journal of Political Economy* 90(2): 295–313.

———. 1993. "Seigniorage and Official Dollarization." In *Proceedings of a Confer-

ence on Currency Substitution and Currency Boards, edited by N. Liviathan. Washington, D.C.: World Bank.

Fisher, Irving. 1933. *Stamp Scrip.* New York: Adelphi.

Flanders, M. June. 1989. *International Monetary Economics, 1870–1960.* Cambridge: Cambridge University Press.

Flandreau, Marc. 1995. "Was the LMU a Franc Zone?" In *International Monetary Systems in Historical Perspective,* edited by J. Reis. London: Macmillan.

Flatt, Horace. 1994. *The Coins of Independent Peru.* Vols. 1, 2. Terrell, Texas: Haja Enterprises.

Foxley, Alejandro. 1983. *Latin American Experiments in Neoconservative Economics.* Berkeley: University of California.

Ford, A.G. 1962. *The Gold Standard, 1880–1914: Britain and Argentina.* Oxford: Calendon.

Forsyth, Douglas. 1993. *The Crisis of Liberal Italy: Monetary and Financial Policy, 1914–1922.* Cambridge: Cambridge University Press.

Frangakis-Syrett, Elena. 1997. "The Role of European Banks in the Ottoman Empire in the Second Half of the Nineteenth and Early Twentieth Centuries." In *Banking, Trade and Industry,* edited by A. Teichova, L. Kurgan-van Hentenryk, and D. Ziegler. Cambridge: Cambridge University Press.

Friedberg, R. 1962. *Paper Money of the United States,* 4th ed. Chicago: Follett.

Fry, Maxwell. 1979. *Money and Banking in Turkey.* Istanbul: Bogazici University Publications no.171.

Fry, Richard. 1976. *Bankers in West Africa: The Story of the Bank of British West Africa Limited.* London: Hutchison Benham.

Gallarotti, Guilio. 1995. *The Anatomy of an International Monetary Regime.* New York: Oxford University Press.

Garber, Peter, and Michael Spencer. 1994. *The Dissolution of the Austro-Hungarian Empire: Lessons for Currency Reform,* Essays in International Finance no.191. Princeton: Princeton University, Department of Economics, International Finance Section.

Gardner, Lloyd. 1964. *Economic Aspects of New Deal Diplomacy.* Madison: University of Wisconsin Press.

Gash, Norman. 1984. *Lord Liverpool.* London: Weidenfeld and Nicolson.

Gesell, Silvio. 1934. *The Natural Economic Order.* San Antonio: Free Economy.

Giddens, Anthony. 1985. *The Nation-State and Violence.* Cambridge: Polity.

———. 1990. *The Consequences of Modernity.* Cambridge: Polity.

Gilbert, Emily. 1998. " 'Ornamenting the Façade of Hell': Iconographies of Nineteenth-Century Canadian Paper Money." *Environment and Planning D: Society and Space* 16: 57–80.

Gilbert, Emily, and Eric Helleiner, eds. 1999. *Nation-States and Money.* London: Routledge.

Giuseppi, John. 1966. *The Bank of England.* London: Evans Brothers.

Glasner, David. 1989. *Free Banking and Monetary Reform.* Cambridge: Cambridge University Press.

———. 1998. "An Evolutionary Theory of the State Monopoly over Money." In

Money and the Nation-State, edited by Kevin Dowd and Richard Timberlake. London: Transaction Publishers.

Goh, Keng Swee. 1972. "Singapore's Monetary System." In *The Economics of Modernization and Other Essays,* edited by Goh Keng Swee. Singapore: Asia Pacific Press.

———. 1995. "Why a Currency Board?" In *Wealth of East Asian Nations: Speeches and Writings of Goh Keng Swee,* edited by Linda Low. Singapore: Federal Publications.

Golay, Frank. 1961. *The Philippines: Public Policy and National Economic Development.* Ithaca: Cornell University Press.

Gold Coast, Government of the. 1955. *Legislative Assembly Debates, 1955.* Accra: Government of the Gold Coast.

———. 1956–57. *Legislative Assembly Debates, 1956–57,* 1st Series, Vol. 2–3. Accra: Government of the Gold Coast.

Goldsmith, Raymond. 1965. *The Financial Development of Mexico.* Paris: OECD.

Goodhart, Charles. 1988. *The Evolution of Central Banking.* Cambridge: MIT Press.

———. 1995. "The Political Economy of Monetary Union." In *Understanding Interdependence,* edited by Peter Kenen. Princeton: Princeton University Press.

———. 1998. "The Two Concepts of Money: Implications for the Analysis of Optimum Currency Areas." *European Journal of Political Economy* 14: 407–432.

Goodhart, Charles, Forest Capie, and Nobert Schnadt. 1994. "The Development of Central Banking." In *The Future of Central Banking,* edited by F. Capie, C. Goodhart, S. Fischer, and N. Schnadt. Cambridge: Cambridge University Press.

Government of Canada. 1870. *Parliamentary Debates,* Dominion of Canada, 1st Parliament, 3rd Session. Ottawa: Ottawa Times.

———. 1967. *House of Commons Debates,* 1st session, 1st Parliament. Ottawa: Government of Canada.

———. 1975. *House of Commons Debates,* 2nd session, 1st Parliament. Ottawa: Information Canada.

———. 1999. *Proceedings of the Standing Senate Committee on Banking, Trade and Commerce, Issue 48—Evidence, March 25, 1999.* http://www.parl.gc.ca/36/1/parlbus/commbus/senate/Com-e/bank-e/48EVB-E.htm.

Government of Italy. 1868 [1862]. "Unification of the Monetary System." Report of the Committee on the Project of Law presented by the Ministry of Agriculture, Industry, and Commerce." In *Report from the Royal Commission on International Coinage,* edited by Royal Commission on International Coinage, 304–7. London: George Edward Eyre and William Spottiswoode.

Great Britain. 1816b. *The Parliamentary Debates.* Vol. 34. London: Hansard.

———. 1817. *The Parliamentary Debates.* Vol. 35. London: Hansard.

———. 1818. *The Parliamentary Debates.* Vol. 38. London: Hansard.

———. 1826. *The Parliamentary Debates.* Vol. 14. Series 2. London: Hansard.

Greaves, Ida. 1953. *Colonial Monetary Conditions.* London: Her Majesty's Stationary Office.

Green Party, The 1994. *European Election Manifesto, 1994.* London: The Green Party.

Greenland, Maureen. 1995. "Compound-Plate Printing and the Nineteenth-century Banknote." In *The Banker's Art,* edited by V. Hewitt. London: British Museum Press.

Griffiths, William. 1959. *The Story of the American Bank Note Company.* New York: American Bank Note.

Grigore, Julius. 1972. *Coins and Currency of Panama.* Iola, Wis: Krause Publications.

Gunasekera, H. A. de S. 1962. *From Dependent Currency to Central Banking in Ceylon.* London: G. Bell.

Guyer, Jane. 1995. "Introduction." In *Money Matters: Instability, Values, and Social Payments in the Modern History of West African Communities,* edited by Jane Guyer. London: James Currey.

Habib, Irfan. 1961. "Currency System of the Mughal Empire." *Medieval India Quarterly* 4: 1–21.

Hamilton, Earl. 1944. "Monetary Problems in Spain and Spanish America 1751–1800." *Journal of Economic History* 4(11): 21–48.

Han, Woo-Kenn. 1970. *The History of Korea.* Translated by Lee Kyung-shik. Seoul: Eul-Yoo.

Hanashiro, Roy. 1996. "The Japanese Imperial Mint and the Issue of Jurisdiction Over Foreign Employees, 1869–75." *Journal of Asian History* 30(1): 1–26.

Hanke, Steve, and Kurt Schuler. 1991. *Monetary Reform and the Development of a Yugoslav Market Economy.* London: Centre for Research into Communist Economies.

Hansen, Leo. 1983. *Official Paper Money of the Kingdom of Denmark 1713–1983.* Copenhagen: Dansk Numismatisk Forening.

Hao, Yen-p'ing. 1986. *The Commercial Revolution in Nineteenth-Century China.* Berkeley: University of California Press.

Hargreaves, R. 1972. *From Beads to Bank Notes.* Dunedin, New Zealand: John McIndre.

Harling, Philip. 1996. *The Waning of 'Old Corruption': The Politics of Economical Reform in Britain, 1779–1846.* Oxford: Clarendon.

Harris, Elizabeth. 1967. *Sir William Congreve and His Compound-Plate Printing.* Washington, D.C.: Smithsonian Institution Press.

Hartendorp, A. V. H. 1958. *History of Industry and Trade of the Philippines.* Manila: American Chamber of Commerce of the Philippines.

Hausmann, Ricardo. 1999. "Should There Be Five Currencies or One Hundred and Five?" *Foreign Policy* (fall): 65–79.

Hausmann, Ricardo, M. Gavin, C. Pages-Serra, and E. Stein. 1999. "Financial Turmoil and the Choice of Exchange Rate Regime." IADB Working Paper. Washington, D.C.: Inter-American Development Bank.

Hausmann, Ricardo, and A. Powell. 1999. "Dollarization: Issues of Implementation." IADB Working Paper. Washington, D.C.: Inter-American Development Bank.

Hawtrey, Ralph. 1928. *Trade and Credit.* London: Longmans, Green.

———. 1932. *The Art of Central Banking.* London: Longmans, Green.

Haxby, James. 1983. *Striking Impressions: The Royal Canadian Mint and Canadian Coinage.* Ottawa: The Royal Canadian Mint.

Hayek, Friedrich. 1990. *The Denationalisation of Money—The Argument Refined*. 3d ed. London: Institute for Economic Affairs.

Hayes, Carleton. 1931. *The Historical Evolution of Modern Nationalism*. New York: Richard Smith.

Hazlewood, Arthur. 1979. *The Economy of Kenya: The Kenyatta Era*. Oxford: Oxford University Press.

Heckscher, Eli. 1930. "Monetary History, 1914–1925." In *Sweden, Norway, Denmark, and Iceland in the World War*, edited by E. Heckscher, K. Bergendal, W. Keilhau, E. Cohn, T. Thorsteinsson, K. Vedel-Peterson. New Haven: Yale University Press.

———. 1955. *Mercantilism*. Vol. 1. Translated by Mendel Shapiro. Revised 2d ed. Edited by E. F. Soderlund. London: George Allen and Unwin.

Heckscher, Eli, and Nils Ludrig Rasmusson. 1964. *The Monetary History of Sweden*. Translated from the 3d ed. by G. O. Matsson. Stockholm: Almqvist and Wiksell.

Heilperin, Michael. 1960. *Studies in Economic Nationalism*. Geneva: Publications De l'Institut Universitaire De Hautes Etudes Internationales.

Helfferich, Karl. 1969 [1927]. *Money*. Translated by Louis Infield. New York: Augustus Kelley.

Helleiner, Eric. 1994. *States and the Reemergence of Global Finance*. Ithaca: Cornell University Press.

———. 1998. "Electronic Money: A Challenge to the Sovereign State?" *Journal of International Affairs* 51(2): 387–409.

———. 1999a. "Historicizing National Currencies: Monetary Space and the Nation-State in North America." *Political Geography* 18(March): 309–39.

———. 1999b. "Denationalizing Money? Economic Liberalism and the 'National Question' in Currency Affairs.'" In *Nation-States and Money*, edited by E. Gilbert and E. Helleiner. London: Routledge

———. 1999c. "State Power and the Regulation of Illicit Activity in Global Finance." In *The Illicit Global Economy and State Power*, edited by R. Friman and P. Andreas. New York: Rowman and Littlefield.

———. 2000. "Think Globally, Transact Locally: Green Political Economy and the Local Currency Movement." *Global Society* 14(1): 35–51.

———. 2002. "Dollarization Diplomacy: U.S. Policy Comes Full Circle?" Unpublished paper.

———. forthcoming. "Towards North American Monetary Union?" In *Changing Canada: Political Economy as Transformation*, edited by W. Clement and L. Vosko. Montreal: McGill-Queen's University Press.

Henriksen, Ingrid, and Niels Kaergard. 1995. "The Scandinavian Currency Union, 1875–1914." In *International Monetary Systems in Historical Perspective*, edited by J. Reis. London: Macmillan.

Hewitt, Virginia 1994. *Beauty and the Banknote*. London: British Museum Press.

———. 1999. "A Distant View: Imagery and Imagination in the Paper Currency of the British Empire, 1800–1960." In *Nation-States and Money*, edited by E. Gilbert and E. Helleiner. London: Routledge.

Hewitt, Virginia, and J. M. Keyworth. 1987. *As Good as Gold: 300 Years of British Bank Note Design*. London: British Museum Publications.

Hilton, Boyd. 1977. *Corn, Cash, and Commerce: The Economic Policies of the Tory Governments 1815–30.* Oxford: Oxford University Press.

———. 1979. "Peel: A Reappraisal." *The Historical Journal* 22(3): 585–614.

Himadeh, Said. 1953. *Monetary and Banking System of Syria.* Beirut: American Press.

Hincks, Sir Francis. 1873. *The Bank of England and the Act of 1844.* Ottawa: I. B. Taylor.

Hobsbawm, Eric. 1983. "Mass-Producing Traditions: Europe, 1870–1914." In *The Invention of Tradition,* edited by E. Hobsbawm and T. Ranger. Cambridge: Cambridge University Press.

———. 1992. *Nations and Nationalism since 1780.* 2d ed. Cambridge: Cambridge University Press.

Hodgskin, Thomas. 1966 [1822]. *Popular Political Economy.* New York: Augustus Kelley.

Hogendorn, Jan. 1996. "McCarthy's 'African Moneys' and Central Principles of Monetary Analysis." *African Economic History* 24: 109–113.

Hogendorn, Jan, and Marion Johnson. 1986. *The Shell Money of the Slave Trade.* Cambridge: Cambridge University Press.

Hogendorn, J.S., and H. Gemery. 1988. "Continuity in West African Monetary History? An Outline of Monetary Development." *African Economic History* 17: 127–46.

Holtfrerich, Carl-Ludwig. 1986. *The German Inflation, 1914–23.* Translated by Theo Balderston. Berlin: Walter de Gruyter.

———. 1989. "The Monetary Unification Process in Nineteenth-Century Germany: Relevance and Lessons for Europe Today." In *A European Central Bank,* edited by M. De Cecco and A. Giovannini. Cambridge: Cambridge University Press.

Holtfrerich, Carl-Ludwig, and Toru Iwami. 1999. "Postwar Central Banking Reform: A German-Japanese Comparison." In *The Emergence of Modern Central Banking from 1918 to the Present,* edited by C. L. Holtfrerich, J. Reis, and G. Toniolo. Aldershot: Ashgate.

Hopkins, A.G. 1970. "The Creation of a Colonial Monetary System: The Origins of the West African Currency Board." *African Historical Studies* 3(1): 101–32.

———. 1997. "Review of *Money Matters.*" *The International Journal of African Historical Studies* 29: 583–85.

Horsefield, J.K. 1953. "The Origins of the Bank Charter Act, 1844." In *Papers in English Monetary History,* edited by T.S. Ashton and R.S. Sayers. Oxford: Clarendon Press.

Hosino, T. 1920. *Economic History of Chosen.* Seoul: Bank of Chosen.

House of Commons. 1817. "A Bill to Prevent the Issuing of Pieces of Copper or Other Metals Usually Called Tokens." May 14, 1817. *House of Commons Parliamentary Papers* 1: 623–30.

Howard, Rhoda. 1978. *Colonialism and Underdevelopment in Ghana.* London: Croom Helm.

Imperial Mint, The. 1923. *A Glimpse of the Imperial Mint, Osaka.* Osaka: Imperial Mint.

International Conference. 1868. *Report of the International Conference on Weights, Measures and Coins, Paris June 1867.* London: Harrison and Sons.

Issawi, Charles. 1982. *An Economic History of the Middle East and North Africa.* New York: Columbia University Press.

Jackson, Kevin, ed. 1996. *The Oxford Book of Money.* Oxford: Oxford University Press.

Jacobsen, Nils. 1993. *Mirages of Transition: The Peruvian Altiplano, 1780–1930.* Berkeley: University of California Press.

James, Harold. 1997. *Monetary and Fiscal Unification in Nineteenth-Century Germany: What Can Kohl Learn from Bismarck?* Essays in International Finance no.202. Princeton: Princeton University, Department of Economics, International Finance Section.

———. 2001. *The End of Globalization.* Cambridge: Harvard University Press.

Jenkinson, Charles. 1880 [1805]. *A Treatise on the Coins of the Realm.* London: Effingham Wilson.

Johnson, David. 1995. *Illegal Tender: Counterfeiting and the Secret Service in Nineteenth-Century America.* Washington, D.C.: Smithsonian Institution Press.

Jones, Geoffrey. 1986. *Banking and Empire in Iran: The History of The British Bank of the Middle East.* Cambridge: Cambridge University Press.

Jones, William. 1976. *Planning and Economic Policy in Mali.* Ph.D. diss., Universite de Geneve.

Joseph, Richard. 1976. "The Gaullist Legacy: Patterns of French Neo-colonialism." *Review of African Political Economy* 6 (May–August): 4–14.

Jucker-Fleetwood, Erin. 1964. *Money and Finance in Africa.* New York: Prager.

Kahn, Eduard. 1926. *The Currencies of China.* Shanghai: Kelly and Walsh.

Kapstein, Ethan. 1994. *Governing the Global Economy.* Cambridge: Harvard University Press.

Karunatilake, H.N.S. 1973. *Central Banking and Monetary Policy in Sri Lanka.* Colombo: Lake House Investment.

Kemmerer, Donald, and Bruce Dalgaard. 1983. "Inflation, Intrigue, and Monetary Reform in Guatemala, 1919–26." *Historian* 46 (1) (November): 21–38.

Kemmerer, Edwin. 1916a. *Modern Currency Reforms.* New York: Macmillan.

———. 1916b. "A Proposal for Pan-American Monetary Unity." *Political Science Quarterly* 31: 66–80.

———. 1926. *Report on the Stabilization of the Zloty.* Warsaw: Ministry of Finance, Republic of Poland.

———. 1973 [1950]. *The ABC of the Federal Reserve System.* Westport: Greenwood Press.

Keyder, Calgar. 1981. *The Definition of a Peripheral Economy: Turkey, 1923–29.* Cambridge: Cambridge University Press.

Keynes, John Maynard. 1936. *The General Theory of Employment, Interest, and Money.* London: MacMillan.

———. 1971 [1924]. *A Tract on Monetary Reform.* Reprinted in *The Collected Writings of John Maynard Keynes,* edited by D. Moggridge. Vol.4. London: MacMillan.

Kim, Byong Kuk. 1965. *Central Banking Experiment in a Developing Economy: Case Study of Korea.* Seoul: Korea Research Center.

Kirshner, Jonathan. 1995. *Currency and Coercion*. Princeton: Princeton University Press.

———. 2000. "The Study of Money" *World Politics* 52: 407–36.

Kisch, Cecil, and Winifred Elkin. 1928. *Central Banks*. London: Macmillan.

Knapp, George. 1924 [1905]. *The State Theory of Money*. Translated by H. Lucas and J. Bonar. London: MacMillan.

Knauerhase, Ramon. 1974. "Some Observations on the Institutional Development of the Reichsbank, 1875–1910." *International Review of the History of Banking* 8: 22–34.

———. 1975. *The Saudi Arabian Economy*. London: Praeger.

Kobrin, Stephen. 1997. "Electronic Cash and the End of National Markets." *Foreign Policy* 107: 65–77.

Kohli, Atul. 1994. "Where Do High Growth Political Economies Come From? The Japanese Lineage of Korea's 'Developmental State.'" *World Development* 22 (9): 1269–93.

Krasner, Stephen. 1993. "Westphalia and All That." In *Ideas and Foreign Policy*, edited by J. Goldstein and R. Keohane. Ithaca: Cornell University Press.

———. 1999. *Sovereignty: Organized Hypocrisy*. Princeton: Princeton University Press.

Krugman, Paul. 1999. "Monomoney Mania: Why Fewer Currencies Aren't Necessarily Better." *Slate* (April 15): 1–5.

Lacaun, M. Guy. 1944. "Capital and Its Circulation." In *The Economic Development of French Indo-China*, edited by Charles Robequain. Translated by Isabel Ward. London: Oxford University Press.

Ladd, George Trumball. 1908. *In Korea With Marquis Ito*. London: Longmans, Green.

Lafaurie, Jean. 1981. *Les Assignats et les papiers-monnaies émis par l'État au XVIIIe Siècle*. Paris, Le Léopard d'or.

Laidler, David. 1991. "One Market, One Money? Well, Maybe . . . Sometimes . . ." In *Federal Reserve Bank of Kansas City, Policy Implications of Trade and Currency Zones*. Kansas City: Federal Reserve Bank of Kansas City.

Lambek, Michael. 2001. "The Value of Coins in a Sakalava Polity: Money, Death and Historicity in Mahajanga, Madagascar." *Comparative Studies in Society and History*: 43 (4): 735–62.

Larson, Karen. 1948. *A History of Norway*. Princeton: Princeton University Press.

Laso, Eduardo. 1957–58. "Financial Policies and Credit Control Techniques in Central America." *IMF Staff Papers* 6: 427–60.

League of Nations. 1920. *International Financial Conference, 1920*. Vol. 1. *Report of the Conference*. Brussels: Printed for the League of Nations, The Dewarichet.

———. 1930. *Proceedings of the International Conference for the Adoption of a Convention for the Suppression of Counterfeiting Currency, Geneva, April 9–20, 1929*. Geneva: League of Nations.

Lee, Sheng-Yi. 1986. *The Monetary and Banking Development of Singapore and Malaysia*. 2d ed. Singapore: Singapore University Press.

Leffler, Melvyn. 1979. *The Elusive Quest: America's Pursuit of European Stability and French Security, 1919–1933*. Chapel Hill: University of North Carolina.

Le May, Reginald. 1924. "The Coinage of Siam: The Coins of the Bangkok Dynasty, 1782–1924." *Journal of the Siam Society* 18: 153–220.

Leslie, Elwin, and A. F. Pradeau. 1972. *Henequen Plantations Tokens of the Yucatan Peninsula*. Tokawa Park, N.J.: Organization of International Numismatics.

Lévesque, Réné. 1979 *My Quebec*. Toronto: Methuen.

Lewis, Bernard. 1961. *The Emergence of Modern Turkey*. London: Oxford University Press.

Lietaer, Bernard. 2001. *The Future of Money*. London: Century.

Lindgren, Hakan. 1997. "The Influence of Banking on the Development of Capitalism in the Scandinavian Countries." In *Banking, Trade and Industry*, edited by A. Teichova, L. Kurgan-van Hentenryk, and D. Ziegler. Cambridge: Cambridge University Press.

Long, Richard. 1969. *The Availability of Twentieth-Century Mexican Coins*. Corpus Christi: Gulf Coast.

Loynes, John Barraclough de. 1974. *A History of the West African Currency Board*. London: West African Currency Board.

Mackenzie, A. D. 1953. *The Bank of England Note: A History of Its Printings*. Cambridge: Cambridge University Press.

Margolis, Richard. 1988. "Matthew Boulton's French Ventures of 1791 and 1792." *British Numismatic Journal* 58: 102–9.

Marichal, Carlos. 1997. "Nation Building and the Origins of Banking in Latin America, 1850–1930s." In *Banking, Trade and Industry*, edited by A. Teichova, L. Kurgan-van Hentenryk, and D. Ziegler. Cambridge: Cambridge University Press.

Martien, Jerry. 1996. *Shell Game*. San Francisco: Mercury House.

Martin, David. 1973. "1853: The End of Bimetallism in the United States." *Journal of Economic History* 33: 825–44.

Martín Aceña, Pablo. 2000. "The Spanish Monetary Experience, 1848-1914." In *Monetary Standards in the Periphery*, edited by P. Martín Aceña and J.Reis. London: MacMillan.

Martín Aceña, Pablo and Jaime Reis, eds. 2000. *Monetary Standards in the Periphery*. London: MacMillan.

Maruyama, Makoto. 1999. "Local Currencies in Preindustrial Japan" In *Nation-States and Money*, edited by E. Gilbert and E. Helleiner. London: Routledge.

Marx, Karl. 1974. *Capital*. Vol.1. London: Lawrence and Wishart.

Masson, Paul, and Catherine Pattillo. 2001. "Monetary Union in West Africa." IMF Working Paper 01/34. Washington, D.C.: IMF.

Mathias, Peter. 1979. *The Transformation of England*. New York: Columbia University Press.

Matsukata, Count Masayoshi. 1899. *Report on the Adoption of the Gold Standard in Japan*. Tokyo: Government Press.

Maxfield, Sylvia. 1990. *Governing Capital*. Ithaca: Cornell University Press.

———. 1992. "The International Political Economy of Bank Nationalization: Mexico in Comparative Perspective." *Latin American Research Review* 27 (1): 75–103.

———. 1997. *Gatekeepers of Growth: The International Political Economy of Central Banking in Developing Countries*. Princeton: Princeton University Press.

McCaleb, Walter. 1920. *Present and Past Banking In Mexico*. New York: Harper.

McGinley, Christina. 1993. "Coining Nationality: Woman as Spectacle on Nineteenth-Century American Currency." *American Transcendental Quarterly* 7(3): 247–69.

McNamara, Dennis. 1990. *The Colonial Origins of Korean Enterprise, 1910–45*. Cambridge: Cambridge University Press.

McNamara, Kathleen. 1998. *The Currency of Ideas*. Ithaca: Cornell University Press.

McPhee, Allan. [1926] 1971. *The Economic Revolution in British West Africa*. London: Frank Cass.

Meier, Katja, and Erich Kirchler. 1998. "Social Representations of the Euro in Austria." *Journal of Economic Psychology* 19: 755–74.

Meisel, Adolfo. 1992. "Free Banking in Colombia." In *The Experience of Free Banking*, edited by K. Dowd. New York: MacMillan.

Mercator. 1867. *A Letter to the President of the Montreal Board of Trade on the Silver Question*. Montreal: John Lovell.

Mevius, J. 1981. *Catalogue of Paper Money of the V.O.C., Netherlands East Indies and Indonesia from 1782–1981*. Vriezenveen: Mevius Numisbooks int. B.V.

Meyer, John. 1987. "The World Polity and the Authority of the Nation-State." In *Institutional Structures: Constituting State, Society and the Individual*, edited by George Thomas, John Meyer, Francisco Ramirez, and John Boli. London: Sage.

Meyer, John, John Boli, George Thomas, and Francisco Ramirez. 1997. "World Society and the Nation State." *American Journal of Sociology* 103 (1): 144–81.

Meyer, Richard. 1970. *Bankers Diplomacy: Monetary Stabilization in the Twenties*. New York: Columbia University Press.

Minai, Ahmad. 1961. *Economic Development of Iran Under the Reign of Reza Shah, 1926–1941*. Ph.D. diss., The American University.

Mitra, Debendra Bijoy. 1991. *Monetary System in the Bengal Presidency, 1757–1835*. Calcutta: K. P. Bagchi.

Moens, Jan. 1991 "The Germinal Franc and the Latin Union." In *One Money for Europe*, edited by J. D Devaeve and J.-M. Duvosquet. Brussels: Credit Communal.

Monroe, Arthur. 1923. *Monetary Theory before Adam Smith*. Cambridge: Harvard University Press.

Moss, David. 1980. *Thomas Attwood: The Biography of a Radical*. Kingston: McGill-Queen's University Press.

———. 1981. "Banknotes versus Gold: The Monetary Theory of Thomas Atwood in his Early Writings, 1816–19." *History of Political Economy* 13 (1): 19–38.

Moynihan, Maurice. 1975. *Currency and Central Banking in Ireland, 1922–1960*. Dublin: Central Bank of Ireland.

Mundell, Robert. 1961. "A Theory of Optimum Currency Areas." *American Economic Review* 51 (3): 657–65.

Mwangi, Wambui. 2002. "The Lion, The Native, and the Coffee Plant: Political Imagery and the Ambiguous Art of Currency Design in Colonial Kenya." *Geopolitics* 7 (1): 31–62.

Nathorst-Boos, Ernst. 1970. "About Swedish Banknotes." *International Review of the History of Banking* 3: 89–96.

Neill, Charles Patrick. 1897. *Daniel Raymond.* Baltimore: John Hopkins.

Neufeld, E. P., ed. 1964. *Money and Banking in Canada.* Toronto: McClelland and Stewart.

Newlyn, W. T., and D. C. Rowan. 1954. *Money and Banking in British Colonial Africa.* Oxford: Clarendon Press.

Nielsen, Axel. 1933. "Monetary Unions." *Encyclopedia of the Social Sciences* 10: 595–601.

Nishikawa, Shunsaku, and Saito Osamu. 1985. "The Economic History of the Restoration Period." In *Meiji Ishin,* edited by Nagai Michio and Miguel Urrutia. Tokyo: UN University.

Nkrumah, Kwame. 1965, *Neocolonialism: The Last Stage of Imperialism,* London: Nelson.

North, Douglas. 1981, *Structure and Change in Economic History.* New York: W. W. Norton.

———. 1985. "Transaction Costs in History." *Journal of European Economic History* 14 (3): 557–76.

Nugent, Walter. 1968. *Money and American Society, 1865–1880.* New York: The Free Press.

Ofonagoro, Walter. 1979. "From Traditional to British Currency in Southern Nigeria." *Journal of Economy History* 39 (3): 623–54.

Oh, Doo Hwan. 1987. "Currency Readjustment and Colonial Monetary System of 1905 in Korea." *Journal of Social Sciences and Humanities* 65: 53–86.

O'Hanly, John. 1882. *On Money and Other Trade Questions, Being a Review of Mr. Wallace's Speech on an Inconvertible Currency.* Ottawa: C. W. Mitchell.

Onoh, J. K. 1982. *Money and Banking in Africa.* London: Longman.

Palk, Deirdre. 1994. "The Old Lady's Women Prisoners." *Off the Record* 6: 4–7.

Parker, Charles Stuart, ed. 1899. *Sir Robert Peel From His Private Papers,* Vol. 3. London: John Murray.

Parry, Jonathan, and Maurice Bloch, eds. 1989. *Money and the Morality of Exchange.* Cambridge: Cambridge University Press.

Pauly, Louis. 1997. *Who Elected the Bankers?* Ithaca: Cornell University Press.

Peck, C. Wilson. 1970. *English Copper, Tin, and Bronze Coins in the British Museum, 1558–1958.* 2nd ed. London: The Trustees of the British Museum.

Pepoli, Marquis. 1868 [1862]. "Project of Law Presented by the Minister of Agriculture, Industry, and Commerce, in the Sitting of 9th June 1862." In *Report from the Royal Commission on International Coinage.* London: George Edward Eyre and William Spottiswoode.

Perlin, Frank. 1987. "Money Use in Late Precolonial India and the International Trade in Currency Media." In *The Imperial Monetary System of Mughal India,* edited by J. Richards. Delhi: Oxford University Press.

———. 1993. *The Invisible City: Monetary, Administrative and Popular Infrastructures in Asia and Europe, 1500–1900.* Aldershot: Variorum.

———. 1994a. *Unbroken Landscape: Community, Category, Sign and Identity: Their Production, Myth and Knowledge from 1500.* Aldershot: Variorum.

———. 1994b. "Changes in the Production and Circulation of Money in Seventeenth and Eighteenth Century India: An Essay on Monetization before Colonial Occupation." In *Money and the Market in India, 1100–1700*, edited by Sanjay Subrahmanyam. Delhi: Oxford University Press.

Perlman, M. 1993. "In Search of Monetary Union." *Journal of European Economic History* 22 (2): 313–32.

Plumptre, A. F. W. 1940. *Central Banking in the British Dominions*. Toronto: University of Toronto Press.

Poggi, Gianfranco. 1978. *The Development of the Modern State*. Stanford: Stanford University Press.

Polanyi, Karl. 1944. *The Great Transformation*. Boston: Beacon.

———. 1966. *Dahomey and the Slave Trade*. Seattle: University of Washington Press.

Pollard, J. G. 1971. "Matthew Boulton and the Reducing Machine in England." *Numismatic Chronicle* 11: 311–17.

Pomeranz, Kenneth. 1993. *The Making of a Hinterland: State, Society, and Economy in Inland North China, 1853–1937*. Berkeley: University of California Press.

Pomeranz, Kenneth, and S. Topic. 1999. *The World That Trade Created*. London: M. E. Sharpe.

Porteous, John. 1969. *Coins in History*. London: Weidenfeld and Nicolson.

Porter, Tony. 1993. *States, Markets, and Regimes in Global Finance*. Macmillan, Basinstoke.

Potter, O. B. 1877. *The National Currency and Its Origins*. New York: J. J. Little.

Pradeau, A. F. 1958. "Store-Cards or Tokens of Mexico." *Centennial Publication*. New York: American Numismatic Society.

———. 1962. *Mexican Patriots and Their Part in Numismatics*. The Numismatist.

Pribam, Karl. 1953. *A History of Economic Reasoning*. Baltimore: John Hopkins.

Price, Arnold. 1949. *The Evolution of the Zollverein*. Ann Arbor: University of Michigan Press.

Province of Canada, Legislative Assembly. 1855. *A Decimal Currency—Weight and Measures*, 3d and 4th Reports of the Standing Committee on Public Accounts. Quebec: Lovell and Lamoureux.

Ramsay, A. A. W. 1928. *Sir Robert Peel*. London: Constable.

Rawski, Thomas. 1989. *Economic Growth in Prewar China*. Berkeley: University of California Press.

Redish, Angela. 1990. "The Evolution of the Gold Standard." *Journal of Economic History* 50 (4): 789–805.

———. 1991. *The Latin Monetary Union and the Emergence of the International Gold Standard*. Discussion Paper no. 91–01. Vancouver: Department of Economics, University of British Columbia.

———. 1995. "The Persistence of Bimetallism in Nineteenth-Century France." *Economic History Review* 48 (4): 717–36.

Regalsky, Andres. 1997. "Banking, Trade, and the Rise of Capitalism in Argentina, 1850–1930." In *Banking, Trade and Industry*, edited by A. Teichova, L. Kurgan-van Hentenryk, and D. Ziegler. Cambridge: Cambridge University Press.

Reis, Jaime. 1995. "Introduction." In *International Monetary Systems in Historical Perspective*, edited by J. Reis. London: Macmillan.

———. 2000. "The Gold Standard in Portugal, 1854–91." In *Monetary Standards in the Periphery*, edited by P. Martín Aceña and J. Reis. London: Macmillan.

Reischauer, Haru Matsukata. 1986. *Samurai and Silk*. Cambridge: Harvard University Press.

Republic of Kenya. 1967. *The National Assembly: Official Report*. 5th Session. Vol. 11. Nairobi: Republic of Kenya.

Richards, J. F. 1987. "Introduction." In *The Imperial Monetary System of Mughal India*, edited by J. F. Richards. Delhi: Oxford University Press

Robinson, M., and L. Shaw. 1980. *The Coins and Banknotes of Burma*. Ringwood: Pardy and Son.

Robson, Peter. 1968. *Economic Integration in Africa*. London: Allen and Unwin.

Rockoff, Hugh. 1991. "Lessons from the American Experience with Free Banking." In *Unregulated Banking*, edited by F. Capie and G. Wood. London: MacMillan.

Rodriguez, Agustin Llona. 2000. "Chile during the Gold Standard." In *Monetary Standards in the Periphery*, edited by P. Martín Aceña and J. Reis. London: MacMillan.

Roll, Erich. 1939. *A History of Economic Thought*. London: Faber and Faber.

Romano, Ruggiero. 1984. "American Feudalism." *Hispanic American Historical Review* 64(10): 121–34.

Rose, John. 1869. *Introducing the Resolution on Banking and Currency, Speech by the Honourable John Rose, Minister of Finance, Canada*. Ottawa: Hunter, Rose.

Rose, Andrew. 2000. "One Money, One Market: Estimating the Effect of Common Currency on Trade." *Economic Policy* 30: 7–33.

Rosenau, James. 1989. *Turbulence in World Politics*. Princeton: Princeton University Press.

Rosenberg, Emily. 1985. "Foundations of U.S. International Financial Power: Gold Standard Diplomacy, 1900–1905." *Business History Review* 59 (2) (summer): 169–202.

———. 1999. *Financial Missionaries to the World: The Politics and Culture of Dollar Diplomacy, 1900–30*. Harvard: Harvard University Press.

Rothchild, Donald, ed. 1968. *Politics of Integration: An East African Documentary*. Nairobi: East African.

Rotstein, Abraham, and Colin Duncan. 1991. "For a Second Economy." In *The New Era of Global Competition*, edited by D. Drahce and M. Gertler. Kingston: McGill-Queen's University Press.

Rowlinson, Matthew. 1999. " 'The Scotch Hate Gold': British Identity and Paper Money." In *Nation-States and Money*, edited by E. Gilbert and E. Helleiner. London: Routledge.

Royal Commission on International Coinage. 1868. *Report from the Royal Commission on International Coinage*. London: George Edward Eyre and William Spottiswoode.

Ruggie, John. 1982. "International Regimes, Transactions, and Change: Embedded Liberalism in the Postwar Economic Order." *International Organization* 36: 379–415.

————. 1993. "Territoriality and Beyond: Problematizing Modernity in International Relations." *International Organization* 47: 139–74.

Russell, Henry. 1898. *International Monetary Conferences.* New York: Harper.

Sahay, Ratna, and Carlos Vegh. 1995. *Dollarization in Transition Economies: Evidence and Policy Implications.* IMF Working Paper no.96. Washington, D.C.: IMF.

Sandham, Alfred. 1869. *Coins, Tokens, and Medals of the Dominions of Canada.* Montreal: Daniel Rose.

Sannucci, Valeria. 1989. "The Establishment of a Central Bank: Italy in the Nineteenth Century." In *A European Central Bank?* edited by M. De Cecco and A. Giovannini. Cambridge: Cambridge University Press.

Savastano, Miguel. 1996. "Dollarization in Latin America." In *The Macroeconomics of International Currencies,* edited by Paul Mizen and Eric Penecost. Cheltenham: Elgar.

Saville, Richard. 1996. *Bank of Scotland: A History, 1695–1995.* Edinburgh: Edinburgh University Press.

Sayers, R.S. 1976a. *The Bank of England, 1891–1944.* Cambridge: Cambridge University Press.

————. 1976b. *The Bank of England, 1891–1944 Appendixes.* Cambridge: Cambridge University Press.

Scanlan, Lawrence. 1994. "LETS Make a Deal." *Harrowsmith* (June): 37–43.

Schacht, Hjalmar. 1955. *My First Seventy-Six Years.* Translated by Diana Pyke. London: Allan Wingate.

————. 1978 [1927]. *The Stabilization of the Mark.* New York: Arno Press.

Schama, Simon. 1993. "Woodland, Homeland, Fatherland: Thoughts on the Ecology of Nationalism." In *The Worth of Nations,* edited by Claudio Veliz. Boston: Boston University.

Schenk, Catherine. 1993. "The Origins of a Central Bank in Malaysia and the Transition to Independence, 1954–59." *Journal of Imperial and Commonwealth History* 21 (2): 409–31.

Schuler, Kurt. 1992. "The World History of Free Banking." In *The Experience of Free Banking,* edited by K. Dowd. New York: Routledge.

————. 2000. *Basics of Dollarization.* Joint Economic Committee Staff Report. Washington, D.C.: U.S. Senate.

Schumpeter, Joseph. 1954. *Economic Doctrine and Method.* London: George Allen and Unwin.

Scott, Sir Walter. 1981 [1826]. *The Letters of Malachi Malagrwather.* Edinburgh: William Blackwood.

Selgin, George. 1992. "Free Banking in Foochow." In *The Experience of Free Banking,* edited by K. Dowd. New York: MacMillan.

Senex. 1922. *One Coin Common to All the World to Stabilize Exchange, to Reduce the Cost of Living, to Give More Employment.* Brighton: Walter Gillett.

Sharkey, Robert. 1959. *Money, Class, and Party: An Economic Study of Civil War and Reconstruction.* Baltimore: John Hopkins.

Shell, Marc. 1982. *Money, Language and Thought.* Berkeley: University of California.

Shinjo, Hiroshi. 1962. *History of the Yen.* Tokyo: Kinokuniya Bookstore.

Shortt, Adam. 1964. "History of Canadian Metallic Currency." In *Money and Banking in Canada*, edited by E. P. Neufeld. Toronto: McClelland and Stewart.

———. 1986. *History of Canadian Currency and Banking, 1600–1880*. Toronto: Canadian Bankers Association.

Silverman, Dan. 1982. *Reconstructing Europe after the Great War*. Cambridge: Harvard University Press.

Simmel, George. 1978 [1900]. *The Philosophy of Money*. Translated by Tom Bottomore and David Frisby. London: Routledge and Kegan Paul.

Smith, Adam. 1976 [1776]. *The Wealth of Nations*. Edited by Edwin Cannan. Chicago: University of Chicago Press.

Smith, Vera. 1990 [1936]. *The Rationale of Central Banking*. Indianapolis: Liberty Press.

Solomon, L. D. 1996. *Rethinking Our Centralized Monetary System: The Case for a System of Local Currencies*. Westport: Praeger.

Spalding, William. 1918. *Eastern Exchange Currency and Finance*. 2d ed. London: Sir Isaac Pitman.

Spufford, Peter. 1988. *Money and Its Use in Medieval Europe*. Cambridge: Cambridge University Press.

Stasavage, David. 2002. "When Do States Abandon Monetary Discretion?" In *Monetary Orders: The Political Foundations of Twenty-first-century Money*, edited by J. Kirshner. Ithaca: Cornell University Press.

Stengers, Jean, and Jan Vansina. 1985. "King Leopold's Congo, 1886–1908." In *The Cambridge History of Africa*, edited by Roland Oliver and G. N. Sanderson. Vol. 6. Cambridge: Cambridge University Press.

Stewart, Ian. 1971. "Scottish Mints." In *Mints, Dies, and Currency*, edited by R. A. G. Carson. London: Methuen.

Stickney, Brian. 1971. *Numismatic History of Republic of Panama*. San Antonio: Almanzar's Coins of the World.

Stokes, Milton. 1939. *The Bank of Canada*. Toronto: Macmillan.

Strange, Susan. 1976. *International Monetary Relations*. London: Oxford University Press.

———. 1995. "The Limits of Politics." *Government and Opposition* 3 (3): 291–311.

Stringher, Bonaldo. 1927. "Unification of Bank-Note Issue and Currency Deflation." In *The Financial Reconstruction of Italy*, edited by Count Volpi and Bonaldo Stringher. New York: Italian Historical Society.

Styles, John. 1980. " 'Our Traitorous Money Makers': The Yorkshire Coins and the Law, 1760–83." In *An Ungovernable People: The English and Their Law in the Seventeenth and Eighteenth Centuries*, edited by John Brewer and John Styles. London: Hutchison.

Subercaseaux, Guillermo. 1922. *Monetary and Banking Policy of Chile*. Edited by David Kinley Oxford: Clarendon.

Suret-Canale, Jean. 1971. *French Colonialism in Tropical Africa, 1900–1945*. Translated by Till Gottheimer. New York: Pica Press.

Swanson, Guy. 1995. "Agents of Culture and Nationalism: The Confederate Treasury and Confederate Currency." In *The Banker's Art*, edited by V. Hewitt. London: British Museum Press.

Takaki, Masayoshi. 1903. *The History of Japanese Paper Currency, 1868–1890*. Baltimore: John Hopkins Press.

Tamagna, Frank. 1965. *Central Banking in Latin America*. Mexico: Centro de Estudios Monetarios Latinoamericanos.

Tannahill, Cecil. 1967. *Trade Tokens of Saskatchewan and Their History*. Ottawa: Canadian Numismatic Research Society.

Tavlas, George. 1993. "The 'New' Theory of Optimum Currency Areas." *The World Economy* 16(6): 663–86.

Taxay, Don. 1966. *The U.S. Mint and Coinage: An Illustrated History from 1776 to the Present*. New York: Arco.

Thailand, Government of, Treasury Department. 1982. *Coinage of the Rattanakosin Era, A.D. 1782–1982*. Bangkok: Rung Slip.

Thakur, Upendra. 1972. *Mints and Minting in India*. Varanasi-1: Chowkhamba Sanskrit Series Office.

Thompson, Virginia, and Richard Adloff. 1969. *French West Africa*. New York: Greenwood Press.

Thomson, Janice. 1994. *Mercenaries, Pirates, and Sovereigns: State-Building and Extraterritorial Violence in Early Modern Europe*. Princeton: Princeton University Press.

Timberlake, Richard. 1987. "Private Production of Scrip-Money in the Isolated Community." *Journal of Money, Credit, and Banking* 19 (4): 437–47.

Toniolo, Gianni. 1990. *An Economic History of Liberal Italy, 1850–1918*. Translated by Maria Rees. Routledge: London.

Touré, Ahmed Sékou. 1979. *Africa on the Move*. London: Panaf.

Triffin, Robert. 1944. "Central Banking and Monetary Management in Latin America." In *Economic Problems of Latin America*, edited by Seymour Harris. New York: McGraw-Hill.

———. 1946. *Monetary and Banking Reform in Paraguay*. Washington, D.C.: Board of Governors of the Federal Reserve System.

———. 1966a [1947]. "National Central Banking and the International Economy." In *The World Money Maze: National Currencies in International Payments*, edited by Robert Triffin. New Haven: Yale University Press.

———. 1966b [1947] "International Versus Domestic Money." In *The World Money Maze: National Currencies in International Payments*, edited by Robert Triffin. New Haven: Yale University Press.

———. 1968. "The Myth and Realities of the So-Called Gold Standard." In *Our International Monetary System*, edited by Robert Triffin. New York: Random House.

Tschoegl, Adrian. 2000. "Maria Theresa's Thaler: A Case of International Money." Unpublished paper.

Tsuen-Hsuin, Tsien. 1954. *Science and Civilisation in China. Vol. 5, Pt. 1. Paper and Printing*. Cambridge: Cambridge University Press.

Twyman, Michael. 1970. *Printing, 1770–1970: An Illustrated History of Its Development and Uses in England*. London: Eyre and Spottiswoode.

Uche, Chibuike Ugochukwu. 1997. "Bank of England vs. the IBRD: Did the Nigerian Colony Deserve a Central Bank?" *Explorations in Economic History* 34: 220–41.

U.K. Government. 1912a. Departmental Committee Appointed to Inquire into Matters Affecting the Currency of the British West African Colonies and Protectorates. *Minutes of Evidence*. London: His Majesty's Stationary Office.

———. 1912b. Departmental Committee Appointed to Inquire into Matters Affecting the Currency of the British West African Colonies and Protectorates. *Report*. London: His Majesty's Stationary Office.

Unger, Irwin. 1964. *The Greenback Era: A Social and Political History of American Finance, 1865–1879*. Princeton: Princeton University Press.

United States Congress. 1830. *Report of Mr. Sanford, from the Select Committee Appointed to Consider the State of the Current Coins*, Senate, 21st Congress, 1st Session, January 11.

———. 1834. *Gold and Silver Coins*, Report by C. P. White from the Select Committee on Coins, 23rd Congress, 1st Session, House of Rep., Feb 19.

———. 1856. *Report to Accompany Bill S.331*, Senate, 34th Congress, 1st session, Rep.Com.No.185, May 23.

United States Federal Reserve. 1944. "New Monetary and Banking Measures in Paraguay." *Federal Reserve Bulletin* 30 (1) (January): 42–51.

———. 1945. "Monetary Developments in Latin America." *Federal Reserve Bulletin* 31 (6)(June): 519–30.

United States Government. 1868. *Message of the President of the United States and Accompanying Documents to the Two Houses of Congress at the Commencement of the Second Session of the Fortieth Congress, Part 1*. Washington, D.C.: Government Printing Office.

———. 1870. *Letter of the Secretary of the Treasury, Transmitting to Congress the Correspondence of the Treasury Department Relative to the Revision of the Mint and Coinage Laws of the US*. Washington, D.C.: Government Printing Office.

———. 1963. *Foreign Relations of the United States—1942*. Vol. 4. *The Near East and Africa*. Washington, D.C.: Government Printing Office.

United States Senate. 1999. *Hearing on Official Dollarization in Emerging-Market Countries*, Senate Committee on Banking, Housing, and Urban Affairs, Subcommittee on Economic Affairs and Subcommittee on International Trade and Finance, July 15.

Vaiá, Dailió. 1980. *Plantation Tokens of Puerto Rico*. New York: Vantage Press.

Van De Putte, Jean. 1920. *A World Currency*. London: Harrison.

van der Berg, N. P. [1895] 1996. *Currency and the Economy of Netherlands India, 1870–1895*. Singapore: Institute of Southeast Asia.

Vice, David. 1983. *The Coinage of British West Africa and St. Helena, 1684–1958*. Birmingham: Peter Ireland.

Vilar, Pierre. 1984 [1969]. *A History of Gold and Money, 1450–1920*. Translated by Judith White London: Verso.

Vinelli, Paul. 1950–51. "The Currency and Exchange System of Honduras." *IMF Staff Papers* 1: 420–31.

von Glahn, Richard. 1996. *Fountain of Fortune: Money and Monetary Policy in China, 1000–1700*. Berkeley: University of California.

von Mises, Ludwig. 1953 [1924]. *The Theory of Money and Credit.* Translated by H. E. Batson. New Haven: Yale University Press.

Wallich, Henry. 1950. *Monetary Problems of an Export Economy: The Cuban Experience 1914–1947.* Cambridge: Harvard University Press.

Wallich, Henry, and Robert Triffin. 1953. *Monetary and Banking Legislation of the Dominican Republic.* New York: Federal Reserve Bank of New York.

Weatherford, Jack. 1997. *The History of Money.* New York: Crown.

Weber, Ernst Juerg. 1992. "Free Banking in Switzerland After the Liberal Revolutions in the Nineteenth Century." In *The Experience of Free Banking,* edited by K. Dowd. New York: Macmillan.

Weber, Eugen. 1976. *Peasants into Frenchmen: The Modernization of Rural France, 1870–1914.* Stanford: Stanford University Press.

Weber, Max. 1968. *Economy and Society.* Vol. 1. Edited by Guenther Roth and Claus Wittich. New York: Bedminster Press.

Webber, Carolyn, and Aaron Wildavsky. 1986. *A History of Taxation and Expenditure in the Western World.* New York: Simon and Schuster.

Weir, William. 1903. *Sixty Years in Canada.* Montreal: John Lovell and Son.

Weishaar, Wayne, and Wayne Parrish. 1933. *Money Without Money: The Challenge of Barter and Scrip.* New York: G. P. Putnam's Sons.

Weiskel, Timothy. 1980. *French Colonial Rule and the Baule Peoples: Resistance and Collaboration, 1889–1911.* Oxford: Clarendon Press.

White, Andrew Dickson. 1933. *Fiat Money Inflation in France.* New York: D. Appleton-Century.

White, Lawrence. 1984. *Free Banking in Britain: Theory, Experience, and Debate, 1800–1845.* Cambridge: Cambridge University Press

Whiting, J. R. S. 1971. *Trade Tokens: A Social and Economic History.* Newton Abbot: David Charles.

Wholesale and Retail Traders, Manufacturers, Brewers, Distillers, and Licensed Victuallers, in London and Its Vicinity. 1814. *Memorial Addressed to the Right Honourable the Committee of His Majesty's Council for Coin, October 18, 1813.* London: House of Commons, April 4.

Whyte, Arthur J. 1930. *The Political Life and Letters of Cavour, 1848–1861.* London: Oxford University Press.

Willem, John. 1959. *The United States Trade Dollar.* New York: Marchbanks Press.

Williams, John. 1920. *Argentine International Trade under Inconvertible Paper Money, 1880–1900.* Cambridge: Harvard University Press.

Willis, Henry Parker. 1901. *A History of the Latin Monetary Union.* Chicago: University of Chicago.

Wills, Antoinette. 1981. *Crime and Punishment in Revolutionary Paris.* London: Greenwood Press.

Woo, Jung-en. 1991. *Race to the Swift: State and Finance in Korean Industrialization.* New York: Columbia University Press.

Woodruff, David. 1999. *Money Unmade.* Ithaca: Cornell University Press.

Woodside, Alexander. 1997. "The Relationship Between Political Theory and Economic Growth in Vietnam, 1750–1840." In *The Last Stand of the Asian Autonomies,* edited by Antony Reid. New York: St. Martin's Press.

World Bank. 1962. *The Economic Development of Uganda.* Baltimore: John Hopkins Press.

Wright, M. 1885. *The "Torpedo," or Ten Minutes on the National Currency Question, "Beaverbacks."* St. Catharines, Canada: E. J. Leavenworth.

Yansané, Aguibou. 1979. "Monetary Independence and Transition to Socialism in Guinea." *Journal of African Studies* 6(3): 132–43.

———. 1984. *Decolonization in West African States With French Colonial Legacy.* Cambridge: Scheckman.

Yeager, Leland. 1990. "Preface." In *The Rationale of Central Banking,* edited by Vera Smith. Indianapolis: Liberty Press.

Young, Arthur. 1971. *China's Nation-Building Effort, 1927–37.* Stanford: Hoover Institution Press.

———. 1983. *Saudi Arabia: The Making of a Financial Giant.* New York: New York University Press.

Young, John Parke. 1925. *Central American Currency and Finance.* Princeton: Princeton University Press.

Zakaria, Fareed. 1999. "Money for Mars." *Newsweek* (Jan.11).

Zelizer, Viviana. 1994. *The Social Meaning of Money.* New York: Basic Books.

Zucker, Stanley. 1975. *Ludwig Bamberger: German Liberal Politician and Social Critic, 1823–1899.* Pittsburgh: University of Pittsburgh Press.

Index

Capital mobility, 13, 189, 226, 228, 230, 235, 241–43
Carey, Henry, 75–76, 128
Carothers, Neil, 72
Central Africa, 166, 169, 187, 209–14. *See also individual countries*
Central African Republic, 209
Central banks, 9, 34–35, 44, 64, 80–91, 116–17, 140–41, 146–57, 165, 175, 228, 234. *See also individual countries*
Ceylon, 174, 178, 188–90, 195, 197, 200, 202
CFA zone, 166–68, 181, 187, 209–14, 218–19, 226
Chad, 209
Chartist movement, 83, 90
Chase, Salmon, 74, 131
Chevalier, Michel, 128
Chile, 127, 147, 233
China
  interwar, 8, 147, 156, 179, 236
  nineteenth-century, 28, 31, 34, 35, 40, 46, 55, 79, 99, 128
  pre-nineteenth-century, 20, 22–23, 25, 28, 30–31, 47–49, 53
  See also Manchuria
Cipolla, Carlo, 27
Cobbett, William, 90
Cohen, Benjamin, 3, 6, 116
Cold War, 194–95
Colley, Linda, 108
Colombia, 147, 154–55, 194, 216
Colonial monetary reforms, 4, 14, 77. *See also individual countries*
Commodity money, 20, 22, 30, 43–44
Common Agricultural Policy, 14, 237
Congo, 209. *See also* Belgian Congo
Congreve, William, 58
Continental Bank Note Company of New York, 103
Cook, Peter, 57
Coppetiers, Emmanuel, 45, 75
Cosmopolitanism, 14, 130–31, 242
Costa Rica, 78, 110, 221
Counterfeiting, 7, 30, 32, 45, 48–49, 55–56, 58–59, 64, 68, 73, 90, 125, 151, 179, 184, 224
Cowries, 20, 22, 24–27, 51, 164, 170–73, 179–80, 205, 208
Cruikshank, George, 56–57
Crystal Place, International exhibition at (1851), 128–29
Cuba, 166, 188, 191
Cullather, Nick, 195
Cunliffe Committee, 148
Currency boards, 165, 168, 174–75, 177–78, 186, 189, 193, 195–96, 198–200, 206, 209, 228, 232, 234
"Currency school," 82–84, 149
Currency substitution
  contemporary, 6, 12–14, 139, 162, 216, 220–21, 226–28, 231–33, 236–37, 240–41, 243
  interwar, 4–5, 12, 140, 157–58, 162, 216, 220–21
  in nineteenth century and before, 21–23
Czechoslovakia, 151, 223

Dahomey, 209
Danzig, 146–47
Darling, J. H., 142, 145
Davis, W. J., 69
DeBeers, John, 188
De Cecco, Marcello, 152
De Gaulle, Charles, 214
De Kock, Michiel, 149
Denmark, 31, 34, 47, 77, 135, 144
Deutsch, Karl, 112
Díaz-Alejandro, Carlos, 233
Dollarization. *See* Currency substitution
Dominica, 215
Dominican Republic, 166, 188, 190–91, 194
Doty, Richard, 47, 68
Drake, Paul, 148, 152
Dutch East Indies, 165, 181
Duus, Peter, 182

East Africa, 168, 181, 199, 204, 206, 219. *See also individual countries*
East Caribbean monetary union, 215, 226
Eastern bloc, 220, 226. *See also* Eastern Europe
Eastern Europe, 223. *See also* Eastern bloc; *individual countries*
Eckert, Carter, 179
E-commerce, 13, 228. *See also* Electronic money
Economic Commission for Latin America (UN), 194
Economic liberalism
  contemporary, 13, 92, 219–20, 230–34, 236, 241, 243
  nineteenth-century, 9, 14, 80–84, 117–18, 124–28, 134–35, 187, 190, 192, 232, 241–42
  1920s, 140–51
  See also "Currency school"
Economist, The, 130, 220
Ecuador, 110, 147, 221
Eggertsson, Thráinn, 45
Einaudi, Luca, 131, 134

Malaysia, 168, 178, 199–202, 204, 206, 208
Maldive Islands, 22
Mali, 8, 211–15
Manchuria, 175–76
Manillas, 27, 60, 170, 179–80, 183
Maria Theresa thaler, 22, 196
Marichal, Carlos, 32
Marx, Karl, 119–20, 161
Matsukata, Count Masayoshi, 86–87, 117
Mauritania, 209, 212
Mauritius, 174
McCaleb, Walter, 74
McPhee, Allan, 184
Melanesia, 183
Menem, Carlos, 221, 228
Mercosur, 219
Mexico, 21–22, 24, 37, 38, 47, 71, 74, 78,
    98–99, 102, 147, 156, 221, 226
Meyer, John, 116
Middle East, 22, 34, 40, 77, 220. *See also in-
    dividual countries*
Mill, John Stuart, 128
Monaco, 216
Monetary unions, 4–5, 12–14
    colonial and early postcolonial, 163,
    168–69, 183, 203–16
    contemporary, 139, 216, 219–20, 227–28,
    231, 233, 236, 240–41, 243
    interwar, 140–46, 162, 234
    nineteenth-century, 39, 128–38, 219–20,
    227–28, 234
    See also Latin Monetary Union; Scandi-
    navian Monetary Union; European
    monetary union
Money, definition of, 20–22
Money doctoring. *See* Britain: foreign mon-
    etary advising; France: foreign mone-
    tary advising; United States: foreign
    monetary advising
Montserrat, 215
Morgenthau, Henry, 188
Morocco, 212
Mughal Empire, 20, 22, 24, 26–28, 48–49
Muller, Adam, 113–15
Mundell, Robert, 6
Mwangi, Wambui, 180–81

Nairobi, 208
Namibia, 216
Naming of currencies, 11, 108–10, 154–55,
    194, 196, 205, 214, 238
Napoleonic wars, 24, 51, 69
National economic autonomy, 75–76, 78,
    213
National identities, 11, 45–46, 127, 132, 137,
    140, 146, 153–56, 186, 194–96, 201–2,

205–6, 209, 212–14, 232, 238–43. *See
    also* Sovereignty
National markets, 8, 62–75, 79, 140, 173,
    227, 229–30
Nation-states, 7, 12, 42–46, 184–85, 224–28,
    234, 243. *See also* National identities;
    National markets; Public receivability
    rules; Taxation
Neoliberalism. *See* Economic liberalism:
    contemporary
Netherlands, 128. *See also* Dutch East In-
    dies
Newlyn, W., 177
New York, financial center of, 178
New York State, 125
New Zealand, 35, 147, 152–53, 155, 216,
    235. *See also* British Dominions
Nicaragua, 35, 78, 110
Niemeyer, Otto, 145, 147
Niger, 209
Nigeria, 170, 172, 174, 177, 180, 185, 199,
    200, 203–4
Nkrumah, Kwame, 214
Nominal money, 20–21, 31, 33
Norman, Montagu, 147, 150, 152, 175, 199,
    203
North, Douglass, 61
Norway, 34, 135, 144
Note issue monopoly, 9, 34–36, 73–74, 78,
    80–94, 97–99, 116, 123–28, 146–57,
    163–64, 174–75, 177–78, 193, 234
Numismatics, 108, 110
Nyerere, Julius, 206

Ofonagoro, Walter, 179
Oldenberg, duchy of, 28
Oman, 208–9
Optimum Currency Area (OCA) theory,
    5–12, 13, 218, 223
Ottawa Commonwealth Conference (1932),
    147
Ottoman Empire, 22, 27, 31, 34, 36, 97, 128

Panama, 110, 166, 216–17, 221
Pan-Americanism, 143
Pan-Scandinavianism, 135
Paraguay, 188, 190–91, 194
Parieu, Félix Esquiron de, 130
Paris conference (1867), 128–33, 142, 220
Parnell, Henry, 126
Parrish, Wayne, 160
Peel, Robert, 82–84, 126, 140, 148, 234
Perkins, Jacob, 58
Perlin, Frank, 28
Petty, William, 117
Peru, 22, 39, 52, 71, 78, 99, 147, 226, 236 n